# What Nudism Exposes

Mary-Ann Shantz

# What Nudism Exposes

## An Unconventional History of Postwar Canada

UBCPress · Vancouver · Toronto

31 30 29 28 27 26 25 24 23 22    5 4 3 2 1

Printed in Canada on FSC-certified ancient-forest-free paper (100% post-consumer recycled) that is processed chlorine- and acid-free.

---

**Library and Archives Canada Cataloguing in Publication**

Title: What nudism exposes : an unconventional history of postwar Canada / Mary-Ann Shantz.

Names: Shantz, Mary-Ann, author.

Description: Includes bibliographical references and index.

Identifiers: Canadiana (print) 20220249121 | Canadiana (ebook) 20220249261 | ISBN 9780774867207 (hardcover) | ISBN 9780774867214 (softcover) | ISBN 9780774867221 (PDF) | ISBN 9780774867238 (EPUB)

Subjects: LCSH: Nudism – Social aspects – Canada – History – 20th century. | LCSH: Nudists – Canada – History – 20th century.

Classification: LCC GV450 .S53 2023 | DDC 613/.194097109045—dc23

---

Canadä

UBC Press gratefully acknowledges the financial support for our publishing program of the Government of Canada (through the Canada Book Fund), the Canada Council for the Arts, and the British Columbia Arts Council.

This book has been published with the help of a grant from the Canadian Federation for the Humanities and Social Sciences, through the Awards to Scholarly Publications Program, using funds provided by the Social Sciences and Humanities Research Council of Canada.

Printed and bound in Canada by Friesens
Set in Garamond and Myriad by Artegraphica Design Co. Ltd.
Copy editor: Deborah Kerr
Proofreader: Helen Godolphin
Cartographer: Eric Leinberger
Cover designer: David Drummond

UBC Press
The University of British Columbia
2029 West Mall
Vancouver, BC V6T 1Z2
www.ubcpress.ca

*To James, for being there through it all*

# Contents

# Illustrations

# Acknowledgments

Having come to the end of a project that spanned more years than I imagined at the outset, it is a great pleasure to acknowledge those who supported and sustained me along the way.

I began research for this book in the History Department at Carleton University, where I found an incredible community of graduate students and professors. Thanks especially to Susan Joudrey and Valerie Minnett for their friendship, and to James Opp for always being ready with astute feedback and sage advice. I am also grateful to Joanna Dean, Patrizia Gentile, Christabelle Sethna, and Josie McLellan for their engagement with and constructive comments on my work. I acknowledge with gratitude the financial assistance of the Social Sciences and Humanities Research Council of Canada, the Ontario Government, and Carleton University.

This project would not have been possible without the cooperation of contemporary naturist organizations. Many thanks to former president of the Federation of Canadian Naturists, Stéphane Deschênes, for providing me access to their archive of records. I also thank the American Nudist Research Library in Kissimmee, Florida, and the volunteers that run it. I am especially grateful to Helen Fisher, who opened the library early for me each day during my visit. The Naturist Education Foundation Research Library provided digital reproductions of many of the photographs featured here, and I am grateful to Doug Hickok for his kind help with this. Thank you also to Ken Puley at the CBC Radio Archives for facilitating my access to radio coverage of the nudist movement, which was an especially rich and enjoyable research experience.

I am grateful for the practical support and encouragement of Ben Bradley, Kristine Alexander, and Jane Nicholas through the process of revising this work. Thanks to Ben for suggesting a conference panel on "Behaving Badly in the Great Outdoors," for sharing article finds on nudists, skinny-dippers, and streakers, and for the chapter edits. Kristine provided opportunities for me to visit the University of Lethbridge as a public lecturer and a visiting scholar, where I benefitted from the space to write and from interactions with the wonderful faculty in the History Department and at the Institute for Child and Youth Studies. Jane invited me to contribute to the collection *Contesting Bodies and Nation in Canadian History* when I was a young scholar, and since then has been generous in her support for my work, including reviewing several chapters.

A number of other scholars took the time to read and provide comments on portions of this work, including Carellin Brooks, Sarah Carter, Sean Kheraj, and Lianne McTavish. Their feedback strengthened this book and I am grateful for their collegiality and generosity with their time. I am grateful to my HIST 261 students at MacEwan University who engaged with a draft chapter and gave me hope this work would connect with an undergraduate audience. I also thank the anonymous reviewers who pushed me to clarify my arguments and expand my analysis. At UBC Press, James MacNevin and Ann Macklem have expertly guided this book through publication, and I am grateful for their responsiveness and professionalism. Deborah Kerr showed me what copy-editing is all about, and this book is better for it.

Since moving to Edmonton in 2007, a circle of friends has made this place home. Thanks especially to Megan Crane, Tracy Deline, and Lauren Wheeler, all of whom encouraged/endured more conversations about nudism than I can count or they deserve. I am also thankful for my Christ Church community, my Westmount neighbours, and the wonderful YMCA daycare staff whose care for my children in their early years gave me the space to pursue this project. Thanks also to my lovely colleagues at the Covenant Health Palliative Institute who make me want to show up to work every day.

After many moves it is both a blessing and a curse to have friends and family spread across the country and beyond. Thank you to: the old friends who continue to cheer me on from afar, including Amy Flint, Andrea Heath,

Shauna McClacherty, and Phuong Truong; my second family, Clifford and Kathryn Lingwood, Daniel Lingwood and Sarah Thompson, Sam Lingwood and Stacey Norton; and my siblings, Amy Shantz, Jenny Shantz, Matt and Emily Shantz, whom I love dearly, not least because they never once asked when this book was going to be done.

I once heard Tina Fey thank her parents for "somehow raising me to have confidence that is disproportionate with my looks and abilities," and I related completely. My parents nurtured my curiosity and love of learning, as well as supporting me in practical ways. My dad, Doug Shantz, taught me how to write and shared his passion for history. My mom, Heather Shantz, showed me how to live and die well, and I know how much she would have loved to hold this book in her hands.

Final thanks go to James, Charlotte, and George Lingwood – for all of the life and love that happened beyond the pages of this book.

# Abbreviations

| | |
|---|---|
| ANRL | American Nudist Research Library |
| ASA | American Sunbathing Association |
| CSA | Canadian Sunbathing Association |
| ECSA | Eastern Canadian Sunbathing Association |
| FCN | Federation of Canadian Naturists |
| TGS | Toronto Gymnosophical Society |
| WCSA | Western Canadian Sunbathing Association |

# What Nudism Exposes

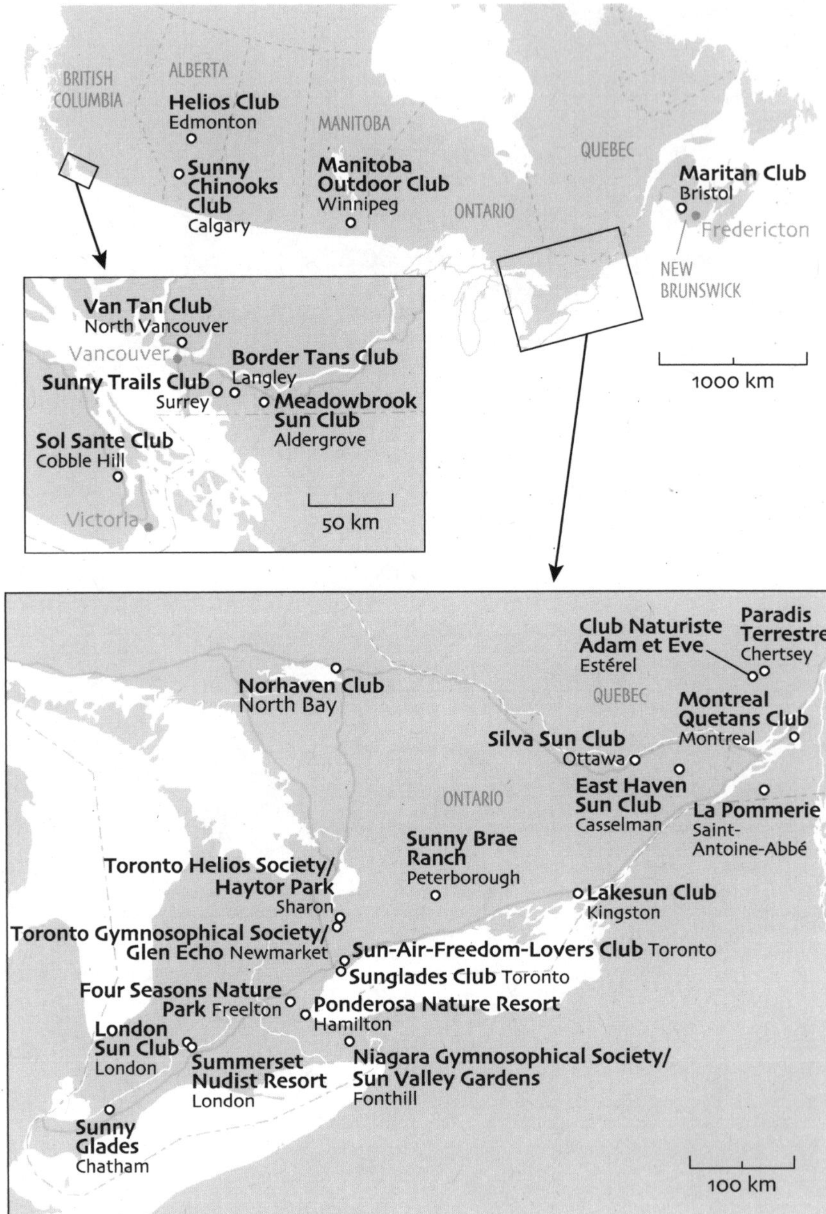


Figure 0.1 Map of nudist clubs referenced in the book

# Introduction

In 1958, *Liberty* magazine ran an article by Peggy Parkes entitled "I'm a Nudist Mother." In it, Parkes introduced herself as a forty-year-old woman from Hamilton, Ontario, with a husband, a son, and a part-time job. Her interests, she said, included detective stories, bowling, and ballet. Her good-humoured husband was keen on gardening and parties, and her fifteen-year-old son, a fan of Elvis Presley and Pat Boone, was "allergic to cats, arithmetic and dishwashing." Parkes insisted that she and her husband were "not prudes," but they were "concerned about juvenile delinquency, and lurid magazines with sexy pictures of undraped females over suggestive captions." In summary, she declared, "I am, except for being a nudist, an average working-class Canadian mother."[1]

What drew a woman like Parkes to join the nudist movement, and why did a person affiliated with something so unconventional nonetheless consider herself "an average working-class Canadian mother"? What led *Liberty,* which billed itself as "Canada's Young Family Magazine," to feature her story? And what did nudism have to do with Parkes's worries about juvenile delinquency? "I'm a Nudist Mother" raises a number of questions that underpin this book. But what is especially remarkable about the article is that nudism provided the occasion for this "average" Canadian woman to reflect on the body, nudity, and sexuality in the pages of a national magazine as she described her first-time experience at a nudist club, recounted conversations with fellow club members about their children's involvement, and explained "how it [was] possible to be clean-minded when beholding the opposite sex in the nude."[2] In short, the nudist movement serves as a lens through which to examine a group of working- and middle-class Canadians reflecting on the place of the body in modern life.

Nudism emerged as part of a far-reaching social movement sweeping Germany at the turn of the twentieth century. Known as *Lebensreform,* or life reform, it also encompassed vegetarianism, hiking, and nature conservation. Common to all of these was the shared objective "to reorient the German people toward nature, and ... thereby to find solutions to the problems of modern [urban-industrial] society." By "nature," as historian John Williams explains, nudists meant "both the nonhuman rural environment and the naked human body."[3] This turn to nature was supposed to address the effects of pollution, overcrowding, and poor working conditions on the health of the German people, problems believed to have physical, mental, and moral consequences.[4] Nudism arose in Wilhelmine Germany as an elitist, middle-class movement, but it blossomed into an ideologically diverse popular phenomenon during the Weimar period that included gymnastics programs, youth hiking groups, and recreational parks.[5] Its pioneers believed that performing these activities without clothes would allow people to take full advantage of sunshine and fresh air, and would also promote greater care for the body. They endorsed social nudism as offering a path to physical, mental, and moral health, with some linking individual renewal to national regeneration.[6] During the interwar period, nudism spread through western Europe as well as to Britain, the United States, Australia, and New Zealand.[7]

Although Canada's oldest nudist club, the Van Tan Club, opened in North Vancouver in 1939, the movement became firmly established in Canada only after the Second World War. European immigrants with nudist experience provided an influx of leaders and members to the fledgling movement.[8] The development of Canadian nudism coincided with the postwar public recreation movement, the proliferation of national and provincial parks, and the "golden age" of the family vacation, which were facilitated by increased leisure time, disposable income, and car ownership, as well as ongoing urbanization. Despite the implication of the common misnomer "nudist colony," the clubs were not permanent residential communities, but weekend and summer recreational sites that served as alternatives to public beaches, parks, and campgrounds.[9] They emerged on the outskirts of many cities but were most numerous in the Greater Vancouver area and southwestern Ontario. By 1960, more than twenty were operating in Canada, ranging in size from ten to more than four hundred members.[10]

This book draws on primary sources created for a non-nudist public, notably the Toronto nudist magazine *Sunbathing for Health,* as well as print, radio, and television coverage of the movement by mainstream media. Though nudism never managed to recruit a significant percentage of Canadians to join its ranks, it did receive considerable press coverage. Twenty-five radio and television interviews from the 1950s, 1960s, and 1970s are particularly rich, and are valuable for what they reveal of how nudists presented their movement to the public.

I also draw on records held by contemporary nudist organizations such as the Federation of Canadian Naturists (FCN) and the American Nudist Research Library (ANRL), as well as the Naturist Living Podcast hosted by naturist club owner and former FCN president Stéphane Deschênes.[11] These sources include internal club minutes and newsletters, private correspondence, and podcast interviews and offer insight into key individuals, interpersonal and club dynamics, and the degree to which public promotion aligned with private views.

In what follows I take seriously nudist critiques of mainstream attitudes toward the body, nudity, and sexuality, while interrogating nudist perspectives and assumptions, particularly the defence of nudity as "natural." As William Cronon asserts, "What we mean when we use the word 'nature' says as much about ourselves as about the things we label with that word."[12] Ruth Barcan puts it another way: the nude body "is never naked, if naked means stripped of meaning, value and political import."[13] The Canadian movement did not exist in a vacuum; rather, it entered broader conversations about what it means to have a body and to interact with others' bodies. What nudism ultimately exposes is the body's position at the intersection of nature and culture, the individual and the social, the private and the public.

## Nudity in Historical Context

German sociologist Norbert Elias's magnum opus *The Civilizing Process,* originally published in 1939, remains the most comprehensive history of body etiquette in Western society. It provides a broad historical context for nudism's emergence. According to Elias, beginning around the sixteenth century, nudity and bodily functions such as urinating, defecating, bathing, sleeping, and sexual relations became confined to the private sphere and removed from the view of others, first among the nobility and then gradually among the lower classes as well. Elias argued that this "civilizing process" was driven by the needs of a society in which individuals lived in increasingly close proximity. Moreover, these changes in behaviour brought a shift in attitudes regarding the body and its functions, notably feelings of shame and embarrassment, which, in turn, reinforced the self-regulation that came to replace external forms of social control.[14]

Nudity's banishment from public space was a slow and uneven process. In his study of Toronto, Dale Barbour points to the period between 1850 and 1930 as the timing for a shift from "vernacular [nude] bathing and the male-dominated swimming hole to the bathing suit and the mixed gender public beach."[15] The rise of the nudist movement, first in Germany and then in North America, coincided with this era and pushed back against the social taboo against nudity. Its members refused to feel ashamed of the naked body and contested the strong cultural correlation between nudity and sexuality. They argued that clothing should be worn for functional or ornamental purposes, not due to a sense of shame. Ontario club owner Karl Ruehle explained,

> The human body is just a body, and whether it is nude or clothed has no influence upon its moral standard ... Most people have no idea what a wonderful work God did. Generally they do not think about it at all unless they are sick and pain forces it to their attention. Did you ever look in the mirror of your bathroom to see your whole body? Did you ever notice those wonderful lines of your limbs and your chest? All the muscles are in the proper place to fulfil their important functions which keep you moving. There is nothing ugly or superfluous. Even your sexual parts have their functions in relation to your entire life and your body ... Their functions are as decent as those of your heart, stomach, or any other organ of your body ... There is nothing evil or disgusting about the sexual organs except in an evil mind.[16]

Nudists challenged cultural perceptions of the nude body as something inherently obscene, shameful, or transgressive. Committed to dissociating nudity from sexuality, their clubs created space for men, women, and children to socialize together in the nude.

Nudism posited a circular relationship between mind and body: the body was as pure as the mind made it, and bodily practices could form a new mental attitude. Throughout the twentieth century, many Canadians expressed concern that looking at naked bodies – in the flesh but also in art or literature – would corrupt the mind, but nudists embraced nudity as a means of exposing, and improving, one's mental attitude toward the body and sexuality.[17] They promoted it as a way to satisfy natural curiosity and loosen the hold of social taboos. Belgian historian Evert Peeters contends that the "perception of the body and sexuality within nudist writing did not simply reflect a discursive message; rather, the physical techniques of nudism became a means of cultural criticism."[18] Nudism was a bodily performance that naturalized nakedness in a society in which mixed-sex social nudity was decidedly unnatural. This is an example of what Michel de Certeau calls "the practice of everyday life," by which social groups or individuals "make innumerable and infinitesimal transformations of and within the dominant cultural economy in order to adapt it to their own interests and their own rules."[19] Going nude and looking at the unclothed bodies of others were both critical components of this process.

In their efforts to broaden their appeal while also levelling a critique of Western attitudes regarding the body, nudists have always been engaged in a complex negotiation of social norms. Even as they transgressed the social taboo against nudity, they sought social respectability. Pioneering Canadian nudist organizer Ray Connett explained, "It goes without saying that to inspire others to try a way of life which is still unacceptable to normal society one must in every other way but this be completely normal, above reproach in all things."[20] This was particularly the case with respect to sexuality. Nudists believed that their movement provided the means to overcome both bodily shame and sexual promiscuity by promoting a healthy respect for the body and sexuality. Bell and Holliday explain that in the nudist philosophy, "the body is re-naturalized and simultaneously de-sexualized; rather than casting off culture/civilization to release animalistic or 'natural' (culturally suppressed) passions ... a strict code of morality is instead *naturalized.*"[21] Nudists argued that it was clothing, not nudity, that heightened sexual tension and that by reducing "artificial stimulation," nudism restored sex to its "natural place," which generally meant safely contained within marriage.[22] In this manner, they simultaneously lauded nudity as natural and championed sexual self-regulation.

Despite their protestations that nudism was not about sex, they devoted a great deal of attention to the subject. Their philosophy was part of the proliferation of sexual discourses that Foucault identified as arising in the eighteenth century. Moreover, it functioned, as Foucault suggests, "to yield multiple effects of displacement, intensification, re-orientation, and modification of desire itself."[23] In her study of German nude gymnastics regimens, Maren Möhring notes that nudists denounced corsets and urged women to build a "muscle-corset." She explains, "instead of *external* constraint, the nudists emphasized *self*-discipline ... Conforming to aesthetic norms was now to be achieved with and on the body itself, not by wearing a corset."[24] In a striking parallel, Canadian nudist leader Karl Ruehle provided the following account of nudist attitudes toward clothing and nudity: "We are working for the day when nudity will not be an invitation for sexual exploitation but a challenge for self-control which is the root of all good beginnings."[25] Nudists abandoned the crutch of clothing as a means of enhancing, not disrupting, sexual self-regulation.

While outlining the long-term trend of removing nudity and bodily functions from public view, Norbert Elias observed a recent "relaxation" of attitudes in some areas. In his opinion, this was "only possible because the level of habitual, technically and institutionally consolidated self-control, the individual capacity to restrain one's urges and behaviour in correspondence with the more advanced feelings for what is offensive, has been on the whole secured. It is a relaxation within the framework of an already established standard."[26] This explanation certainly applies in the Canadian context of the 1950s and 1960s, where the practice of nudism occurred within a highly regulated environment. As Ray Connett declared, "It's total freedom we want, but this does not mean permissiveness." Indeed, nudist clubs had a "Sunday school picnic ... morality."[27] Clubs demanded that people regulate themselves even more carefully than they would in public. As individuals shed their clothes, they substituted other forms of containment, notably their club screening process, strict standards of behaviour, and an emphasis on gender and sexual norms. Respectful of the Canadian Criminal Code, which made it a criminal offence to be nude in a public place or in a place visible to the public, they confined their activities to shielded private properties.

### Nudism and Health

The nudist movement has consistently attempted to rehabilitate the nude body and render it compatible with modern life, but it also evolved over time. Prior to the Second World War, its predominant focus was physical health. Early nudist writers extolled the health-giving effects of the sun and fresh air and endorsed nude sunbathing as the way to obtain optimum benefit. Nude hiking and gymnastics were especially popular. In Weimar Germany and interwar England, nudists claimed that performing these activities without clothes enabled men and women to adopt a "rational," "objective" view of their own bodies and those of others by exposing them to the "scrutinizing gaze."[28] This, they believed, would motivate members to work to achieve idealized strong and healthy bodies, and also allow them to completely and honestly assess the physical fitness of potential marriage partners. Together, these measures would lead to a stronger, healthier society by promoting individual physical health and "eugenically purposeful sexuality."[29]

This interwar preoccupation with physical health reflected the values of society more broadly. The era saw the advent of heliotherapists, who embraced "sun cures" as a means of treating diseases such as rickets and tuberculosis. Citizens also formed Sunlight Leagues in industrial cities such as London to agitate for the reduction of coal pollution and to champion urban planning that would maximize the presence of sunlight.[30] Open-air schooling, rural recreation, and camping movements were all initiated during this period, with the shared goal of improving health through a reconnection with nature. At the same time, physical culture and amateur sport emerged as popular forms of leisure. Charlotte Macdonald explains,

> So central had the pursuit of the "better body" become by the 1930s that it seemed almost to define the modern condition ... What was portrayed as new-found freedom for the body was celebrated in enthusiasm for "natural" places and pursuits. Exercising with bare feet; exposing skin to fresh air and sunlight; walking, hiking, camping and cycling in the outdoors were all taken up with gusto.[31]

Physical fitness and outdoor recreation became modern obsessions, what one scholar has labelled an "extraordinary modernist preoccupation with physicality."[32]

If the interwar period was focused on improving bodies, the era that followed the Second World War was concerned with improving minds. This was a result of parallel developments: better standards of living and overall physical health, and heightened attention to the warnings of psychologists that modernity brought both benefits and new problems. Improved sanitation and the development and availability of antibiotics and vaccines to treat and prevent infectious disease meant that Canadians enjoyed better health and longer lives than ever before. But as the field of psychology ascended to a position of social authority, it raised public anxiety that mental health, juvenile delinquency, and sexual "deviance" were critical problems in modern society.[33]

Postwar Canada presented more opportunities than ever to pursue recreation, and the health justification for doing so nude was increasingly tenuous. Anne-Marie Châtelet suggests that the curing of tuberculosis through the use of antibiotics rendered open-air schooling obsolete – and by extension, dealt a blow to the practice of "nature cures."[34] Gymnastics, which in Weimar Germany had been "the least controversial and most accepted and practiced of all the nudists' reform ideas," was almost entirely absent from Canadian nudism, which tended to embrace a philosophy of bodily acceptance (though physical attractiveness was not without import, especially for women).[35] As the language of eugenics dropped out of popular usage in the aftermath of the Holocaust, nudists likewise abandoned any discussion of racial improvement.[36] Nevertheless, the whiteness of Canadian clubs shored up their claims to normalcy and respectability, and was perpetuated by the screening practices of some clubs.

Moving away from the physical culture of early nudism, postwar Canadian nudists engaged with contemporary psychological discourse to present their movement as encouraging healthy, "normal" psychological development. They argued that delinquency and deviance were rooted in repressive social attitudes that cultivated shame and inhibitions, and they offered nudism as the antidote – a way of becoming comfortable in one's own skin. Furthering society's romance with the nuclear family, they cast their practice as strengthening, not undermining, marriage and family life.[37] In the midst of the baby boom, they promoted themselves as family friendly and offered nudism as a means of raising psychologically healthy, well-adjusted citizens – and therefore something that every parent should be willing to try.

Although they were not primarily concerned with reshaping the body, they did situate it as an important source of self-identity. Over the course of the twentieth century, the rise of physical culture and amateur sport and the democratization of fashion and beauty culture increasingly defined the body as a source of self-identity and pleasure. One individual described the attraction of nudism as being the

> deep experience that I haven't lost myself in the crowd – that I am still an individual ... that detached from all the trappings of civilization there is a me left, not just a cog in a wheel ... something to offer as proof of individuality, some reason to feel that I have a life, a being, apart from the civilization of which I am an infinitesimal part.[38]

Nudists were engaged in a balancing act, offering people the chance to take part in a unique social practice while simultaneously asserting their normalcy and respectability. Ironically, sociologist Joanne Entwistle argues that fashion exhibits this same tension, "express[ing] the contradictory desires to fit in and stand out."[39]

## A New History of Postwar Canada

On first glance, it may be surprising that nudism blossomed in Canada in the 1950s, given that the decade is often associated with conformity and conservatism. L.B. Kuffert explains that "modern life connotes a set of conditions in which the social foundations of culture undergo significant and accelerated changes, and culture itself becomes on the whole more uniform."[40] Although these developments emerged out of industrialization, which began in Canada after about 1850, they were accentuated by improved standards of living, rising consumerism, and the growth of mass culture that followed the Second World War. The ultimate symbol of social homogeneity was the sprawling suburb, and Richard Harris characterizes suburbanization as a process of "creeping conformity, not only of the suburbs but also of certain aspects of Canadian society."[41] The baby boom and the "intense pro-family climate" that developed in the aftermath of the Great Depression and the Second World War were closely related elements of this process.[42]

The postwar period was also the age of the expert; psychologists and physicians, among others, enjoyed a particularly influential place in society and, as scholars Mary Louise Adams and Mona Gleason demonstrate, many of them reinforced hegemonic social values through the promotion of "normal" socialization. Gleason argues, "the normal family that was constructed through psychological discourse ... entrenched and reproduced the dominance of Anglo/Celtic, middle-class, heterosexual, and patriarchal values."[43] In other words, the "ideal" family became the standard against which all others were judged. Moreover, conformity itself became a shared value. In both private and public life, the ability to find consensus, to fit in, and to get along was highly prized. Conversely, "deviance from any number of mainstream norms" was seen as threatening to the social order.[44]

Canadian nudists sought public approval and embraced the normalizing discourses analyzed by scholars such as Gleason and Adams. But *What Nudism Exposes* complicates the image of the postwar years as dominated by conformity and reveals that groups such as nudists could employ the rhetoric for their own ends. Their use of psychology to reinforce their philosophy speaks to the pervasiveness of that discourse and of contemporary concerns about mental health, juvenile delinquency, and deviant sexuality. But it also demonstrates that they navigated normalizing discourses to promote something that psychologists did not endorse. Adams observes that "the point of studying dominant cultural discourses – mainstream ideals ... is that we all have to negotiate them, whether we subscribe to them, are marginalized by them, or actively resist them."[45] Despite its unconventionality, the nudist movement serves as a case study of how a group of working- and middle-class Canadians responded to, and made use of, expert advice. At the same time, the tolerance extended to nudists by Canadians who did not engage in their practice undoubtedly rested on the whiteness of the movement and the limited nature of its cultural critique.

As Canada underwent dramatic social and cultural changes during the late 1960s and the early 1970s, the movement suffered something of an identity crisis. It had made a point of affirming sexual and gender norms and of enforcing strict standards of behaviour on club grounds. Now it risked being perceived as behind the times. In response to the "swinging" sixties, clubs began to re-evaluate their messaging and policies. In particular, they grappled with how to deal with social drinking, the sexual revolution, second-wave feminism, and environmentalism. Many loosened their restrictions on alcohol and their bans on separated or divorced individuals. Some launched provocative pageants that attracted publicity and helped fund extensive property development, emphasizing greater openness to sexuality while doubling down on the objectification of women. Other nudists found their purpose through re-emphasizing the connection between nudity and the natural world, vaguely aligning themselves with environmentalism. By 1980, Canadian clubs had settled into a new normal, abandoning some of their most radical innovations while permanently relaxing rules regarding drinking and heterosexual marital norms. Nudism resists simple "liberal" or "conservative" labels; instead, the clubs adopted a range of responses to cultural change and the challenge of moving with the times while maintaining social respectability.

My purpose is not to offer an organizational history of nudism, but instead to provide a cultural history of the movement and of postwar attitudes toward the body more generally. Although it never entered the mainstream of Canadian life, this examination of the nudist movement reveals how a subset of Canadians navigated the social and cultural changes of the postwar period – stretching from the immediate postwar years through the end of the 1970s – and in doing so offers new perspectives on society at large.

# PART I
# Nudism Comes to Canada

# 1
# Building a Movement

> When we were still in Germany we tried to get some land to start our own camp somewhere in Germany, but land was so scarce, and the trouble to be a club in the bigger cities took quite a bit of time. So after quite a few things came together we decided to go to Canada, where there was plenty of land and immigrants were welcome. So we came in '53 to Canada. Not actually planning to have a camp here in Canada, but to live somewhere in Canada on a piece of land, in the nude as much as possible, make a living, and go from there. That it developed into what we have now we have never dreamt about.
>
> – Karl Ruehle, *Identities*

Canadian nudism emerged as part of a transnational movement. This included the circulation of nudist books and periodicals, as well as the flow of people through travel and immigration. The most significant factor in its growth was the arrival of hundreds of thousands of European immigrants in the aftermath of the Second World War. A national movement took shape with the creation of the Canadian Sunbathing Association (CSA) in 1947, aided by the publication of *Sunbathing for Health* magazine in Toronto from 1947 to 1959. At the local level, individual clubs played an important role in promoting nudism, and a few of the more ambitious ones launched publicity campaigns such as open house events that put a spotlight on nudism. Clubs varied significantly in size, amenities, and atmosphere. They also had the largest impact on individual Canadians' experiences with nudism. The chapter that follows explores the Canadian movement as an international, national, and local phenomenon, and how it became established on a firm footing in the decades after World War II.

## Canada in a Transnational Context

Prior to the establishment of the organized movement in Canada, some Canadians encountered nudism through literature. For example, they may have read *Among the Nudists* and *Nudism Comes to America,* published in the early 1930s by Americans Frances and Mason Merrill. Or they may have perused Maurice Parmelee's *Nudism in Modern Life* (featuring a foreword by noted psychologist Havelock Ellis) and works by British nudists Reverend C.E. Norwood and William Welby.[1] Ray Connett, the most influential nudist in western Canada during the 1940s and 1950s, first encountered the movement when he picked up a copy of *The Nudist,* an American magazine, while on a cross-border trip from his Vancouver home to Bellingham, Washington in the 1930s.[2] He also became a reader of *Health and Efficiency,* an English nudist magazine, which enabled him to decode a discreetly worded ad in the personals section of a 1939 issue of the *Vancouver Province:* "Member of N.S.A.A. wishes to form similar club here."[3] The ad alluded to the British National Sun-Air Association. This sort of coded language was a means of overcoming the refusal of many publications to openly advertise nudist activities or groups. In responding to the ad, Connett became a founding member of the Van Tan Club, Canada's oldest operating nudist club. As more Canadian clubs were established, many developed small library collections to make nudist literature available to members, which connected them to a wider network of like-minded people.

Just as the publications circulated internationally, so did nudists themselves. Besides Connett, other founding members of the Van Tan Club were Hardy and Lenore Kaye. According to James Woycke, "He was English, she Australian; both were en route from a vacation in England – where they had just experienced nudism for the first time at the Arcadians club – back to Australia when they got stranded in Canada at the outbreak of the war."[4] Though the declaration of hostilities meant that the Kayes became early members of the Van Tans, the war soon interrupted the club's development by limiting the resources and leisure time of its members. At the same time, some Canadians serving overseas had the opportunity to visit British clubs, including Ray Connett.

But it was European immigration, especially from Germany, that played the greatest role in advancing the nudist movement in Canada. Between 1946 and 1962, 2.1 million migrants came to Canada, the vast majority of them from Europe, a massive influx of people into a country whose 1941 population consisted of just 11.5 million. Across Europe, millions had been displaced by the war, and farms, factories, and infrastructure lay in ruins. Franca Iacovetta explains that though the federal government was cautious in its approach, "a combination of factors – including economic self-interest, labour shortages, international pressures, and pro-refugee lobbies – eventually encouraged and cajoled the Canadian government into prying open its doors to immigrants."[5] Initially, Canadian officials were reluctant to admit Germans, but in 1950 Canada removed them from the "enemy alien" class – the wartime designation for citizens of hostile nations. By the early 1960s, approximately 270,000 Germans had come to Canada, making Germany the third-largest source of immigrants in this period, surpassed only by Britain and Italy. In part, the policy shift was driven by the growing tendency to distinguish between culpable war criminals and average Germans.[6] But Alexander Freund explains that it also reflected "the privileges [Canadian] bureaucrats conferred upon [Germans] as white, Christian, Northwest Europeans," considering them "first-class citizenship material" at a time when Canadian immigration policy openly persisted in the objective of keeping Canada white.[7] This approach stands in marked contrast to Canadian attitudes regarding another class of enemy aliens, people of Japanese descent living in Canada. Ottawa eventually stepped back from forcefully "repatriating" British Columbians of Japanese origin to Japan following the war, most of whom were in fact Canadian-born, and in 1949 it ended its 1942 prohibition against anyone of Japanese descent living in the coastal province. But as Pamela Sugiman explains, "the government's racialized [postwar] policy of repatriation and its unmaking of this community both rested upon and reinforced a belief in the sameness of all persons 'of the Japanese race.'" It was "guided by the notion that transnational loyalties [to Japan] cross[ed] generations."[8]

In contrast, after a brief wartime interruption, Ottawa renewed its long-standing belief that Germans were generally ideal immigrants who would readily adapt to their new environment. According to the white settler mythology that informed Canadian immigration policies, to be Canadian was to be of European origin. Sherene Razack describes the rationale: "It is believed that white people came first and that it is they who principally developed the land; Aboriginal people are presumed to be mostly dead or assimilated. European settlers thus *become* the original inhabitants and the group most entitled to the fruits of citizenship."[9] While introducing amendments to the Immigration Act in 1947, Prime Minister King stated that "large-scale immigration from the Orient would change the fundamental composition of the Canadian population" in a way that European immigration would not.[10] Franca Iacovetta indicates that the Canadian press also generally expressed a high regard for German immigrants: "The cheerful reports on the many happy arrivals met by excited crowds of relatives and compatriots largely sidestepped the complex subjects of Italy's Fascist and Germany's Nazi past." Germans were frequently praised for their work ethic and ability to assimilate.[11]

Despite the assumption that Europeans easily became Canadian, they brought cultural differences with them, including nudism. Lisa Stein, a German immigrant who established two nudist clubs in Ontario with her husband during the 1960s, told a CBC interviewer that nudism in the United States originated with German immigrants. Unwilling to relinquish the practice, they "decided to not give it up but to show North America what nudism is all about."[12] This was also true of many German nudists who came to Canada after the war. Rather than give up nudism, they cultivated a movement in Canada as they uprooted their lives and re-established themselves in a new country. In Canada they encountered a society in which "a fundamentally conservative Cold War consensus had taken hold ... one that transformed all forms of criticism and nonconformist behaviour into attacks on democratic decency," according to Dirk Hoerder. Yet German immigrants played a critical role in establishing an unconventional, and potentially threatening, movement on a firm footing. They provide an apt example of the "transcultural agency" of migrants, in this case ones who operated from the position of a preferred white immigrant group, though no doubt facing significant challenges in building new lives.[13]

Although they became active in nudist clubs across Canada, it was in Ontario in particular that they led the transformation of nudism from a couple of clubs comprised of just a few individuals to a full-fledged movement that attracted thousands of members and visitors. Beginning with Karl and Marlies Ruehle, German immigrants spearheaded the establishment of nudist camps and resorts across southern Ontario during the 1950s and

1960s. After relocating to Canada in 1953, the Ruehles acquired property in the Niagara peninsula the following year, named it Sun Valley Gardens, and took over leadership of the local nudist group, the recently formed Niagara Gymnosophical Society. The Sun Valley club was launched in the 1954 summer season with eighteen adult members. By the end of the 1950s, it boasted more than three hundred, making it Canada's largest nudist club.[14] Its members went on to found clubs of their own throughout southwestern Ontario, including the London Sun Club in 1955, Ponderosa Nature Resort, which opened outside Hamilton in 1964, and the Four Seasons Nature Park, which opened near Guelph in 1969.[15] Ponderosa and the Four Seasons were also established by German immigrant couples. In addition, Hans and Maria Behrmann, who came to Canada in 1951, opened the Lakesun Club outside Kingston, Ontario, in 1959, though Woycke numbers them among "the few nudists of German/Austrian background to learn of nudism *after* reaching Canada." The Behrmanns became acquainted with nudism through a Hamilton radio program on the subject, probably one of a number of programs that featured Karl Ruehle or Sun Valley member Peggy Parkes.[16] German immigrants also helped the movement along in western Canada. Helga and Dietrich Wesemann, for example, met at a German nudist camp before emigrating to Canada and founding the Helios Club outside Edmonton in 1963.[17]

Historian Pascal Maeder recounts the story of a postwar Eastern European immigrant who redefined her DP (displaced person) status as "delayed pioneer." This definition aptly characterizes the attitude of several German Canadian nudist club owners in Ontario.[18] Karl Ruehle took pride in the fact that when he and Marlies acquired the twenty-five-acre property for Sun Valley Gardens in 1954, "it was for the most part thorn-filled bush and some swampy areas, and there was a lot of clearing out and weeding and hard work to do to get something out of it."[19] Hans Stein, who founded the Ponderosa Nature Resort with his wife, sister, and brother-in-law, explained,

> There was absolutely nothing here. The volleyball and the tennis courts and all these things, this was one big field with oats planted ... And there was not even a road coming in here ... a car could never get through. So then we started building, building a road first, then we did a clubhouse and a swimming pool ... It was all solid rock here, bedrock, so we had to blast a swimming pool, 14 feet deep, out of the rock with dynamite.[20]

In 1971, Lakesun owner Hans Behrmann reflected, "Looking back on our eleven-year history we have come a long way. Out of sheer rock we have over the years created a haven for naturists to spend their weekends and holidays."[21] In relaying the history of their clubs, Ruehle, Stein, and Behrmann cast themselves in the tradition of Canadian pioneers, clearing land and domesticating space. Some Canadian-born nudists also subscribed to this rhetoric. Stan Wortner, who founded the Sunny Glades club near Chatham, Ontario, in 1959, described his early days as its owner:

> I've got two kids, one dog, and a wife, I'm living in a little cottage 16×24, with my running water consisting of a pipe coming up through the floor running cold water, my outdoor toilet was on skids and I dug a hole underneath of it. I actually virtually pioneered ... really and truly pioneered. You know, we enjoyed it, but we were without a lot of things. We had one telephone and one television, you know, that type of thing.[22]

But German Canadian nudists took particular pride in simultaneously laying the foundation for successful clubs while building new lives in Canada. Reflecting on the beginning of the Ponderosa Nature Resort fifty years earlier, Hans Stein noted, "I don't think we could have done any better than we really did, because we started off with basically nothing, it was just hard work. You know, we worked seven days a week, and we worked 14 and 16 hours every day, all of us, in the teamwork here."[23] German Canadian nudist leaders laid claim to a settler Canadian identity even as they transplanted a European practice to North America.

German and other European immigrants also provided a pool of members for the new clubs. In a 1974 CBC Radio interview, for example, the Ruehles noted that they first advertised their club in German-language newspapers. Ontario leaders observed a strong European presence at their clubs, counting German, Dutch, French, English, and Scottish immigrants among their members.[24] Doug Beckett recalled the first time he and his wife visited Glen Echo Nudist Park, outside Toronto, in 1958, to which they would belong for fifty years:

> We were family number twenty-three. And they, uh, one of the chaps that we were talking to, because we were new to the group, said, "Well, where did you come from?" Well we said, "We're Canadians. We've always been here." And he turned around and shouted out to the gang, "Hey

> gang, this thing's going to catch on. Here come a couple of Canadians!" Because at that time the membership was English, German, French, a few French ... and Dutch.[25]

The growth of nudism in Canada was fed by postwar immigration, but as it slowed and the profile of the movement grew, the ratio of European to Canadian-born members would shift.

## Creating a National Movement

Belonging to a transnational movement, Canadian nudism also developed into a national community. *Sunbathing for Health,* published in Toronto between 1947 and 1959, played a prominent role in its creation. The magazine sold on select newsstands across the country and was also available by subscription.[26] It was published by the Rex Book Company, a division of the Sinnott News Company based in Scarborough, Ontario. Between 1939 and 1947, Sinnott had produced *Sunbathing and Health,* a magazine comprised of reprinted articles by English nudists and stock nude photographs. But in 1946, Ray Connett, back from overseas service and employed by Canada Post, approached Sinnott about the possibility of contributing an original column. Titled "Sunny Trails: A Nudist Call to Canada," it first appeared in the December 1946 issue, and it ran in every issue thereafter. The following April the magazine was relaunched with significant Canadian content under the slightly modified title of *Sunbathing for Health.* It also featured Connett's wife, Mildred Harris (writing under her maiden name), as contributor of the "Woman's Page." Together, the two reported on the state of nudism in Canada, offered advice on its practice and club organization, and responded to readers' questions, some of which were published on the "Readers' Page." The magazine provided a forum for individuals and small, isolated groups from across Canada to exchange news and ideas, to organize, and to promote their philosophy to a wider public audience. During the interwar period, there had been rumoured nudist activity in locales ranging from Vancouver Island to Edmonton to Toronto, though little evidence remains of these. In his first *Sunbathing for Health* column, Connett put out a cross-Canada query: "Is there a nudist in the house?" At the time, the country had only two formal clubs, the Van Tans in BC and the Sun-Air-Freedom Lovers in Ontario.[27] But individual nudists, would-be nudists, and small, informal sunbathing groups of three or four also responded to

Connett. He began forwarding letters from prospective nudists to club organizers in their areas, and eventually club listings and contact information were published in the magazine. Over the years, club leaders such as Gaetan Couture from Montreal and Karl Ruehle contributed reports and articles on nudism, but Connett was the dominant voice of the movement in *Sunbathing for Health*. When it folded in 1959, he declared, "What there is of the Canadian nudist movement probably owes its existence to this magazine."[28] Though his claim is perhaps something of an overstatement, *Sunbathing for Health* certainly played an important role in the growth of Canadian nudism during the postwar years.

In the fall of 1947, less than a year after Connett's column debuted, he also participated in the creation of a national nudist body, the Canadian Sunbathing Association (CSA), in Vancouver. Those present at this gathering composed a constitution and elected an executive, including a president and national secretary. Connett was chosen as national secretary, a role he held for close to a decade. During this time, his advice was frequently sought by national and local nudist leaders (and was sometimes offered unsolicited). As a founding member of the Van Tan Club and the CSA, and as someone who had attended American and English clubs and conventions, he had a wide experience with the movement. The formation of the CSA signalled the development of a national nudist community. The association gathered annually, with conventions held in eastern or western Canada on an alternating basis. However, given the vast size of the country only a few members were able to attend any given convention. Thus, the community was largely maintained through correspondence. The CSA executive and club leaders exchanged letters updating one another on developments in their clubs and regions, and discussed ideas and concerns about the challenges of nudist organization in Canada.

One shared concern was the Criminal Code prohibition against public nudity. Section 205A made it a criminal offence to be nude in a public place or in a place visible to the public. This clause was a legacy of the federal response to the Sons of Freedom Doukhobors, who used public nudity to protest state authority and to express community dissent.[29] John McLaren explains that Section 205A was a 1931 amendment to the Criminal Code that resulted from pressure by the British Columbia and Saskatchewan governments, whose provinces were home to Doukhobor communities. It "effectively made public nudity a political crime" by increasing the maximum penalty from six months to three years of jail time.[30] Canadian nudists had no desire to challenge the law. In his *Sunbathing for Health* column, Ray Connett frequently outlined the Criminal Code provision on nudity and explained how clubs and individuals could ensure that they obeyed the law while practising nudism in the club setting and at home. He advised leaders to select secluded grounds for their clubs that were naturally screened from the view of neighbouring property, public roads, and waterways. At home, he suggested that nudists take care to pull their blinds and plant trees or build fences to shield their backyards from the eyes of neighbours. Stan Wortner, owner of the Ontario Sunny Glades club, noted that before establishing his club in 1959, he took the step of consulting a lawyer and visiting the local Ontario Provincial Police (OPP) detachment:

> I had a lawyer in Chatham go through the statutes to see what the Canadian law had to say about nudity in public or private, and uh, you know, its consequences. So he researched it. And there was nothing that said, there was a lot of things that said if you were an exhibitionist or in view from public property, then you could be charged, but not on private property. We also ... went around to see the, he was district inspector of the OPP headquarters for ... Essex and Kent County. Had an audience with him, told him who we were and what we were going to do. And he said, oh, he said, wouldn't have any problem from their side of the force. Thanked us for coming in, and gave us a word of advice. And his advice was, if you can get along with your neighbours you'll get along with us.[31]

Many clubs specifically mandated that their members respect the law. The Toronto Gymnosophical Society, for example, required them to "abide by the Laws of Canada, taking no risk of exposing themselves, while nude, to view from adjoining property or public places."[32] So long as CSA members were "properly engaged in private or group sunbathing," the association would provide legal aid and advice if they were arrested or prosecuted.[33]

Because they took such careful precautions, Canadian nudists rarely faced criminal charges. Their main concern, in this respect, was to distance themselves from the Doukhobors and the association of nudity with political dissent. Canadian nudism's emergence coincided with renewed Sons of Freedom activism in the late 1940s, including nude demonstrations, which culminated in the seizure of Doukhobor children by the British Columbia government in 1953.[34] Although the Sons of Freedom were a small religious group, their protests and the institutionalization of their children were widely reported across Canada. According to Ashleigh Androsoff, "*Time, Life, Newsweek, Maclean's,* and *Saturday Night* printed over 40 articles about Canadian Doukhobors during the 1940s, 1950s, and 1960s," and newspaper coverage was also extensive.[35] Members of the Canadian nudist movement objected to media characterization of Doukhobors as "nudists" and wished to rehabilitate the meaning of the term. A man who hoped to found a club in the Kootenays, where the Sons of Freedom were most numerous, informed CSA secretary Hazel McKague, "We will have to be very careful not to get any landowners against us as they will surely brand us as the Sons of Freedom."[36] This meant establishing an identity of who nudists were as well as who they were not. Mildred Harris declared, "Most of all we wish to be law abiding people who may enjoy the goodwill of the general public. We cannot expect tolerance if we flout the law like Doukhobors."[37] Nudists defined themselves as law abiding and respectful of Canadian institutions. They were not Doukhobors and did not espouse what that stood for in the public mind: politically dissident, exhibitionist, alien.[38]

The cultural context in which clubs operated varied across the country. The only criminal prosecution for club activity occurred in Montreal, then Canada's largest city, following a police raid on the Montreal Quetans Club in 1951. The Quetans had formed in the fall of 1948, after prospective members from the Montreal area were put in touch with one another via *Sunbathing for Health* and Ray Connett.[39] Lacking property, the group visited the Sun-Air-Freedom Lovers at their newly-acquired North Bay–area campground in the summer of 1949. In spring 1950, leader Gaetan Couture was happy to inform *Sunbathing for Health* readers that they had secured a property and begun developing it. Thirty-five adults and twenty children belonged to the club, and he expressed optimism that it would have as many as a hundred members by the end of the summer season.[40] But a police raid in July 1951 brought an abrupt end to its activities. Nine undercover officers conducted a covert operation, reportedly crawling through the grass of the seventy-acre property to reach the clearing where six club members were raking and cutting hay. Connett offered a dramatic interpretation of events for *Sunbathing for Health* readers based on the account he had received from Couture:

> As the ladies ran screaming to their tent to hide from the foul intruders, nine stalwart Provincial Police arose from the bushes, and bravely advanced

> upon the lone man who remained to face them. Gaetan Couture, leader of the Quetans, clutched a towel about his middle and challenged them. His only thought was that they must be reporters and cameramen from some scandal sheet. He shouted that they were trespassing on private property, that they had no right to be taking pictures, and that they should leave at once. Finally, after what seemed minutes, one flashed a badge that showed him to be a police officer.[41]

Couture was arrested on the charge of "promenading in the nude on his property in public view." He was convicted and sentenced to six months in prison; upon finding him guilty, Judge Oscar Gagnon offered the legal interpretation that a group of unrelated persons, such as those at the club, constituted "the public." He also made a point of noting that "this is a Catholic province, and here we observe certain beliefs and adhere to certain practices."[42] On appeal, Couture's conviction was quashed on a technicality: charges under Section 205A of the Criminal Code required prior approval of the attorney general, which had not been obtained.[43] Despite Couture's acquittal, Quebec nudist organization abruptly ceased in the wake of the incident, and for nearly twenty years afterward Quebec nudists travelled to Ontario and the United States rather than establishing new local clubs.[44] As a result, several clubs near the Quebec border drew a large number of members from Quebec during the fifties and sixties.[45] Clubs began to re-emerge in Quebec only in 1969, following significant political and cultural shifts.[46] Expressing concern for Couture and the implications for nudism in Quebec, CSA members established a defence fund to cover his legal costs. Despite the lower court conviction, nudists remained confident that club activities were legal and that unique factors were at play in Quebec.[47] In fact, Couture's trial remains Canada's only instance of criminal prosecution for nudist activity on private club property.

In Toronto, nudists faced different obstacles. Small groups had gathered there since the mid-1940s, but evidence suggests that the city's reputation as "Toronto the Good" and its enthusiastic policing of morality laws posed challenges. Nudist Doug Beckett recalled that *Sunbathing for Health* could not be sold in city limits: "It was published in Toronto, but ... you couldn't buy it in Toronto, but you could buy it in Thunder Bay and you could buy it in Barrie. You could buy it just about anywhere then, speaking [of] Canada, but Toronto."[48] For one early organizer, harassment by the Toronto tabloid *Flash* resulted in his loss of employment as an artist at *Maclean's* magazine.[49] The threatened exposure of other local nudists, high property values in the region, and internal club conflict stymied organization. After years of stops and starts, the Toronto Gymnosophical Society (TGS) formed in 1954 and found a home the following year when member couple Eddy and Mary Todorowsky purchased a hundred acres outside Newmarket, Ontario. Once established at this site, known as Glen Echo, TGS experienced rapid growth. By 1958, its records listed 134 members, and by 1971 it had expanded to more than 400.[50]

Unlike in Montreal and Toronto, the Maritan Club was well received in the small town of Bristol, New Brunswick. Its organizer, Marcus Meed, ran a machine shop, served as a church deacon, and was a respected member of his community, and when the Maritan grounds were not being used by the club they were occasionally used by local school groups.[51] The Maritans, however, remained small, and they existed only as long as Meed offered space and leadership to the group.

Despite shared objectives and concerns, the challenge of developing a nationally integrated movement in a country as vast and regionally diverse as Canada was great. The end of the 1950s proved to be a turning point. In 1959, losing money on the venture, Sinnott News ceased publication of *Sunbathing for Health,* and almost thirty years would elapse before another national nudist periodical was produced in Canada.

The following year, in another blow to national organizing, the CSA was dissolved and replaced by two bodies, the Western Canadian Sunbathing Association (WCSA) and the Eastern Canadian Sunbathing Association (ECSA). By this time, small clubs had been established on Vancouver Island, in the prairie cities of Edmonton, Calgary, Saskatoon, and Winnipeg, in Kingston and Ottawa, and in New Brunswick, but the BC Lower Mainland and southwestern Ontario were the clear hubs of Canadian nudism. They were two of Canada's most population-dense areas, they were the destination of most postwar European immigrants, and they subsequently had the largest pool of potential nudists from which to draw.[52] Furthermore, clubs tended to spring up in clusters, as members broke off to form new ventures of their own, either to serve an outlying area or because of dissatisfaction with the original club. During the postwar decade, two new clubs had branched off from North Vancouver's Van Tan Club: former members Ron and Stella Walker founded the Border Tans Club in Langley in 1948, and Ray and Mildred Connett spearheaded the establishment of the Sunny Trails Club in Surrey in 1952. In Ontario, Glen Echo outside Toronto and Sun

Valley Gardens in the Niagara region both opened in the mid-1950s; the latter gave rise to a number of clubs in the Golden Horseshoe, as noted above. The displacement of the CSA by the WCSA and the ECSA reflected the geographical gulf separating BC and Ontario nudists. It was also driven by a lack of organizational cohesion. The change was initiated by Ontario nudists, who disliked the bureaucracy, the membership fees, and the internal dissension of both the CSA and the American Sunbathing Association (ASA), with which it was affiliated. The split occurred at the 1959 eastern CSA convention, whose minutes record,

> It was stated that Club Members resent the rule of officials who do not represent their Clubs, and who have been elected or appointed by Conventions which only a fraction of the Membership can attend. It was stated that CSA had been spoiled by squabbling and by publication of squabbling. A feeling was expressed that trouble results from appointing or electing people to mind other people's business; that Clubs should run their own business, and be represented in all business concerning them.[53]

However, the new organizations were no more successful than their national predecessor at avoiding infighting or negotiating a structure that would satisfy the various member clubs, and they would play a largely inconsequential part in growing the Canadian movement.

Finally, a third significant change occurred around this time: Ray and Mildred Connett left their jobs and home in the Vancouver area and travelled around Canada and the United States before settling in California, where they founded the Glen Eden Sun Club in 1963. Although they maintained ties with the Canadian movement, their relocation south of the border brought an end to an era, as the pair no longer played the integral leadership and promotional roles that they had held within the Canadian movement through the forties and fifties.[54]

### Nudism at the Local Level

The most significant form of nudist community before and after 1960 was the local club. Regional, national, and international organizations were loose affiliations of independent clubs that cooperated in promoting the philosophy and agreed to uphold a shared standard of behaviour. But the clubs acted as gatekeepers – determining who was, and was not, granted entry –

and they played the most prominent part in shaping people's experiences of nudism. They also proved most active in attracting new members. During the 1950s, Sunny Trails and Sun Valley Gardens undertook particularly bold promotional campaigns. Ray Connett had left the Van Tan Club in part because he wished to advertise nudism more openly than some of his fellow Van Tans. At Sunny Trails, he played a leading role in promoting an attitude of openness and transparency to public scrutiny. Connett believed that secrecy implied shame, the very thing nudists claimed to reject. He therefore encouraged clubs to cultivate respectful and open relationships with local officials and the community. He also suggested that club leaders build connections with the media by issuing press releases and inviting journalists to attend their major events. At its official opening in July 1953, Sunny Trails hosted its first annual open house. It was attended by 250 members of the public and 125 nudists, whose numbers were bolstered by visitors from nearby Canadian and American clubs.[55] The nudists wore clothes for the occasion. However, the following day an invited group of clergy and municipal leaders toured the camp while its members went nude. Both events were widely reported in local media and nationally broadcast on CBC Radio. The shift from concern over privacy and anonymity to more open public relations parallels the changing strategy of American gay and lesbian organizations in the 1950s, something that historian Martin Meeker sees as indicative of a changing cultural climate.[56]

In Ontario, Karl Ruehle took inspiration from Connett's methods, launching an extensive publicity drive of his own in the Hamilton area. Like Connett, he issued press releases and gave interviews with local media. Sun Valley Gardens staged its first open house in 1956, and the club held its largest public relations event when it hosted Canada's first nude open house in May 1959. Before being granted admission, guests signed a declaration that "at no time and in no way will we object to – or feel offended by – the nudity and activities of the people whom we see or meet."[57] Two years later, in a televised interview with June Callwood that aired on *Close Up,* a CBC prime time current affairs program, the Ruehles outlined the reasoning behind hosting the event. Marlies Ruehle told Callwood that at the original open houses,

> we admitted the general public and we found lots of just fellows coming in and it wasn't the kind of material we wanted for members, so we thought we could try it out and be in the nude as we really are because some people

> asked, well why did you get dressed when we come? Do you do something that we don't see, you know? ... So we figured if we admit couples only and have them sign a statement that they won't be offended we'd give it a try. And we did last year for the first time and it has been a tremendous success ... Over a thousand people signed in. And most of them were so much interested when they came that a big percentage joined within the course of that summer.[58]

The Ruehles reported that more than ninety people joined Sun Valley Gardens as a result of its first nude open house.[59] This time, Sunny Trails followed Sun Valley Gardens' lead and held its own nude open house a few months later, in the summer of 1959. Whereas the original clothed open houses had drawn hundreds of visitors, the first nude open houses reportedly attracted thousands.[60] These events were designed to fulfill a dual purpose: to serve as a membership drive and to cultivate a good public image for the movement. The March 1960 Sun Valley Gardens newsletter noted, "We would be fools not to repeat Nude Open House, and we hope that more and more clubs take up this idea for the good of gaining new members and to demonstrate how clean and natural it is to be nude for recreational purposes."[61] Nudists wanted to win the acceptance of mainstream society, and they hoped that opening their grounds to public view would provide reassurance that they were ordinary, respectable people.

At the same time, clubs sought to balance publicity campaigns with the protection of members' privacy. Nudists combined their club involvement with jobs, family responsibilities, and other social activities. In many cases, their extended family, friends, co-workers, and neighbours were unaware of their nudist affiliation. Fear of social censure or loss of employment were motives for keeping their membership under wraps. For every nudist like Ray Connett or Karl Ruehle there were many more who were less forthcoming about how they passed their leisure time. Sunny Glades owner Stan Wortner observed,

> I had some couples, some people from the United States, driving great big Cadillacs and things like that, and they'd park their car and cover their license plates. That's one of the things that you kind of wonder whether their positions were in jeopardy. But we had some people here too that wanted anonymity, just absolutely total anonymity. And I think it's still, there's still a twinge of that here ... They may live in Chatham,

and they'll go to the Four Seasons, the United States someplace, down in Florida, and they never come here. Simply because they're either business people, or it's too close to home, and what if somebody sees them who knows them?[62]

Club protocol was to use first names only, and discussion about places of employment was discouraged to protect members' identities, even from each other. Some clubs even kept their location private. In 1958, two families who were TGS members caused consternation to Peterborough's Sunny Brae Ranch when they sought directions to the property from the Peterborough Chamber of Commerce and local and provincial police, unaware that its location was not public knowledge. After learning of the incident, the TGS secretary apologized on their behalf: "I think there are very few among us who do not realize the discretion which has to be observed in Nudist matters in Canada. Certainly the strictness of our own enrolment procedure and other rules would demonstrate this to all."[63] Within the club context, nudists substituted their private location and the confidentiality of membership for the privacy of clothing.

Sensitive to the countercultural aspects of their movement, they took great pains to stress that they were not socially deviant. In her 1961 interview with the Ruehles, Callwood gave them the opportunity to correct this perception. She remarked, "You are regarded in many places as uh, people practicing some strange kind of cult, or that, perhaps there is a great many orgies, or strange behaviour goes on in nudist camps. How do you answer this sort of charge?" Karl replied, "That's all in the mind of those people. If these people would go and find out for themselves they would find out very soon it's so different. People who come for open houses also, they see it really different and they go home with a different idea."[64] In his club newsletter, he also informed prospective Sun Valley Gardens members that "you will find that we are just average and normal people, but claim that we have overcome the complex of false shame by accepting nudity as the natural state of our body and nothing else."[65] The Silva Sun Club presented a similar explanation to potential members, describing a nudist park as "very similar to a country club or public resort, offering swimming and recreational facilities of all descriptions. The main difference is that clothing is not required."[66] Nudists believed that if they could "cease to be strange" in the public imagination, they would make great progress toward widespread acceptance. Connett's advice to them was "Be ordinary! People resent outsiders because they are *different.*"[67] Interviewed just prior to the first open house at Sunny Trails, Connett declared, "We're ready to show people that after all there was nothing to be afraid of and that we're really very ordinary people. In fact, when they come down Saturday night, they'll have a hard time deciding who are nudists and who aren't, because of course we'll be wearing clothes also."[68] Lisa Stein told a CBC Radio reporter that she was won over on her first visit to a nudist club when she found that "the people were very nice, they were my kind of people, they weren't dirty old men or dirty old women, they were just ordinary people, like my neighbours."[69]

Although the movement stressed the ordinariness of its members, its difference appealed to some. One *Sunbathing for Health* contributor extolled the joy of finding freedom from the "struggle for survival" and the conventional "narrow-minded outlook."[70] Connett too noted that the clubs possessed "a spirit of gaiety generated by taking part in something which is a little unusual."[71] In the midst of modern life, these individuals found nudism to be a refreshing respite and a source of a distinctive identity and community.

NUDISM FOUND A FOOTHOLD in Canada in the years following the Second World War, spurred on by the promotional activity of Ray Connett, Karl Ruehle, and the pool of leaders and members who emigrated from Europe. A national magazine, *Sunbathing for Health,* and a national organization, the Canadian Sunbathing Association, facilitated its growth through the 1950s. By the end of 1960, both no longer existed, reflecting the challenges of organizational unity in such a large country. Nevertheless, local clubs took the reins, some pursuing innovative public relations campaigns while others were content with slower growth. Local clubs acted as gatekeepers and offered varied experiences of nudism at camp sites across the country.

# 2

# Constructing Community at the Club

When one enters a nudist club he sheds not only his clothes but also the sham, the conceit and the pretence that they typify. He is wholly himself, not what the clothes he can afford make him ... When a nudist sheds his unnatural garb, he is his own natural self.

– Hilliard Macdonald, "Naturism – A World Need"

As in every fraternal movement there is the magic spark of hospitality and friendship wherever you go – once you're in. But because we have such a radical new idea, this clothesless life, we must be so very careful who gets in.

– Ray Connett, Sunny Trails

Nudism developed as a philosophy, a lifestyle, and a social movement. Its clubs served a practical function – the pooling of resources and the development of shared facilities for sunbathing and recreation – but more importantly, they provided space to practise nudism in a social setting. Solitary nudism was hardly nudism at all; seeing the bodies of others and being seen by them in return was essential. Nudists critiqued clothing as a barrier to human interaction and believed that their movement encouraged closer social relations. As Hilliard Macdonald's comment above suggests, they perceived clothing as a literal and figurative cover, masking both the body and the "natural self." Removing clothing in social situations enabled people to interact on a deeper, less superficial level. Whereas mainstream society viewed public nudity in a negative light – as exhibitionist – nudists turned the tables and cast clothing as the negative, as masking or concealing, ultimately redefining nudity as an act of truth and self-revelation. No longer could one hide behind clothing and the identity assumed through it. Despite the suggestion of many Canadians that nudity would be distracting in social interactions, nudists argued that it enabled them to focus on character rather than appearance.

And yet, as Connett's remark above indicates, forming clubs and recruiting members were not straightforward undertakings. This was especially true given nudism's position on the margins of society. Its Canadian pioneers concentrated on growing the movement and fashioning its public image. The two were linked, as clubs attempted to attract members who would reflect well on the movement as a whole. Throughout the postwar period, winning social approval was their overriding concern, one that lay at the centre of their policies and practices. Through club operations, particularly admission and behavioural standards, nudists articulated self-perceptions of who or what they were, but just as importantly, of who or what they were not. This chapter explores themes of inclusion and exclusion as they developed in the clubs. How did clubs attract and screen new members? How did nudism challenge or reinforce social divisions of race, class, gender, and sexuality? And how did this all align with its claim to break down social barriers and promote more open human relationships? In their clubs, nudists juggled competing priorities: the philosophical imperative to be inclusive and to extend the movement's benefits to as many as possible, the aspiration to earn mainstream acceptance, and the desire to socialize with like-minded people in an intimate setting. Most clubs continually sought new members – to grow the movement, to compensate for membership losses, and to provide greater revenue for the development of facilities – but they were selective. Each one established a screening process to assess applicant suitability, and this was more than a mere formality: many clubs reported that their membership figures could be much higher if they were less discriminating. Philosophically, they presented their movement as "democratic," "tolerant," and socially inclusive, judging people only on "moral" fitness. But their concern to protect their limited rights, the desire to gain social approval, and the more basic interest in admitting only compatible individuals meant that identities of race, class, gender, and sexuality emerged as factors in determining moral suitability.

This chapter approaches the movement in terms of community. John Walsh and Steven High highlight three components of this concept: "community as imagined reality, community as social interaction, and community as process."[1] These permeate my discussion as I consider the identity that nudists articulated, the social dynamics of their clubs, and the boundaries they constructed.

## The Ideology of Inclusivity

Nudists believed that "you are more open when you are naked," that shedding their clothes enabled them to shed social pretense and accept people for their true selves. A *Sunbathing for Health* contributor declared, "Artificiality is discarded with the clothes, and people are real and genuine."[2] Interviewed on the CBC Radio program *Assignment* in 1962, Calgary Sunny Chinooks Club member Betty told interviewer Fred Skelton, "Well in a nudist camp people talk to the face and, if a person happens to have a scar, a bit overweight, something like this, it's not noticed, because we take a person, first of all we judge them by their character ... The way they're accepted in camp is the most important thing." As a result, Betty suggested that relationships at the club were closer and more lasting than those outside of it. She concluded, "Nudist friends are your truest friends – I believe there's a companionship, a very definite bond."[3] In a similar vein, a teenaged member of the Sunny Trails Club told a reporter that one of her favourite aspects of belonging to it was "the good sociability in the club, and the friends – they're real friends, they're not like some others."[4]

Related to the idea that nudists discarded social pretense with their clothes and accepted people for their true selves was the claim of social inclusivity. As Karl Ruehle informed potential recruits, "We are interested in all kinds of people of all professions, races, faiths and shapes and sizes. In all these things nudists may differ, but one thing they have in common is the belief that a clean and healthy mind can live and grow best in a clean and healthy body."[5] Canadian nudists did not employ the eugenic discourse decrying physical degeneration and encouraging racial fitness that some European nudist organizations had espoused before the Second World War, and their club brochures and newsletters often presented their membership as diverse. In its letter of introduction to potential members, the Ottawa Silva Sun

Club noted, "Our membership is drawn from most walks of life and of all ages, shapes and sizes. We make no test of race, religion or politics. We simply require a good moral character and an ability to get along with other people."[6] In fact, it was a principle of the Canadian and American Sunbathing Associations that the clubs not discriminate on the basis of "race, colour, or creed," and the constitutions of many Canadian clubs reaffirmed this policy and expressed the desire that nudism "be representative of the whole social order."[7]

In the interests of inclusion and group harmony, clubs discouraged the discussion of religion and politics. When religion was mentioned, however, there was frequently the presumption that members, or prospective members, subscribed to at least a nominal Christian faith. Over the years, several articles in *Sunbathing for Health* addressed the subject of nudism's compatibility with Christianity, and it was also raised in letters published on the "Readers' Page." Nudist promoters highlighted the presence of practising Christians of all stripes – Protestant and Catholic – among their members, and *Sunbathing for Health* columnist Mildred Harris identified herself as a "devout Anglican."[8] Christian ministers were often invited to attend open house events, along with municipal councillors, members of women's organizations, and school trustees – groups whose approval was especially valued. Canadian clubs rarely held religious services on their grounds, in contrast to the United States, where it was not uncommon for clubs to offer Sunday morning services so that members need not choose between practising nudism and practising their faith. Yet the compatibility of nudism with any religion besides Christianity was never raised in Canadian nudist sources.

The subject of race was also rarely broached, and when it was, it was often in a circumspect manner. Interviewed on CBC Radio in 1960, Peggy Parkes, then serving as national secretary of the CSA, characterized the movement as a "very United Nations effort," declaring, "we have members of all faiths and creeds and races."[9] What Parkes did not make entirely clear was whether this observation applied to Canada or the international movement as a whole. Betty of the Sunny Chinooks generalized in a similar way when asked by a reporter whether nudists were all "one colour." She responded, "We have no discrimination along that line. Uh, Orientals, Negroes, uh, every nationality is a part of nudism."[10] However, the findings of two Yale University students who conducted a sociological study of five southern California nudist clubs in the summer of 1961 painted a different picture. They observed hardly any visible minorities, despite the ASA's inclusive principle. In their entire summer of research, they encountered one Mexican American family and one single man, as well as two teenagers "of Oriental descent."[11]

In 1954, Connett wrote disapprovingly in his "Sunny Trails" column of racial discrimination, noting that the admission of two Black men had split a Seattle-area club. He also took issue with remarks made by an American nudist leader at the 1954 convention of the Northwest Sunbathing Association, who advised that clubs take care to avoid the charge of racial discrimination, not by accepting Black members but by steering clear of announcing that Black applicants had been rejected on the basis of their colour. Connett regretted the divisiveness "the race problem" had caused in the American movement, calling it "a sad day when nudists who need tolerance themselves should be so guilty of intolerance." He tempered his criticism, however: "We Canadians do not understand some of the thoughts and feelings of our cousins south of the border ... Some of my best friends have very strong feelings on the subject, and the Seattle Club lost a number of good solid couples, some original founders of the club, over this matter."[12] His comments suggest that Connett saw race as a relative non-issue at Canadian clubs. They serve as an example of what legal historian Constance Backhouse labels "the ideology of Canada as a 'raceless' nation," displaying a naïveté about the realities of racial discrimination in Canadian society.[13] Connett authored this column while living in Greater Vancouver, a region with a long history of Chinese, Japanese, and Indian immigration, and where less than a decade earlier more than twenty thousand Japanese Canadians had been forcibly relocated to internment camps and had their property seized. Connett's remarks may also be interpreted as an indication that very few non-white Canadians expressed an interest in nudism, allowing the clubs to avoid confronting the issue head on and facilitating the illusion that Canada was a racially harmonious country. A photo published in *Sunbathing for Health* shows that visible minorities were admitted to at least one club (Figure 2.1). Under a shot of four children who appear to be of South Asian descent enjoying themselves at a creek, the accompanying caption read, "Sunshine and a happy outdoor life are shared by all nudists, regardless of race, colour or creed. Members of Sunny Trails find this coloured family to be very desirable members."[14] But the language also suggests that their presence was a novelty rather than a commonplace occurrence.

Canadian nudists spoke most often about inclusivity in terms of class rather than ethnicity. To convey the message that all social classes were

**Figure 2.1** Nudist children at the Sunny Trails Club in Surrey, British Columbia | *Sunbathing for Health*, January 1958, courtesy of Naturist Education Foundation Research Library

welcome, they liked to offer examples of various occupations held by their members. The New Brunswick Maritan Club reportedly included a "Civil Servant, Cook, Police Officer, School Teacher, Laborer, Public Accountant, Housewife, Packing Plant Foreman, Machine Shop Manager, Proof-reader on a large Daily, Professional Musician, Members of the Army, Navy and Air Force, Poultry Farmer and Postal Employee, to list a few."[15] A member of the Calgary Sunny Chinooks told a reporter, "There are mechanics, there are postmen, there are doctors, there are salesmen. Take your pick, somebody is represented."[16] The Sun Valley Gardens newsletter explained, "By being nude all people are equals. No matter whether you are a doctor, a scientist or just a plain labourer. What counts is the way one behaves, not what one claims to be."[17] The philosophical underpinnings were nicely spelled out by Ron and Stella Walker, who owned the Border Tans: "Money and social standing are not necessary qualifications. We have no objections to patched clothes and apple-box chairs. We do insist that the clothes and apple-box are neat and clean."[18]

In a November 1955 letter to a Montreal man who hoped to establish a club, Connett professed his belief that "the foundation of nudism in this country rests on the working class and middle class peoples."[19] Although privacy concerns at the time mean that surviving records including personal information on rank-and-file members are limited, judging by the occupations of club leaders Canadian nudism did have a strong working-class presence. Ray Connett was a sorting clerk for Canada Post, and his wife, Mildred, worked in retail. Gerald Eaton, who served a term as CSA president in the early 1950s, was a ferry deckhand. Another one-time CSA president and leader of the Maritans, Marcus Meed, owned a machine shop, and Lakesun owner Hans Behrmann worked in a Kingston department store. Hans Stein, who started the Ponderosa Nature Resort with his wife, sister, and brother-in-law, eight years after immigrating from Germany, noted, "three of us, we all worked night shifts in Hamilton – in the Steel Company, United Gas, Otis Elevator, and so on – we all did night shifts" while building their club from the ground up by day.[20]

This strong working-class involvement deviates from statistics on American club composition. Various sociological studies undertaken in the 1950s and 1960s found that American nudists were more highly educated and better paid than the average American, and they depicted most of them as middle and upper-middle class.[21] Researchers Ilfeld and Lauer attributed this to the prohibitive cost of membership for the working class, but Donald Johnson suggested another reason: "that persons of limited education are more likely to stick to fixed opinions, lacking the broadened viewpoint which education achieves."[22] This echoed Alfred Kinsey's observation in his influential 1948 study, *Sexual Behavior in the Human Male,* that nudity was more taboo among people with lower educational levels.[23]

Clearly, this was not true for the working-class leadership of the CSA. Though fees and the virtual necessity of possessing a car to travel to a club were real financial barriers, making membership affordable was a priority of many clubs during the early years. Montreal Quetans organizer Gaetan Couture bluntly noted that its dues "are generally quite low and well within the means of all but the poorest."[24] Harris also emphasized the affordability of nudism, promoting the clubs as "so much cheaper than going to expensive resorts where the kids want hot dogs or chips or ice cream every time you turn around."[25] Long-time nudist Doug Beckett explained that in 1958 "there was very little camping equipment because before the war camping just wasn't done." Describing the early years of Canadian nudism, Beckett stated, "There was less worry about conveniences. Nudism was much more simple ... Our accommodation was tents, and uh, some of the Germans were amusing, because the German style at that time was how long can you have a holiday in the outback with the minimum of equipment that you can carry in one trip."[26] In addition, the early clubs were often co-operative: members contributed their labour so that recreational facilities could be constructed at a reasonable price. Ray Connett commended nudist clubs to people "of middle-class or lower income bracket," suggesting "it makes a regular holiday camp but it's all provided ... through the efforts of our own members."[27] Over time, many clubs began charging higher fees in exchange for providing and maintaining amenities such as pools, clubhouses, and lodging, but rising wages and the improved standard of living during the postwar period meant that membership remained financially accessible to a large percentage of Canadians, comparable to the cost of spending summer holidays camping or road-tripping.

In depicting their inclusivity, nudists revealed a naive understanding of the relationship between dress and social class. As a possible response to the question, "What, exactly, is a nudist?" one club newsletter suggested the following:

> We are factory workers, business executives, secretaries, ministers, and policemen. We're simply a slice of society. When we take off our clothing, we also take off any phony postures and status symbols of the everyday world. Without adornment, the wife of a clerk is the social equal of a corporation president, and many people find this the most rewarding part of nudism.[28]

Clothing was treated as synonymous with class, and class with clothing. This was aptly illustrated in a *Sunbathing for Health* article entitled "A Glance at Nudism." Declaring nudism to be "the most democratic institution in the world," the writer explained, "It is impossible for a social barrier to exist between unclothed persons. If a laborer does not look any worse than a duke (and most laborers have a better physique than dukes) all social barriers melt away. Nudism gathers its members from all classes."[29] Nudists presented the simple step of doffing their clothes as the solution to class division.

## Membership Screening

Despite the simplistic equation of class and clothing that they espoused, nudists were much more sophisticated when it came to evaluating their membership applicants. Sociologist Erving Goffman's ideas about "the presentation of the self" provide a useful point of departure here. Goffman argued that "everyone is always and everywhere, more or less consciously, playing a role ... It is in these roles that we know each other; it is in these roles that we know ourselves." He identified a significant aspect of this performance as one's "front," which could be comprised of "insignia of office or rank; clothing; sex, age, and racial characteristics; size and looks; posture; speech patterns; facial expressions; bodily gestures; and the like."[30] The nudist philosophy focused on clothes as a person's main "front" or cover, from which derived the belief that the shedding of clothing led to the shedding of pretense. And yet the screening process employed by clubs relied on a much more comprehensive assessment of applicants, with attention to numerous outward forms of self-presentation, as highlighted by Goffman.

The standard procedure for individuals who were interested in joining a club was for them to write a letter of introduction to the owner or membership committee. In his *Sunbathing for Health* column, Ray Connett offered tips on how best to go about this. Applicants should inform themselves about nudism and should provide as much detail as possible about themselves, such as "your marital status, your ideas on nudism and life in general. Only thus can one form an opinion of a prospective correspondent and friend."[31] Connett warned his readers,

> Nothing will hurt you more in your first letter than poor handwriting and bad grammar. I do not mean that a person with poor education cannot join a nudist club ... But I must be honest and say that, since almost all applications are first received and considered by mail, the chances of an uneducated person being accepted are less than those of a person who can write clearly and legibly, and whose letters read fluently and easily, as if he were talking ... Appearance in your letters is as important as appearance in your dress.

For those who could not write an effective letter, Connett suggested hiring a stenographer. He reflected, "This would be cheating so to speak, but at least if I could persuade a group leader to meet me, he would then have the opportunity of judging me face to face on my physical appearance, my manner and my speech, which might be considerably better than my letters."[32]

If the letter proved sufficiently impressive, the next step was to arrange an interview with the applicant. This step in the screening process was intended to enable a first-hand assessment of applicants and their motivation for joining, as well as to answer their questions about nudism generally or the club in particular. Unmarried men were usually interviewed by a male club member and couples and single females by a member couple. The interviewers decided whether the applicants would be invited to visit the club on a trial basis, which in most cases would lead to acceptance into membership. Interviews were conducted in a clothed state, preferably in the homes of applicants, as this provided additional insight into their character and social standing. The 1964 by-laws of the Toronto Gymnosophical Society outlined the thinking: "The interview should be at the applicant's residence if at all possible, because the way their place is kept is one of the best guides to their character and habits."[33]

Connett counselled *Sunbathing for Health* readers on how to prepare for the interview and alerted them to the factors that might influence the final decision:

> Naturally you will give careful attention to your appearance, cleanliness, and tidiness in your clothes. There is no need to be a fashion plate, in fact this could prejudice one against you. But your clothes must be neat and clean, you must be shaven, and your body must give an appearance of cleanliness, and betray no odour, which would reveal you as careless of body cleanliness. If you are a married couple or a family, you are almost sure to be accepted in most clubs, unless your surroundings are impossible. If you have children it is to be hoped their manners will stand you in good stead. That is a matter of training, and will reveal much about you.[34]

In contrast to the philosophical aim of nudism – enabling people to look beyond the surface to the "natural self" – the screening process focused on external markers such as appearance, clothing, physical and domestic cleanliness, and the conduct of children as signs of moral suitability. In essence, before stripping away the barrier of clothing, nudists erected a new barrier: the screening process itself. The privilege of joining a club was premised on the successful navigation of this hurdle. Years after joining Glen Echo, Eric Jarvis recalled, "Before you were allowed to be a member you were interviewed in your own home. So we were interviewed by a couple, and I guess they found we were happily married, we had a child, and we had some experience of nudism, and so were accepted and we were able to go and we joined."[35] Only after a successful interview were applicants permitted to visit the club, shed their clothes, and participate in the inclusive, classless setting that it purportedly provided.

Those who faced the most discrimination in the screening process were unmarried men. Throughout the postwar period, clubs grappled with "the problem of the single male." In point of fact, many more men than women inquired about membership, including unmarried men and those who wished to join without their wives. Connett once estimated that half of the letters inquiring about membership came from single men, and of those who pursued the application process there were approximately eight men for every couple or family.[36] According to Brian Hoffman, a historian of American nudism, this sprang from the fact that wartime nudist magazines had used suggestive images and content to increase their readership, and veterans who had purchased them began pursuing club membership after returning home.[37] Nudists themselves offered other explanations, mostly pointing to the differing ways in which men and women were socialized, a topic discussed at greater length in Chapter 4.

The concern for most clubs was to prevent their membership from becoming overwhelmingly male; this, they feared, would scare off the female members and deter couples and families from joining. In 1950, Gaetan Couture informed *Sunbathing for Health* readers that at the request of its married couples, his club would no longer accept single men. As he reported, when "the Quetans resolved that they would no longer accept unaccompanied single men, either as members or as visitors, several married couples immediately joined us."[38] Many clubs accepted men only if they had a female companion, whether that be a spouse, girlfriend, sister, or friend. Over time, however, most introduced a gender ratio for new members, such as admitting five men for every three women. Nevertheless, they continually grappled with how many men to accept independent of women and how to assess their suitability for membership.

In an early edition of his "Sunny Trails" column, Connett explained that clubs were likely to prefer a young single man to a husband who hoped to join without his wife. When considering an application from an unmarried man, Connett wrote, club leaders "see the added work and enthusiasm the single man will put into the club, and they assume that in a year or two he will probably bring into the club a girl of his choice, worthy of being a nudist wife and mother." In contrast,

> In the case of the married man seeking admittance without his wife, no such vision can be conjured up ... The club would not want a member who would neglect his family, home and garden for nudism. He may offer the promise of later bringing his wife and children with him but in the face of obvious risks involved most clubs prefer to pass up this hope.[39]

The single men who aroused the least suspicion were those who were judged most capable of finding a girlfriend and wife. According to Connett, "It usually amounts to this; the youngest, most intelligent looking, personable fellows are chosen."[40] During the 1960s, Sun Valley Gardens accepted single men "of good character" but did not renew their membership if they failed "to win a female partner within reasonable time."[41] The spectre of homosexuality was unacknowledged but loomed large over such attitudes. A man who lacked a significant attachment to a woman was subject to suspicion. In other words, he had the difficult task of convincing club leadership that despite his unmarried state, he was both desirous and capable of forming a romantic heterosexual relationship, as a testament to his respectability and suitability for membership.

Nudists took care to avoid bad publicity by rejecting anyone who might bring scandal. This was a major factor in their exclusion of homosexuals or those suspected of being homosexual. In 1948, Toronto organizer Reg Nicholls interviewed a single male applicant, forming the impression that he was "rather a fine looking man and seemed to be the type we are looking for." But during their meeting, the man inquired about the possibility of bringing homosexual friends to visit the club and asked about its attitude toward them. Nicholls recounted his response in a letter to Connett. Initially, he seemed inclined to give the applicant the benefit of the doubt: "At first I wondered if [his] tolerance might be due to reading that widely circulated review on the Kinsey Report, but he said he hadn't read it." Subsequently, "I told him that such characters are DEFINITELY NOT acceptable ... There is no definite evidence that he engages in these practices, but I think you will agree that there would be too great a risk in accepting him."[42]

Many more single men who asked about joining a club were not offered so much as an interview, let alone membership. As well as reflecting concerns about the public perception of the movement, this exclusion was grounded in the comfort level of club members. Connett sent mixed messages about whether men or women were most threatened by the presence of single men at the club. In 1948, he suggested that "old bachelors" made female members uncomfortable:

> Possibly they resent the independence of a man who has learned to live without a woman in his life, or scorn the inadequacy of the man who is not able to win a wife or sweetheart. I don't know, I can only guess. Perhaps they fear for the safety of their children, and they seem to object to the curiosity of middle-aged singles. I think this is pure imagination because I can't recall ever seeing anyone *stare* at women in a nudist club ... But there it is, that feeling in the ladies of being "looked at." Right or wrong, if she feels that way about it you can bet she and her husband will vote against middle-aged singles.[43]

But in a 1952 column, he changed his tune about single male applicants:

> The women do not object to their presence. Confidentially, the only people who do object are men, and I am ashamed to tell you why, for I am ashamed to admit that some men who are, or claim to be, bona-fide nudists, are still burdened with shame complexes, curiosity phobias, etc., which make them suspect others of their sex of having improper attitudes.[44]

Connett left to his readers' imaginations what these "improper attitudes" might be and whether the men who objected were concerned for themselves, their wives, or children. Karl Ruehle was more forthcoming in a 1962 club newsletter, attributing the discrimination to male members who did not wish their wives to be seen in the nude by other men without exchanging the same privilege. He defended Sun Valley Gardens' relatively high proportion of single male members:

> Some married men object to them because THEY LOOK AT THEIR WOMEN. We say: be glad that someone finds your wife attractive enough to look at her, and after all a real nudist does not mind by whom he or she is seen, because to a real nudist the entire body is pure and wholesome. Because a fellow is single does not mean that he is immoral, nor does a married fellow automatically become a saint.[45]

Nudists boasted about the stringency of their screening process and expressed confidence in their ability to judge applicants. Gaetan Couture of the Montreal Quetans advised single women who wished to meet "real gentlemen" to join a club, bragging, "Even in your church organizations, men are not put through such strict and searching tests before being accepted for membership!"[46] Asked by a CBC Radio interviewer whether "there is any chance or possibility of any lady member being bothered by a stranger in a nudist camp," Betty of the Calgary Sunny Chinooks responded categorically: "Certainly not in any camp. Our standards are the highest, and we will only take people and families of the very highest calibre."[47] Fellow club member Fred expressed equal assurance that the screening process enabled the club to accurately assess character. Asked about "how deep the screening process go[es]" and how a club determines "what type of person" an applicant is, Fred conceded, "This is a difficult thing to do." But, he continued,

> We have been very fortunate so far in that we have, we have not made a wrong selection. Uh, it's pretty easy to tell by a person's home life and family life and whatnot, as to just what type of an individual he is. And in most cases, as I say 100% of the cases so far, we have not been wrong.[48]

Likewise, the secretary of the Toronto Sunglades boasted, "Our screening policy is so strict that no undesirable elements can possibly enter."[49] Passing the screening process and gaining admittance to a club signalled to other members that the membership committee had certified an individual's suitability. In fact, closeness of community arguably owed at least as much to the screening process as it did to the shedding of clothes. Connett suggested as much: "Nudists are, as a general rule, friendlier than non-nudists. Membership in any nudist club is only granted after careful investigation and screening so members feel safer and have greater trust in others they meet at a club than they could with any person met, for instance, at a dance or on a public beach."[50]

## Protecting the Reputation of the Movement

The screening process was partially driven by the concern to protect the social reputation of the movement. Once admitted, members in a sense became its ambassadors. In 1947, Connett wrote that "nudism is a reform movement. Just as surely as the Salvation Army or the W.C.T.U. it insists on clean living, clean thinking, decency and morality. Outsiders judge its worth by the conduct of its members. Will you help or hinder nudism in your district?"[51] In his column two years later, he voiced a similar refrain:

> Our movement is yet so young and poorly organized. We are like the early adherents of any movement feeling our way cautiously lest we upset a hornet's nest of opposition which might set our progress back a century or so. Still we are not silent. We have our nudist magazines, we have our associations; we have printed pamphlets to give to prospects. We have our local clubs whose members, like the early Christian congregations, each carry on the missionary work of the movement, converting friends and relatives by example and by argument till the circle widens.[52]

The marginal social status of the movement thus lent a great deal of import to the screening of applicants. Interviewers considered whether prospective members would reflect positively on nudism and their fellow nudists.

As far as Connett and most club leaders were concerned, erring on the side of exclusion was better than risking scandal. In 1949, Gaetan Couture wrote,

> We must be very careful as to the type of persons who are admitted to membership in our groups, in order to avoid any possibilities of misconduct and therefore, of scandal. One single scandal could very well lay to waste all the good work that has been done during the last few years by our group leaders and our earnest pioneers: the C.S.A. officers. Consequently, it is much better for a group to remain small and without blemish, than to grow too quickly and run the risk of a scandal being caused by some members who were admitted just for the sake of trying to make the group larger and apparently stronger ... If we [Quetans] had admitted to our membership all those who applied for it, we would have reached well over 100 members ... As it is, the Quetans have only 34 members so far, but these have been carefully screened and we are quite certain that none of them will ever cause a scandal. If a nudist scandal occurred in the province of Quebec, it would probably set back the nudist movement in this province by about 10 years, and perhaps more.[53]

Couture's words proved prophetic: as discussed in the previous chapter, when Couture himself was arrested two years later organized nudism halted in Quebec for almost two decades.

In the early 1950s, the Toronto Sunglades Club developed a reputation for the exclusive attitude of its members. Boasting that the Sunglades screening policy "has given us the best results, not in quantity, but in quality," its secretary, Albert, explained its approach:

> We are very careful with the applications from the declining districts of Toronto, and particularly the downtown section, firstly, because the living quarters located there consist to a large part of slums, and secondly, because the majority of its population is communistic ... We have a pretty good reputation right now, not with regard to wealth of members, but with regard to moral, intellectual and educational standard, and we do not want to lose this reputation just by admitting a few undesirable characters.[54]

Despite Albert's assertion that screening was not based on wealth, his reference to the declining slum districts of downtown and his concern about communistic groups read as coded references to Eastern European immigrants in the city. It suggests that the Sunglades did take class and ethnicity into account as they assessed applications, hoping to establish a particular image for their group and to associate only with people who shared their social and ethnic background. Although Albert's attitude sparked controversy and elicited opposition from Canadian nudists, it conveyed just how a preoccupation with reputation could lead to exclusionary screening policies. Aware of the controversy, Sunglades leader Reg Nicholls wrote to reassure Connett that not all members shared Albert's discriminatory views: "DON'T PAY TOO MUCH ATTENTION TO ALBERT – we are frequently amazed at the things he does – and writes. Sometimes I'm on edge wondering what he'll write next!" He declared, "As far as I know, *only one couple* has indicated disapproval of Jews, Chinese & coloureds." But he followed this up with a candid reflection of his own: "Personally, I wouldn't care to see Sunglades *overwhelmingly* of any of these races or types because it would inevitably affect the club's growth ('for the greatest good'). Does that make me prejudiced?"[55]

The expulsion of a member from the Ottawa Silva Sun Club offers another good example of anxiety about members' potential impact on the public image of the movement, as well as calling into question the success of the screening process. The minutes of a March 1965 Silva Sun board meeting raised concern about a member, Art, who was reportedly "arrested on the streets of Ottawa in the early morning hours of December 4, 1964, thoroughly intoxicated and wearing only shoes and a windbreaker." The minutes noted that Art was charged with indecent exposure, committed to hospital for thirty days of observation, and subsequently charged with drunk and disorderly conduct, at which point he was released on the basis of time already served. The minutes continued, "Art has since given up drinking and seems to be living a more quiet and orderly life. But because of his actions and to forestall any subsequent action that might endanger the good name and reputation of the club a motion was made ... that [his] membership be cancelled effective December 1, 1964 ... Carried by a majority vote."[56] The board took such pains to insulate the club's reputation that it cancelled Art's membership retroactively, four days before his drunken stroll on the streets of Ottawa. An amendment to the Silva Sun by-laws shortly thereafter suggests that in the fallout from the situation, the club had developed a heightened awareness of the connection between members' conduct and the reputation of the club and the movement more broadly. The amendment added a new by-law: "Each member shall act at all times in such manner as will bring no discredit to the club or to the National Association."[57]

The darkest chapter in postwar Canadian nudism emerged from this same desire to protect the reputation of the movement. In 1956, former nudist Gerald Eaton was charged with the sexual assault and brutal murder of eight-year-old Carolynne Moore. A founding member and secretary of the Border Tans Club, Eaton had served as CSA president in 1952 to 1953. However, according to notes by Ray Connett, Eaton and his wife had not been active as nudists since 1953, when they became foster parents with the BC Children's Aid Society. When Eaton was arrested and the story broke in the spring of 1956, the leadership of the CSA and of clubs in Greater Vancouver feared the consequences for nudism if his former association became public. Connett, as national secretary, strategized damage control in letters and meetings with other local CSA leaders. He also updated leaders, including Marcus Meed in eastern Canada and Norval Packwood, president of the American Sunbathing Association, of the steps he was taking to contain the threat. Connett reached out to his local media contacts to persuade them not to report on Eaton's affiliation with nudism. Together with Rex Craig, CSA publicity director and Van Tan member, he also drafted a press release for later use if required. The official line Connett offered was to stress that Eaton "was to all appearances a solid and respectable citizen at the time he left the movement," that nudist organizations could not be expected to have guessed otherwise given that the Children's Aid Society had failed to do so, and "that the slightest hint of misdemeanor would have resulted in his expulsion from any club." He advocated for "what seems to be a perfectly logical sequence," that "possibly Gerald's downfall began when he left the movement to devote his full spare time to the care of children from the Aid Society." Finally, Connett proposed the suggestion be made that "had Gerald Eaton stayed in the nudist movement ... the story might have been considerably different."[58]

Though Connett's approach might seem reasonable, his correspondence reveals that he was willing to go much farther in shielding the movement. He informed his fellow leaders of a recent discovery regarding Eaton:

> Unfortunately we now have evidence from three different nudist girls that he had been guilty of misdemeanor before he left the movement, though never is he said to have done anything wrong at camp. We can only hope desperately that no hint of this will come to the attention of the authorities. To this end I hastily shelved one thought which was to contact the RCMP and offer, on behalf of the nudist movement, any cooperation they might desire.

Clearly, Connett was more concerned with the reputation of the movement than with the impact of Eaton's behaviour on the three girls. Even more damning was his "top secret" note, appended to Rex Craig's copy of his letter, in which he confessed that he had known of the girls' allegations against Eaton for the past three years. He asked Craig to contact one of them, by then a young married woman, "to ascertain whether she has been in contact with any press sources," and he advised Craig to warn her "of grave consequences to many people she respects and admires if she uses this situation merely to hurt Gerald."[59]

This defensive reaction was the worst manifestation of the preoccupation with advancing the reputation of nudism. In this, Connett was not alone; in fact, his fellow leaders approved of his actions. ASA president Norval Packwood praised CSA leaders' handling of the crisis and, ignoring the allegations of the three girls, agreed that the wisest line of reasoning was to suggest "that Eaton does not appear to have gone wrong until after he left nudism." In all of this, fear was the overriding motivation. Packwood described the situation as "a powder keg and all we can do is to hope to keep it from becoming a real explosion. Nudism throughout the North American continent could suffer to the extent it would take us years to recover."[60] Connett noted a climate of public concern regarding sex offenders in the Vancouver area and worried about its consequences for the movement. He observed, "At present there is a strong feeling throughout the Lower Mainland, women's groups are holding meetings and even suggesting emasculation or permanent incarceration of all known deviates. How soon nudists will be lumped with them remains to be seen!"[61] Rather than being categorized as "deviant," Connett looked forward to the day when "membership in a nudist club [is] a matter of character reference similar to membership in a lodge."[62]

Historians Elise Chenier and Estelle B. Freedman describe the growing social anxiety over "sex crimes" in postwar Canada and the United States. Freedman observes that the public image of a sex criminal was of "a drifter, an unemployed man who lived beyond the boundaries of familial and social controls," despite growing statistical evidence to the contrary.[63] Gerald Eaton did not fit the stereotype: a married father to one son, he had stable employment and community ties. His conviction for the murder of Carolynne Moore cast doubt on nudist clubs' ability to screen members, but these policies reflected the perception of the broader society in which they were situated. Regardless, the panic triggered by the Eaton case among the nudist leadership appears to have been for naught. Eaton was tried and convicted in 1956, lost his appeal later that year, and was hanged in the summer of 1957. All of this was reported in the press, but his prior nudist activity went unexposed, with the exception of a sly remark from *Vancouver Sun* columnist Jack Wasserman the day after Eaton's execution: seemingly thumbing his nose at the CSA, Wasserman advised "the publishers of certain U.S. nudist magazines" to "change your listings because Gerald Eaton is no longer the president of the Canadian Sunbathing Association."[64]

## Nudism as a Social Club

Whereas the screening process enabled clubs to protect their legal rights and the wider reputation of nudism, nudists also wished to admit only those who were well suited to their group. They often spent their summer weekends and holidays at the club. Many clubs also ran events in the off-season, both to encourage the practice of nudism and to keep members engaged. Popular winter activities included monthly sauna or swim nights, held at the club if it possessed indoor facilities or at public pools rented for private use after hours. Some hosted the occasional outdoor nude skating party for members who were daring enough to participate. Clubs also held gatherings such as parties and dances that members attended clothed. For many, the club became a major social outlet.

The screening process allowed members to make decisions about whom to admit on the basis of any number of personal characteristics. In outlining the reasons for joining a club, the Meadowbrook Sun Club newsletter explained that nudists "want the social pleasure of being with like-minded people. They want to make certain that every other nudist has similar high purposes, and has been screened by a membership committee to keep the obvious nuts away."[65] Marcus Meed noted that the New Brunswick Maritans had many interested applicants, but that they were selective in admitting them to ensure good behaviour and a cohesive community. He wrote to Connett, "We have a personal interview with all prospects and they are carefully screened. Every one is a real lady or gentleman, a good mixer, and a lasting friend."[66] Connett summed up the attitude of many nudists when he listed the criteria for club membership to Vancouver's CKNW Radio host Les White: "The important thing is that a person must be of good moral character. And we check their background carefully and uh, they have to be able to get along with people, and we don't want those who stick out like a sore thumb or, who might, shall we say, be called 'queers.'"[67]

Connett made no secret of the fact that nudists wanted to spend their free time with like-minded people and sometimes had rather weak philosophical justifications for their exclusive attitude. Elaborating on the clubs' unwillingness to admit single men, particularly those who did not appear to be "normal, well balanced individuals," Connett stated, "Being a lonely individual he is ill at ease in company, finds it difficult to express himself, or else to cover his nervousness talks too much ... Of course such a man if he gets in a club, soon becomes a nuisance, not a moral pest, but certainly a social one."[68] Connett expressed the belief that "a doubtful prospect often can be 'educated' into the right channels and become an entirely suitable prospect," and yet he acknowledged that more often than not the "odd 'character'" would not be admitted to a club.[69] Mildred Harris acknowledged a problem of "cliquiness" among founding club members, which could lead them to decide they "prefer not to take in strangers, especially black, brown, yellow or single ones."[70] Many clubs, as Connett explained, were run on the principle of "majority rules," which was not without its problems: "The danger of democratic clubs is the exclusion of minorities, single men, yes, and women, coloured people, even class discrimination when one class or type gains power or office and are thus able to exclude all others."[71] In the interest of fostering cohesion, some nudists preferred their clubs to remain small and intimate, and were resistant to opening their doors to new members. Doug Beckett identified this attitude among some fellow members of Glen Echo once it had been firmly established: "There were people who said, well gee, we've got fifty members, maybe that's enough. Maybe we can just close it for us."[72] Even at large clubs such as Sunny Trails and Sun Valley Gardens, which engaged in ambitious promotional campaigns, race, class, gender, and sexual orientation, as well as personality, all factored into whether an applicant was deemed both morally suitable and socially compatible with members. While noting that "the natural [membership] losses each year have to be made up and a true increase achieved if our most progressive Park is to prosper," Karl Ruehle called on Sun Valley Gardens members to help recruit new ones, but to exercise good judgment in doing so:

> Bring us good and honest people as new members – not drunkards and stinkers. This makes me think that we can afford to be choosy. Yes, rather a few people less, but nicer people instead. Not necessarily "Better Class People." Far from it. We do not wish to be snobs, but we do not want "Riff-raff" either. So the middle way of this is to accept all decent and thinking people. I am sure that the majority belongs to that category – and they are welcome at SVG. Bring your friends, acquaintances and relatives now, if you know that they fit into the frame of our Park. But if you know that they are no good, don't try to bring them. We are no Reformatory Institution.[73]

Ruehle's concern seemed to go beyond ensuring the safety of members to protecting them from awkward or unpleasant encounters.

Nudists extolled the relationships fostered by their movement, but these could also be a hindrance, even to the point of undoing a club. The

Meadowbrook Sun Club, which broke off from Sunny Trails in 1963 and established itself in nearby Aldergrove, British Columbia, was racked by serious internal strife during the 1970s. Issues included cliques within the group, gossip, and lack of volunteers for club operations and maintenance. The editors of the newsletter openly criticized the atmosphere:

> It should have come to almost everybodys [sic] attention that this club has to be (as a group) the most apathetic, picky, clique ridden club in existence. With a few (thank God) exceptions everyone here seems to want the club to grow and expand but when the time comes to do a few hours work, no one seems that interested ... One reason some members do not attend dances is that although at the dance everyone seems to enjoy themselves the nit picking (who wore what, who did what) after is so rampant that they figure it is not worth the hassle ... If it does not stop we are going to cause hard feelings which will split this club into cliques of unrest, until we lose what we are here for. A place to be with friends in comfortable and congenial surroundings, away for a few minutes from the picky, apathetic and clique ridden world we live in.

Despite all these apparent problems, the editors maintained that they had "never been at a location, like Meadowbrook, where we can relax most of the time, and this is not a commercial for Meadowbrook ... Let's hang on to and improve what we have."[74] Their plea was in vain. When the property lease expired the following year, three-quarters of the members voted to dissolve the club. Reflecting on what went wrong, long-time nudist and founding Meadowbrook member Joan Detwiller observed,

> Something to remember about nudists generally is that they are very forward thinking, dominant people or they would not have taken that step to become a member of a social nudist group. This accounts for the numerous points of friction that arise within the groups from time to time. Everyone has strong thoughts and when they are not the same thoughts there are abrasive areas. Despite our disagreements, let's try to remember all the lovely things about Meadowbrook.[75]

In a movement that demanded a strong sense of individualism, cohesion was an ongoing challenge.

In interviews and publications, Canadian nudists projected an image of themselves as democratic, law abiding, and respectable. Conversely, they rejected negative cultural definitions of social nudity as politically dissident, exhibitionist, or perverse. In their efforts to establish the movement, they sought numerical growth and public acceptance, objectives that sometimes worked at cross-purposes. Despite their claims to accept people for who they "really are," they evaluated membership applicants on the basis of their appearance, dress, place of residence, and, most importantly, gender and marital status, to determine whether they would project the right image and be congenial companions.

# 3
# Regulating Sexuality

> Today the importance of sex is exaggerated. It is sometimes made to appear the one vital factor of our existence. On the other hand, there is sometimes such a suppression of sex that it amounts to a pretence that no such thing exists. Both extremes are equally absurd ... [Nudism] enables one to appreciate the anatomical differences at their proper value and in a perfectly natural way. It puts sex in its proper place as a natural function without artificial stimulation ... While nudism does not destroy the natural impulses of sexual sympathy, neither does it promote sexual excitement.
>
> – R.B. Prosser, "Naturism in Relation to Sex"

Since its origins, a central premise of nudism, and also its most radical claim, has been that nudity is not inherently sexual. Nudists posited that men and women could socialize together in the nude without any sexual arousal or activity taking place. They argued that they were neither "prudes" nor "perverts," and that, in contrast to the extremes of sexual ignorance and hyper-sexualization that were prevalent in mainstream society, their practice restored sex to its "proper place" – generally defined as heterosexual marriage. But the mixed-sex social nudity that occurred at clubs was a double-edged sword, operating as a basis for, and a threat to, claims to respectability. The presence of both men and women at clubs signalled an embrace of heterosexual norms, but in departing from the conventional relegation of nudity to the private sphere of the home, it carried subversive potential. In order to embody the philosophical conviction that nudity could be divorced from sexuality, but also to combat any perception of deviance, efforts to normalize nudity generally coupled mixed-sex club composition with the strict regulation of sexuality.

Early nudists were aware that the most controversial aspect of their practice was the mingling of naked men and women, given the strong cultural correlation between nudity and sexuality. However, the basis on which they justified the practice evolved over time. Through the interwar period, nudism bore the taint of sexual impropriety, and its adherents often reluctantly addressed the subject only because they felt compelled to defend themselves.[1] But in the late 1920s, as historian John Williams argues, charges of moral subversion directed at German nudists by the Catholic Church and other conservative groups became more forceful, and as a result the movement's leaders "began to assert ever more vigorously that their everyday turn to nature ... controlled sexual desire."[2] Interwar nudists were also increasingly influenced by the new fields of sexology and psychology, and became more closely aligned with the sex reform movement.[3] Nevertheless, this function remained subordinate to their preoccupation with physical improvement: British nudist William Welby cast the movement as primarily affording "a means to [physical] health" and expressed regret "that the question of sex seems to have formed so large a part in discussions on Nudism."[4]

In the postwar context, however, a "well-adjusted" sexual identity and marital happiness emerged as a primary benefit that nudism offered. At Canadian clubs, it was not what one did in the nude, but the act of going nude and seeing the naked bodies of others – male and female – that was seen as transformative. In this chapter, I consider how nudism reflected and responded to mainstream messaging about sexuality and what insight this offers into postwar Canadian society. In doing so, I recognize that there was a diversity of experiences, attitudes, and desires among nudists. Men and women were attracted to the clubs for a variety of reasons, some consistent with, and others departing from, official nudist messaging. Whereas rhetoric and reality lined up for some, this was not always the case. Individuals navigated not only broader cultural norms, but also club values and regulations, which set parameters for what they did on the premises and for what they said about their experiences.

## The Rationale for Mixed-Sex Club Composition

Canadian nudist clubs went to great lengths to maintain a numerical balance between the sexes in the face of far more membership applications from men. These efforts were consistent with their aim to be "representative of the whole social order."[5] But the presence of both men and women at clubs was fundamental to the philosophy and practice of nudism in a way that the inclusion of different classes and "races" was not. Why was this the case? As American nudist Herbert Webb acknowledged in his 1957 book on nudism, *Eden Regained,* "all the purely physical effects [of nudism] could be obtained by segregated groups of men and women."[6] But the practice was about more than full exposure to sunshine and fresh air. The insistence on mixed-sex clubs was grounded in two beliefs. First, the natural affinity and compatibility between men and women provided a strong foundation for the clubs. In the late 1940s, Connett flirted with the notion of male-only clubs as a solution to the problem of overwhelming male interest, but he soon set this idea aside:

> The man who thinks he would love to roam in the outdoors without clothing, to play games and swim and lie in the sun, with only the company of his own sex, is either mistaken, or abnormal. Certainly soldiers did these things in their time off in warmer climates during the last war and enjoyed themselves, but it was a substitute for mixed activity.[7]

Despite receiving letters from men who expressed interest in a male-only club or suggested it as a solution to their exclusion from clubs with stringent male-female quotas, Connett believed that same-sex clubs were bound for failure. He reasoned that

> a basic fact of human nature ... is the desire of both men and women to talk to, to see and to engage in various social activities with members of the opposite sex. This does not mean that sex activities have any part or place in a nudist club, but the fact remains that in any activity, nudist or others, man seeks the company of woman, and vice versa. This is ... even more true in a nudist club.[8]

In a similar vein, nudist Gerald Craig reflected,

> Human nature being what it is, nudism is not a completely sexless business and this is certainly not to its discredit. It is perfectly natural that all of us, men and women, young or old, clothed or unclothed, do take an interest in the opposite sex ... All is well so long as this is a healthy interest, and in nudism anything else is a rarity.[9]

Postwar nudists, along with many of their contemporaries, contributed to a culture that exalted heterosexuality, partially in reaction to the homosocial environment that many Canadian soldiers had experienced during the war.[10]

The second rationale for mixed-sex nudity was that the mingling of men and women was a crucial component of the aim to normalize nudity and to de-eroticize the body. Even as Connett and Craig promoted male and female camaraderie as the foundation of nudism, they made it clear that sexual activity had no place in the club. Nudists believed that "nudity does not create sex feeling, at least not in the natural state which is practiced in well-operated clubs. The average person ... is sure that the act of removing all of one's clothing is automatically a prelude to sex activity. This simply is not so."[11] Connett and Craig denied a causal relationship between nudity and sexuality, arguing that any connection between the two depended on the context in which nudity occurred and the attitude with which it was approached. Connett explained,

> If you make up your mind to take off your clothes for the sake of health, greater freedom of movement in the water, more enjoyment of the sun or any of the countless number of healthful, sincere, and decent reasons, then you experience no sex thrill. But if you take off your clothes to incite sex then you may perhaps not be disappointed.[12]

## Critique of Clothes

In seeking to dissociate nudity and sexuality, nudists levelled a cultural critique of conventional assumptions about clothing. They dismissed the truism that it facilitated sexual modesty, although they accepted that it had protective and ornamental functions and offered reassurances that their goal was not to create a clothesless society. They did, however, object to wearing clothes due to a sense of shame. Fashion historian Valerie Steele traces the "modesty" or "lust-shame" theory of clothing to Saint Augustine, who contended that Adam and Eve clothed themselves when they first experienced lust as a result of the Fall, a feeling that transformed their nakedness from innocent to erotic. The perspective that clothing originated in lust and shame dominated Western thought for centuries.[13] And yet, the Christian tradition also displayed ambivalence toward clothes and the naked body. Ruth Barcan states, "The story of Adam and Eve invokes two forms of nakedness – an original, sinless form (now lost) and a postlapsarian form that is a shameful reminder of sin and of alienation from God. In consequence, clothing too is ambiguous – both a 'solution' to and a perpetual reminder of the problem of the naked body." She suggests that this "made it possible for some Christians to put aside traditional suspicion of the body in favor of an argument for the innocence of nudity and the corruption of clothing."[14] Embraced by nudists who defended the compatibility of their practice with Christianity, this logic informed the nudist critique of clothing.

Nudists argued that, far from upholding modesty, clothes functioned as a form of sexual display:

> No matter how plain and drab, clothes cannot eliminate the natural curiosity aroused by the human body being covered and unfamiliar, nor the erotic impulses created by the act of their removal. Those familiar with primitive peoples have observed that clothes covering bodies that once went naked have contributed to the natives' moral decadence by stimulating an unnatural curiosity which never before existed ... Modesty has never really had anything to do with it but has simply been a rationalization supporting the fact that clothing exists.[15]

Romanticizing "primitive" innocence was more typical among early European nudists than postwar Canadian ones, but the comment nevertheless conveys a core belief: clothes, not nudity, heighten sexual desire by cloaking the body in mystery. Canadian nudists more commonly made this point with a modern reference, arguing that nakedness was not sexually stimulating but that revealing attire such as a "tight clinging bathing suit" certainly was.[16] *Sunbathing for Health* columnist Mildred Harris wrote, "I've found after several years of naturism that men don't *look* near as much in a nature camp as they do where clothes give a hint of something mysterious and secret, something hidden."[17] Occasionally, nudists praised the less concealing fashion of the period as a positive step in the right direction, but more often they condemned it because it eroticized the body. In their opinion, the belief that the simple act of concealing certain body parts, such as the genitals, would deflect attention from them amounted to "false modesty." In fact, they held that clothing contributed to a hyper-sexualized attitude toward the body. Moreover, the cultural relativity of which forms of dress were considered decent or indecent provided additional fodder for refuting the notion that clothes were about modesty. As Ray Connett observed, "Certainly we ourselves appear now on the public beach in garments which would have been inconceivably shameful in our childhood."[18] That standards of modesty in clothing were not fixed or absolute affirmed the nudist perspective that modesty was defined not by one's clothes but by one's attitude.

Nudists were not the first group to question the necessity and function of clothes in Western society. In the mid-nineteenth century, women's dress reformers in Britain, the United States, and, to a lesser degree, Canada, began to criticize contemporary fashions as impractical and oppressive. They took particular aim at corsets that constricted women's diaphragms and at heavy skirts that inhibited movement. Men's dress reformers, most active in Britain in the interwar period, also questioned the form and purpose of clothing, while simultaneously criticizing the drabness of male dress and arguing that women should not have a monopoly on beautiful clothes.[19] In 1930, English psychoanalyst and dress reformer J.C. Flugel published *The Psychology of Clothes,* a book that stemmed from a series of radio talks he gave through the British Broadcasting Corporation. In it, he extended a Freudian analysis to clothing, and his ideas overlapped significantly with the nudist philosophy. Citing publications by German nudists Richard Ungewitter and Hans Suren and American nudist Maurice Parmelee, he also engaged with contemporaries such as sexologist Havelock Ellis and fellow dress reformer and English Sunlight League founder Caleb Saleeby. He argued that the function of clothing was characterized by a tension between display and modesty. Valerie Steele effectively sums up his thinking:

> The key words here are "displacement" and "ambivalence." Originally, both the desire to display oneself and the reaction formation of modesty or shame were related to the naked body. The unconscious conflict between exhibitionism and modesty is displaced – shifted away – from the naked body onto clothing, which then functions as a "compromise," since it both covers the body and attracts attention to it. Ostensibly used to "frustrate" exhibitionist tendencies, clothing actually provides a means of gratifying them with "far less opposition from modesty."[20]

Concluding his study with a call for a more rational approach to dress, Flugel noted that his thinking "points ultimately, not to clothing, but to nakedness." He reflected on

> the possibility that dress is, after all, destined to be but an episode in the history of humanity, and that man (and perhaps before him woman) will one day go about his business secure in the control both of his own body and of his wider physical environment, disdaining the sartorial crutches on which he perilously supported himself during the earlier tottering stages of his march towards a higher culture.[21]

Like nudists, Flugel did not believe that modesty was the primary purpose of clothing or that it was essential to the maintenance of the social order, including the regulation of sexuality.

Nudist attitudes toward clothes and nudity constituted a reversal of conventional assumptions. In responding to a reader who asked for clarification on the "philosophical basis for *complete* exposure of the human body," Connett explained,

> It is not a question of exposure, on our part, but of hiding, on the part of the everyday world ... Clothes are not actually a part of us, and we do not so much take them off, or expose our bodies to the view of others, as that we actually put clothes on, and conceal our bodies in normal life.[22]

Nudists equated concealment with shame. *Sunbathing for Health* contributor Wayne Johnston stated, "The big difference between the nudist and the average person is that the former does not believe that sex organs are objects of shame, something to keep hidden under cover. He is not ashamed of his body."[23] From the nudist perspective, therefore, clothing did not resolve, but contributed to, feelings of bodily shame.[24]

### Attitudes toward the Body and Sexuality

Whereas nudists viewed the confinement of nudity to the private sphere as a function of shame, this perspective did not extend to bodily functions.[25] They envisioned somewhat greater openness in the nuclear family toward these, but they also felt that "there are several body functions which are just 'not done' in company of others."[26] For example, clubs did not possess communal toilets the way that some hippy communes did in the late 1960s. Rather, they created space for social nudity while maintaining privacy for bodily functions, especially sexuality. In an article titled "The Natural State," Karl Ruehle juxtaposed the nudist approach to nudity with sexuality:

> Nudity is the natural state of the human body. Exposure of it obligates us to keep our body as clean as possible, to control our feelings towards the opposite sex as much as social life requires, and maintain an open mind for the natural functions of the body. Sexual relations are necessary for the maintaining of human life for future generations, and for the well-being of our own lives, but they are a sacred and completely private affair and should be regarded as such. Nude persons in society will never display any inclination toward sex, if educated in the proper way.[27]

For nudists, keeping sex behind closed doors was not evidence of shame. In fact, open nudity was justified because it did not correspond with open sexuality. Though they rejected the argument that clothing was essential to modesty and to the containment of sexual desire, nudists accepted that the social order demanded that sexuality be appropriately channelled, that the "stronger emotions of anger, hatred and sex ... must be guided as one would guide a spirited horse."[28] The purpose of nudism was not to promote uninhibited behaviour but to call people to a higher standard, where people's conduct was regulated by respect for the body, not by social taboo. As one writer explained, its purpose was "promoting the discipline from within," not without.[29]

Free from the "artificial" stimulation of dress, sex could assume "its proper place in the nudist life." According to the Connetts (Figure 3.1), "its proper place" was "a relatively infrequent activity, confined to the privacy of the home and the marriage bed."[30] The two fervently articulated this position in their *Sunbathing for Health* columns, drawing on their own experiences to explain the effects of nudism on the marital relationship and to elucidate the relationship between nudism and sexuality. Responding to a female reader who had expressed concern about "sex problems" at nudist clubs, Harris offered reassurance. She claimed that her enjoyment of her sexual relationship with her husband had increased as a result of their nudist lifestyle. Furthermore, she confided, "From talking to other wives I think too that it can be said with confidence that a nudist club is the best place in the

**Figure 3.1** Mildred and Ray Connett pictured in *Nude Living*, February 1962 | Courtesy of Naturist Education Foundation Research Library

world to reclaim an erring husband." She proposed nudism as an antidote to a "shaky domestic situation," suggesting "couples who are no longer happy together, seeking freedom elsewhere can find happiness together in our clubs if they will but try our life."[31]

Ray Connett also affirmed the positive impact of nudism on his marriage, contrasting his frame of mind before becoming a nudist with his attitude since:

> After the [first nudist] outing and increasingly after subsequent outings I felt somehow that my wife was better than any other woman in the world. She appeared to me on a pedestal, I wanted no other. And I will be honest now, for with the years come honesty, and admit that such had not always been the case ... Nudism put all that behind me ... Nudist

> husbands and nudist wives enjoy the companionship and pleasures of married life, as thoroughly and completely but with considerable more frankness and decency than do non-nudists. I know, for I have been both. And I have read letters from non-nudists, I get them still, which reveal the shocking attitude of so many towards that which should be so fine and beautiful, that is the sex side of life. The non-nudist who sometimes never even sees his mate unclothed, must attach to sex an imaginary excitable aura which is at once unwholesome and, but for the holy sacrament of marriage, bordering on the indecent. The nudist, who knows every inch of his mate's body by sight admires and respects, even reveres his mate. And sex to them is a chaste, beautiful, almost holy experience.[32]

From this couple's perspective, far from encouraging superficial or short-term sexual liaisons, nudism promoted authentic and honest relationships based on a true knowledge of one another. It enhanced intimacy between husbands and wives by freeing them of pretense and enabling them to know and respect each other in a deeper way. The Connetts held a romantic view of marriage and stressed that nudism would enhance the sexual fulfillment and emotional intimacy that was fundamental to such a marriage.

The establishment of the nudist movement in Canada on a firm footing during the 1950s and 1960s preceded the sexual revolution, but despite the buttoned-up stereotype of the 1950s that persists in the cultural imaginary, important changes in sexual behaviour had already occurred over the first half of the twentieth century. On the basis of cultural analyses, birth rates, and sexual surveys, such as those conducted by Alfred Kinsey and his researchers in the 1940s, a number of historians have cited the 1910s and 1920s as an important turning point in the history of sexuality in Canada and the United States. Education rates for women increased, white women won the right to vote, and men and women mingled as never before at work and at leisure. Birth rates, which had begun to drop in the last quarter of the nineteenth century, continued to decline through the end of the Second World War; men and women increasingly "disentangle[ed] older associations between sex and procreation," and Protestant churches began to abandon their theological opposition to contraception.[33] As "dating" replaced "courting" and moved "from front porch to back seat [of a car]," couples had more freedom and privacy to engage in premarital sex, from necking and petting to intercourse.[34]

This period also saw a reduction in the sexual double standard, with a growing expectation that both male and female sexuality be confined to a monogamous heterosexual relationship. According to the Kinsey Reports, *Sexual Behavior in the Human Male* and *Sexual Behavior in the Human Female,* published in 1948 and 1953 respectively, women born between 1900 and 1920 were twice as likely to report engaging in premarital intercourse than women born before 1900 (36 percent up from 14 percent), whereas men born after 1900 were far less likely than those of earlier generations to report having engaged in sex with prostitutes.[35] Nevertheless, "technical virginity" and the association of women's value with their sexual "virtue" remained significant and were accommodated by a drop in the average age of first marriages following the Second World War, which provided social licence to married teenagers and young adults to have sex.[36] At the same time, expectations rose that marriage would provide not only economic and social stability, but individual emotional and sexual fulfillment. Rebecca Davis argues that "the definition of a successful marriage had transformed from an early twentieth-century ability to avoid divorce 'failure' to a late twentieth-century model of mutual emotional, financial, and sexual gratification."[37]

The views of Ray and Mildred Connett were consistent with what historians John D'Emilio and Estelle B. Freedman describe as the sexual ethic that was dominant by the mid-twentieth century: the affirmation of sexual pleasure in its own right, apart from reproduction, and sharp differentiation of "normal" heterosexuality from that perceived as threatening or deviant.[38] In postwar Canada, psychologists, church leaders, and sex educators affirmed marriage as the fundamental adult relationship and as the place in which sexuality would, and should, find ultimate expression.[39] The Connetts espoused these values and believed that nudism, far from undermining the institution of marriage, reinforced it. Connett declared, "Marriage is as natural and proper to nudists as it is among clothed people. Why not? Nudists are completely normal in every respect. They observe the same laws and in most respects have the same feelings as the more conventional folk."[40]

But changes were percolating. American historian Alan Petigny points to "exploding levels of premarital sex during the forties and fifties," based on an analysis of premarital and out-of-wedlock pregnancy rates in the United States. Petigny rejects the assertion of scholars such as Elaine Tyler May, John D'Emilio, and Estelle Freedman that levels of premarital intercourse remained constant from the 1920s to the 1960s, arguing that a lack of cultural candidness masked real increases in such activity during the immediate postwar years.[41] In Canada, pregnancy rates for unmarried teens rose between 1945 and 1961, and gay and lesbian subcultures also grew in size and visibility.[42]

Nudists tread a careful line where sexuality was concerned. They sought to convey that they were not swingers or deviants, but they were not asexual or prudish either, and that social nudism could go hand in hand with a "normal" sex life. Navigating this territory could be tricky, however, in a context where sexual norms were shifting. Although clubs officially marketed their membership primarily to heterosexual couples and nuclear families throughout the fifties, sixties, and seventies, and promoted it as improving the marital relationship, they sometimes quietly signalled greater openness to other sexual practices. In 1960, Karl Ruehle reprinted an article from a Danish nudist magazine in the Sun Valley Gardens newsletter in which the author called out his fellow nudists for exhibiting greater intolerance toward extramarital sex than mainstream society.[43] Another reprinted article alluded to the work of Freud, Krafft-Ebing, and Havelock Ellis and concluded that "sex in any form that's mutually enjoyable between consenting adults, and not excessively physically harmful to either, should be considered normal and acceptable for the parties involved."[44] Ruehle did not go so far as to voice agreement with these articles, but it is significant that he printed them at all and that they engaged with ideas circulating outside the movement that differed from those of the Connetts. But it is also notable that Ruehle did so in the context of a private newsletter circulated among club members, rather than in a more public forum such as a magazine sold on newsstands or a radio or television interview.

Most telling, however, are sentiments conveyed by Ray Connett in letters dating from the late 1940s. Responding to correspondence from Toronto leader Reg Nicholls, Connett wrote,

> Regarding your personal observations re: members of your club, I am inclined to think that, like many "new nudists" who have not been tempered by several years of nudism and visits to several camps, you may be a little narrow or over critical in what you expect of fellow nudists ... Your member who sees nothing wrong in sexual intercourse between single people, is surely with the majority in this modern age. I don't think you could find many club members anywhere, Reg, who would disagree with

him or think him an undesirable so long as such activities were kept entirely outside the club. We had an instance of a man who was a very worthwhile member except that we were afraid his philandering might reflect on the club. We finally had to tell him bluntly that he must keep the two separate, that is, he must not use club contacts to serve his ends, and he must not be known commonly as a nudist where he wishes to play around. So far as we know he has adhered to this ruling and is otherwise an asset.[45]

Connett supported this man's membership as long as he kept his sexual activity separate from the club. In doing so, he expressed, not a moral concern but a desire to preserve a respectable image for the movement.

## Controlling Behaviour

Notwithstanding significant discussion of the subject, sex was purportedly a non-issue for nudists because they saw the naked body as "natural" and not erotic in and of itself. In a 1962 CBC Radio program, interviewer Fred Skelton raised "one question I think a lot of people are wondering about as far as nudism is concerned ... the question about sexual emotions being aroused." He was speaking with a Calgary nudist named Jack, who replied,

> We feel there must be a little switch or something in the human mind, that when you go into camp and see the naturalness of the people around you, that is, the ordinary every day activities that are going on and sports and people just loafing in the sun, and you take your clothes off yourself, something clicks on, if I use that term, and there is no emotional arousement [sic] at all of any kind. That the average mind suddenly realizes that this is not the time or place where sex becomes involved at all and therefore the subject is forgotten completely.[46]

This idea, that the club setting and matter-of-fact attitude regarding nudity freed it of its association with sexuality, was commonly espoused by nudists.

But clubs did not place complete faith in the outlook of their members. Writing in *Sunbathing for Health,* Gerald Craig noted,

> Those who organize and run nudist clubs can't really ignore sex completely. Officially they do, but actually they watch their members very carefully,

> for a single nudist scandal would do the movement an immeasurable amount of harm. There is little danger of any such trouble arising, for the members are carefully screened before they are admitted. The ideal theory is that all members should act like perfect ladies and gentlemen; that they should behave exactly as they would if they were clothed; that nudity should make no difference at all. Actually, in order that there should be no cause for misunderstanding, they are just a little more careful about their actions than they would be if they were clothed.[47]

Both to ensure good behaviour and to project an image of a movement that was above reproach, clubs adopted rules to govern members' conduct. They demanded that people comport themselves even more carefully than they would in most public contexts. The reasoning was clear: "Our strongest weapon against the ignorance, prejudice and backwardness that are opposing us is the high standard which we maintain."[48] Upholding this standard depended on careful monitoring by club leaders. Long-time nudist Doug Beckett reflected on what this entailed:

> I think it takes a certain amount of, uh, talking to. Because as this one club owner said, I congratulated him on it, it was a small club and either he or his wife made a circuit about nine o'clock in the nude, rain or shine, and said what the activities would be of the day. And I said that really made us feel a part of it. You always had your cheery smiles. He said, I always did, but he said, did you see my eyes? And I said not particularly. He said, I'm watching, for people who don't obey the club rules or don't seem to fit in. And then, he said, we have a little talk, tell them that perhaps they don't quite get the message here.[49]

Such monitoring was undertaken both to protect the reputation of the movement and to ensure that club members were not made uncomfortable by someone's behaviour.

Thus, the practice of mixed-sex social nudity at clubs occurred within a highly regulated environment. As described in Chapter 2, the first and perhaps most powerful form of regulation was the screening process. Single men were often rejected, both to ensure a rough balance between the sexes and to exclude anyone who might be joining for sexual gratification – generally assumed to be an unmarried man.[50] Clubs also stepped carefully where marital problems were evident or suspected. The 1959 Toronto

Gymnosophical Society constitution, for example, required married couples to join together, treated divorced applicants as singles (making it difficult for divorced men to gain admittance), and barred separated individuals from membership. This kind of regulation, common in the 1950s and 1960s, underscored support for the sanctity of wedlock but also displayed concern that unstable marriages were a potential threat to the movement. Evidently, despite Mildred Connett's optimism that club involvement would ease matrimonial problems, this was not always the case, and clubs had no desire to appear to have aided the dissolution of a marriage.

Clubs worked to disabuse potential members up front of any notion that they were places to meet sexual partners or engage in sexual activity. The early Ontario group, the Sunglades, declared in its constitution, "We regard the body as neither an object of shame, nor as a subject of levity or erotic exploitation. Any behavior inconsistent with this view is contrary to the whole purpose of this club, and the persons leaving this track of thought have no place among us."[51] The message on a Ponderosa brochure simply stated, "For those persons who believe this is a place for sexual adventure, we most heartily advise you to forget us. This does not exist here."[52]

This kind of messaging responded to popular misperceptions about the movement, as well as inquiries from potential members who were not as keen to divorce nudity and sexuality. Sunny Glades owner Stan Wortner recalled "problems ... that almost brought [his] club down" shortly after opening in 1959:

> I guess maybe as knowledgeable as I was, out in the railroad working, I didn't realize that some people had a taste for swapping wives, and swapping husbands, and whatever, and promiscuous in that sense, and I did run into that element. And, but I found that very discouraging the first couple years, at least when it happened. These were married couples, church-going, professional people, engineers and school teachers, and all that kind ... Not that I was, you know, setting them up on a pedestal, but these were the ones that were the instigators of the whole thing. And I was approached, said well I could make a lot of money if I just run the park as they seen fit. Anyway, we came to parting ways. And I made that quite clear, the one fellow from Detroit, he probably, he was an engineer and had money and everything else. And I said, why don't you buy your own property? Well, the answer was, well, we don't want to own property we just want somebody else to run it.[53]

Wortner's remarks indicate that people who wished to pursue extramarital liaisons could be attracted to a nudist club and that he was committed to screening them out.

The clubs also generated certain rules for conduct whose purpose was to prevent sexual contact or arousal, or the suggestion of it. The first rule of many North American clubs was that members must act "as ladies and gentlemen." The clearest application of this rule was to men: they were advised that erections were not acceptable and could be avoided through physical activity and mental discipline.[54] Members were also expected to refrain from swearing or making sexually suggestive comments or jokes. In addition, the following regulations designed to clearly detach nudity from sexuality were standard at Canadian clubs throughout the 1950s and 1960s: no alcohol consumption, no physical contact between members, and no clothes worn when conditions permitted, with some exceptions.[55] The stricture against alcohol originated in the first German clubs as a health measure, alongside bans on tobacco and meat. Canadian clubs did not forbid meat or smoking, and members felt free to drink in their personal lives, but initially alcohol was strictly prohibited on Canadian club grounds. TGS member Doug Beckett recalled that his club strictly banned it and linked the ban to owner Eddy Todorowsky's concern that it facilitated bad behaviour: "Eddy said, 'I have been a bell captain in the Royal York Hotel for some years,' and he said, 'I've seen so many degraded drunks in my life, and people who were well up in business who, just on an hour or two off, would get sloppy drunk.'"[56] Connett elaborated for *Sunbathing for Health* readers on why "liquor and nudism do not mix": "we feel that alcohol, even in moderate amounts, tends to loosen the bonds of propriety."[57] This was a widely shared sentiment: Canadian strip clubs, for example, were not initially licensed to serve liquor.[58] The practice of nudism hinged on the self-control of members, and nudist groups believed that the use of alcohol potentially placed this in jeopardy.

The rule against touching was more unevenly applied. Connett noted that "nearly every club I have ever studied or visited prohibit[s] 'undue familiarity or intentional touching,'" but "in practice ... this rule is broken to various degrees in various clubs." The rationale behind the regulation was that physical contact in the nude could be easily misinterpreted by either members themselves or visitors. Technically, this included contact between a married couple or a parent and child. Though many nudists evidently looked the other way when members disregarded this injunction,

Connett advocated a harder line. Paradoxically, he believed that "intimate contact is simply one of the things we give up in return for that glorious freedom we call nudism."[59] Although selectively enforced, this rule occasionally resulted in disciplinary action. In one documented instance, a male club member in his fifties reportedly subjected a fellow member – a teenaged girl – to unwanted attention, including putting his arm around her on two occasions. He was expelled from his club.[60]

The third standard regulation was that clothing be worn only for functional purposes. This meant that it could be worn for warmth, but not out of a sense of modesty; for example, a cold nudist might put on a shirt but not pants. Nudity was generally expected for sunbathing and sports activities, and bathing suits were seen as serving no useful function and were not permitted at all. The requirement that members go nude as much as possible derived from concern with voyeurism and the desire to cultivate a shared, non-sexualized way of seeing the body. A 1949 issue of *Maclean's* magazine featured Vancouver journalist Jack Scott's visit to a Seattle-area nudist club to report on the Northwest Sunbathing Association convention, which was attended by Canadian and American nudists. While there, Scott observed an interesting incident. Two "Peeping Toms" – which he described as "sharp-faced, middle-aged men in city clothes" – were caught hiding in the bushes by the pool area. The nudist men who spotted the interlopers offered them the choice of stripping down voluntarily for a dip in the pool or being thrown in fully clothed.[61] This incident conveys the significance of nudism as a participatory practice: mutual nudity neutralized the voyeuristic act by subjecting everyone to observation. Nudism disrupted both the power of the voyeur and the objectification of the subject by making everyone both – and consequently, from a nudist perspective, neither. The fact that nudity was the standard condition at clubs went a long way toward normalizing it. However, gender stereotypes came into play in determining the enforcement of the regulation. If prospective and new male members did not quickly join in nude activity, they risked arousing suspicion and possible denial or removal of membership, whereas women were given more leeway. It was also accepted that they might choose to wear shorts during menstruation.

## Changing Regulations in the 1960s and 1970s

During the late 1960s and early 1970s, the nudist movement began to re-evaluate its messaging and policies in response to significant social change.

First, many clubs revoked their alcohol bans. Clubs such as Sunny Trails and Ponderosa Nature Resort led the way in permitting liquor on their grounds as early as 1964 and 1965 respectively, at a time when the American Sunbathing Association (ASA) – the umbrella organization with which many Canadian clubs were affiliated – still opposed it. In 1970, the ASA reversed its position, however, and many more Canadian clubs, including the Four Seasons and the Sunny Chinooks, also began to permit drinking on the premises. By this time, there was a strong cultural association between alcohol and camping – sitting around a fire with beer in hand was increasingly an essential part of summer leisure for many Canadians – and the relaxed regulations enabled nudists to participate in this popular ritual. Nudist resorts with clubhouses also began permitting liquor to be consumed there after hours when children were not expected to be around (typically 9:00 p.m.), creating a space for it to be used as a social lubricant as long as other rules were respected.[62] In the lead-up to a 1972 vote on removing the alcohol ban at the Sunny Chinooks Club, minutes from a 1971 board meeting offer insight into the rationale for doing so:

> Mugs suggested that after the experience of the winter wine and cheese parties there could be little doubt that alcohol would present no problems on club grounds. Serena emphasized that the present rule was being broken in any case and that greater problems were created by unenforceable rules than by what they were supposed to overcome ... Jack said that none of the clubs that had permitted alcohol after the change in the ASA rule last year had reported problems ... Laura mentioned the Canadian, US and European clubs she had visited where alcohol had been permitted, none of which had given evidence of drunkenness or improper behavior. In any case, conduct becoming a lady or a gentleman would still be required, and any problems arising could just as well be dealt with under that rule.[63]

Not all clubs reversed their stance, however. Kingston's Lakesun Club, for example, doubled down on its prohibition against liquor and credited its "peaceful" atmosphere in part to this regulation.[64] In 1975, owner Hans Behrmann wrote in the Lakesun newsletter, "Alcohol and social nudism do not mix ... The press, radio and TV is reporting this tragedy with increasing frequency. Lakesun will remain a place where families can bring their children without being exposed to this."[65]

Less common, and more controversial, was a loosening of the ban on physical contact between members. In 1964, the Sunny Trails Club – no longer under the leadership of Ray and Mildred Connett, who had relocated to California in 1958 – abolished regulations against touching, as well as against drinking and "colourful language." But for some, the changes did not go far enough, and in 1969 "the club split over the issue of 'touchy-feely' sessions. Sympathizers argued that the club should make room for a 'non-verbal communications seminar' and become a 'progressive' club which would 'grow and expand with the times,' while opponents denigrated the 'crazy sessions' and 'Love-Ins.'"[66] Ultimately, those opposed to such changes broke off to form the Meadowbrook Sun Club. In the 1970s, Sun Valley Gardens also began allowing body contact as well as offering a health club with communal bathing and massage.[67]

Another experimental change at some clubs was switching from a strict nudist environment to a clothing-optional one. Sunny Trails also made this transition.[68] Its members were required to be nude in the pool, sauna, and hot tub, but they were otherwise free to wear clothes whenever they liked. This change was driven by a desire to step back from the heavy-handed regulation of behaviour, but some nudists worried that it would encourage voyeurs who came to look rather than participate.[69]

Over the course of the 1960s and 1970s, obtaining membership also became somewhat easier for single, separated, and divorced individuals. In 1964, the Toronto Gymnosophical Society amended its constitution to permit legally separated people to apply as singles and added, "In common-law marriage particular scrutiny will be applied to its stability and once acceptable this marriage will be considered equal to a legal marriage."[70] Sun Valley Gardens began accepting singles or couples regardless of whether they were married, divorced, separated, or married but attending without their spouse.[71] By this time, divorce between nudist couples had become more common, though the messiness of a divorce between club members could have consequences for operations and public relations, particularly in situations where the couple owned the club. A bitter child custody dispute between owner Dietrich Wesemann and his ex-wife, Helga, put the Edmonton-area Helios Club in the news during the 1960s.[72] The Sunny Chinooks were also thrown into turmoil by the divorce of the property owners, who stopped attending during their separation, in compliance with club rules.[73] Both clubs eventually overcame these challenges but the dissolution of these marriages complicated matters for club members in the interim.

In 1973, the Meadowbrook Sun Club adopted the following rule: "Any member who, to prospective members or visitors, promotes or engages in 'swinging,' i.e. wife swapping, on the club grounds shall have his or her membership terminated."[74] It is telling that the executive found such a regulation necessary. Moreover, though ostensibly casting swinging as incompatible with membership, the wording seemed primarily concerned with preventing the public from associating the club with wife swapping. The prohibition was against promoting or engaging in swinging with "prospective members or visitors" at the club, leaving members free to engage in extramarital hook-ups with each other.

Canadian clubs had always been somewhat willing to turn a blind eye to sexual activity outside the marital norm so long as it took place off-site and did not result in negative publicity, whether Gerald Eaton's contact with minors or a member's consensual "philandering," while simultaneously promoting nudism as a marital salve. During the 1960s and 1970s, some clubs began demonstrating greater tolerance for members who were not part of a monogamous heterosexual marriage. Nevertheless, as a whole the movement continued to embrace heterosexual marriage and the nuclear family as the basis for club stability and social respectability. Throughout this period, newspaper ads for clubs such as the Silva Sun and Helios Club appealed exclusively to "Families and Couples" to consider joining, often specifically directing their call to "Married Couples" or those of "good character."[75]

Clearly, applicants and club members displayed a range of motivations and attitudes regarding sexuality, from sincere agreement with the nudist philosophy to titillation at the sight of naked bodies to more active sexual intentions. The movement's commitment to dissociating nudity and sexuality hinged on vetting applicants and policing member behaviour. Its public messaging emphasized both that nudity was not inherently sexual and that club involvement contributed to matrimonial well-being. Respectability was a constant concern, which helps to explain why clubs focused so exclusively on marital sexuality, though in practice leaders exhibited varying degrees of tolerance for extramarital sexuality, so long as it remained discreet.

# 4
# Navigating Gender Norms

THE BELIEF THAT GOING nude did not necessarily facilitate sexual arousal held different implications for men and women, given the different cultural associations with male and female nudity. Nudism held the potential to liberate women from sexual objectification and from the expectation that they act as gatekeepers of sexual purity, and it provided a rare setting in which male nudity figured as non-threatening and non-exhibitionist. Just as they believed that nudism broke down class distinctions, some suggested that it promoted gender equality and enabled men and women to relate "as people." However, nudism did not entail a rejection of masculine and feminine gender identities. As with sexuality, it sought to assign "the anatomical differences" to their "natural place," which typically amounted to an affirmation of gender difference and complementarity. The movement challenged the equation of nudity with sexuality, but it did not disrupt sexual and gender norms, nor did it seek to. Nudism comprised a complex mix of liberatory and disciplinary rhetoric and practices. Informing the analysis that follows is Patricia Vertinsky's suggestion that embodied practices provide "an opportunity to examine the tensions between the performance of agency with its potential capacity for self-transformation, and the effects of discipline and cultural conformity through movement." In other words, bodily practices may be sources of agency, self-identity, and transformation, on the one hand, and a means of materializing cultural norms, on the other.[1]

## Gender Ideology

Canadian nudists inherited a mixed legacy with respect to gender ideology. On one end of the spectrum, German nudist pioneer Richard Ungewitter has been characterized as "decidedly antifeminist" for his emphasis on women's primacy as mothers and his belief that their education should be confined to domestic skills.[2] On the other end, in the socialist branch of German nudism, "the individual body remained sexual ... but its gendered character seemed to all but disappear," and equality between men and women was stressed, John Williams argues.[3] Historically, nudism had broad appeal to women as well as men. Physician Bess Messendieck inspired many German women to take up nude gymnastics, promoting it as a means to health, beauty, and self-confidence.[4]

During the interwar period, American Maurice Parmelee offered the most extended consideration of the topic among English-speaking nudists. In his *Nudism in Modern Life,* Parmelee made the bold assertion that nudism "is a powerful aid to feminism, because it abolishes the artificial and unnecessary sex barrier and distinction of dress." He believed that it "weaken[ed] sex solidarity and strengthen[ed] human solidarity," establishing companionship between men and women that was free of sexual innuendo. Moreover, he noted, "I have observed in [nudist] circles that men and women tend to become more alike, because artificial barriers and distinctions are removed," though he concluded that "the genuine sex differences can, of course, never disappear, nor is it desirable that they should, because they add greatly to the variety and savour of life."[5]

Unlike Parmelee, Canadian nudists never went so far as to associate nudism with feminism, although they did occasionally suggest that it promoted equality between the sexes. In 1946, *Sunbathing and Health* – before it was rebranded as *Sunbathing for Health* – published an excerpt from British nudist William Welby, who authored several books on nudism in the 1930s. In it, Welby informed readers that "most Nudists become automatically oblivious to outward and visual differences in sexual anatomy ... The camaraderie and community of interests which is engendered between the sexes in a Nudist camp breaks down the antagonism or indifference to the opposite sex which exists in some individuals. It brings about a better understanding."[6] In 1956, a special edition of Mildred Harris's "Woman's Page" echoed this perspective. It featured a letter from Harris's friend Joan, who described her experience with gender relations at her club. Joan explained that "one of the pleasantest things [about nudism] ... is the fact that I am accepted as a *person* by both men and women." Despite finding it difficult "to believe that men could be with women in the nude without entertaining erotic thoughts," she was put at ease after her first visit to a club. Its atmosphere was "one of relaxed companionship and close friendship ... Men and women work together; there is no need for segregation. There is great beauty in this and great dignity." Harris could not resist following up with her own reaction, agreeing that instead of being treated as "a symbol of sex" at clubs, women "actually come into our own. We are someone loved and respected, admired for what we are of ourselves, and not just as clothes horses."[7] Similar sentiments appeared in a *Sunbathing for Health* piece on "the ordinary married naturist couple." It suggested that nudism fostered equality and companionship between men and women:

> They are bound together by ideals unknown to those outside the movement. They have complete confidence and trust in each other. They feel a measure of equality ... Naturism encourages both men and women to keep fit and retain their youth, therefore they have equal interests in sports and the ordinary everyday pleasures. There is between them a happy comradeship that is often lacking in marriage.[8]

Despite the emphasis on equality, sexual difference remained significant. Nudists considered it essential that their clubs, like marriage, be comprised of men and women. Many Canadian clubs were managed through the joint undertaking of a married couple, such as Ray and Mildred Connett, Hans and Lisa Stein, Karl and Marlies Ruehle, and Eddy and Mary Todorowsky. Hans and Lisa Stein founded the Ponderosa Nature Resort in 1964 together with Hans's sister, Ernie, and her husband. Years later, Hans nostalgically recalled the hard work required of all four and the division of labour they adopted: during the first year of ownership, Hans, Lisa, and Ernie's husband worked night shifts in Hamilton and constructed an outdoor swimming pool by day, while Ernie handled the cooking and housework for the families.[9] Ray and Mildred Connett were founding members of the Sunny Trails Club, which was co-operatively run. While they held paid jobs elsewhere, Ray as a postal worker and Mildred as a part-time retail employee, they both played integral volunteer roles in their club as well as in the Canadian movement.

Another couple, Eric and June Jarvis, founded the Toronto Helios Society at Haytor Park (near Newmarket, Ontario) in 1972. Both worked full-time jobs while gradually developing their property. Eric recalled of June,

> She was a teacher and so she had a full-time job, but she used to help me and she'd done a lot of the cutting down of the original woods in order to make the hole for the lake. And uh, and she helped me in every way possible, and she was very very good with the members, and they all liked her, she was very, very, very pleasant to everyone.[10]

Gender roles feature in the accounts of these prominent club owners, with men frequently highlighting their own physical labour. However, as the comments of Eric Jarvis and Hans Stein reveal, women also did the heavy work of clearing land and building pools, especially in the early days of club development.

Through their efforts to maintain a balanced sex ratio and their belief that social nudism required the unclothed bodies of both men and women, Canadian clubs highlighted sexual difference. A crucial component of their practice was "the presentation of the male and female figures in their entirety and completeness."[11] The Meadowbrook Sun Club newsletter declared, "We, more than any other group of people, realize that humans ... come in two varieties, male and female."[12] Though these policies and beliefs might be interpreted as merely reflecting biological "facts," the work of scholars such as Thomas Laqueur reveals "that almost everything one wants to *say* about sex – however sex is understood – already has in it a claim about gender."[13] An observation made by Ray Connett demonstrates the conflation of sexual difference with gender:

> Many nudists say, and are derided for saying, that there is no sex in nudism. But it would be folly to say that there is no sex, for sex means more than just the act of mating. Sex is all the differences which exist between the male and female. And sex thus gives to life many more pleasures than the momentary experience of copulation.[14]

In part, nudists believed that men and women must go naked together to undo the damage inflicted by social taboos – taboos that affected them in different ways and carried different consequences. Their critique of mainstream society as promoting a sense of shame about the body suggested that it was particularly felt by women. According to many leaders, the reason that more men than women inquired about membership was that society lauded modesty as a feminine virtue, and from a young age women were taught to be modest. Several nudist women said that they had been "reared more guardedly [than men] and instilled much more with the idea of the shame of exposing the nude body."[15] A member of the Ottawa Silva Sun Club contrasted his experience at the YMCA, where men swam in the nude, with his wife's experience at the YWCA – where bathing suits were worn in the pool and where "they are quite fussy when they put their clothes on after, in the locker room."[16] The Connetts mentioned female acquaintances or letter-writers who had never been entirely nude in front of their husbands; they offered no examples of the reverse scenario.[17] During a 1960 interview for the CBC Radio program *Assignment,* nudist Peggy Parkes was asked how it felt to experience nudism for the first time. She asserted, "It's a little bit awkward the first time because you're really afraid that something terrible is going to happen; you've been taught all your life that when you take your clothes off something is going to happen – you shouldn't be in the nude in front of the other sex – and um, so you do hesitate, particularly a woman."[18] The suggestion was that women had more inhibitions to overcome than men as a result of their socialization.

In addition, insecurity over physical appearance was identified as a greater hurdle for women. Prospective members who raised the issue were assured that nudist women represented the spectrum of shapes, sizes, and attractiveness, and they would be welcomed and accepted regardless of their appearance. Harris urged women,

> Look at yourself again and say, I know I am just like ten thousand other women. Maybe not as good looking or with such a good figure as some ... but then we can't all be good looking, can we? ... If you can get that far, ladies, if you can look at yourself without shame and without self-consciousness then rest assured you can enter our happy healthy sun life and feel at ease.[19]

Though nudists suggested that the socialization of modesty and concern with physical appearance made entry into the movement a greater challenge for women, they believed that women could, and should, throw off these inhibitions. The result would be a sense of liberation and greater self-confidence. One woman explained the impact of nudism on her life:

> As for your figure, you find there are some who look better than you do and some look worse ... You find that it's the individual, the personality that is important ... Their body is unimportant ... Best of all [is] the freedom – *the utter freedom* ... In order to take the first step, you have already cast out some inhibitions and old conventionalities. And you get rid of more as you go along.[20]

## Enhancing Femininity

Despite nudism's promise to free men and women from bodily taboos and enable them to relate as people, its practitioners did not reject normative gender roles. They were anxious to assure the public that they were just like everyone else, excepting their involvement in a nudist club, and depicted themselves as "normal" men and women. Articles in *Sunbathing for Health* often made note of the activities that men and women performed at clubs and the ways in which nudism benefitted both. A story about one of the best-known English clubs, Spielplatz, reported that, unlike most of its North American counterparts, it had year-round residents. Given this, "one may drop in and find the housewife busy at work; cooking, washing, mending, or maybe nursing the baby – all very much the same as her town or suburban sister, except – a very significant exception – that she wears no clothing and finds life all the brighter."[21] A feature on a nudist couple who lived at a California camp picked up on the same refrain: "Edgar was employed in a nearby large city with his duties keeping him mostly inside. Jeannie, contented to be a good housewife, spent most of her time at home in the trailer."[22] Though nudism offered an escape from the everyday world, it did not upset the gendered division of labour that organized that world. Assuring a dubious reader that it did not feature women "parading" nude in front of men, Harris wrote,

> The men in our club spend most of their time working at improving the club property. If I started parading in front of them they'd probably hand me a rake and say, "How about a helping hand?" When we call them to dinner they sit down to eat and all the parading I or any other wives do is over to the stove and back for more coffee.[23]

The point here was that far from being on display in a club, nudity receded into the background; what is most telling about her comment, however, is what it reveals about the respective roles played by men and women at a club.

There was also an assumption that despite shedding their clothes, women possessed an innate desire to be beautiful, and female grooming did not disrupt the "naturalness" or "body freedom" of social nudity. A series for women entitled "The Fine Art of Being Lovely," which ran in *Sunbathing for Health* in the fall of 1947, conveyed this perspective:

> Whatever else a woman's ambition may be, she longs to be lovely. She desires it for her own satisfaction, she desires it in order that her family and friends may be proud of her, she desires it so that she may appear most desirable to the eyes of the man she loves. The secret source of a woman's loveliness is the constant realization that she is a woman, for the very fact of womanhood implies the potentialities of beauty. The world craves beauty; beauty of mind and of body, and she who possesses it is a constant source of joy to those with whom she comes in contact.[24]

There was no critique of the expectation that women discipline their bodies to conform to aesthetic norms and to cultivate sexual desirability. Another *Sunbathing for Health* series that targeted women appeared from 1952 to 1954. Titled "7–11 Morning Exercise Club" and written by American nudist Marguerite Bosc, it offered beauty and exercise tips, which ranged from advice on how to enhance femininity and attain a "well-balanced figure" to such tidbits as "a beautiful smile, which can be most appealing and heart-warming, is beautiful only so long as the teeth which it displays are presentable." Bosc encouraged women to send in photos of themselves for "a complete figure analysis," promising to reply with recommendations for "a series of exercises to correct the apparent deficiencies."[25] Although nudists claimed to judge people on their character, not appearance, and made a point of reassuring women that their bodies would not be subject to scrutiny, Bosc invited them to submit themselves to her critical gaze for the purpose of improving their looks.

Articles about nudist women often emphasized that they took the time to apply their makeup and style their hair at the club. Whereas makeup and grooming might seem to be artificial aids that, like clothing, masked one's "true self," their use was construed as natural for women. The *Sunbathing for Health* article about Edgar and Jeannie, who lived at the California club, concluded by discussing her morning beauty ritual: the application of lipstick. It quoted her as saying, "even though here at camp I am not dressed up when I step outside, still I've got to appear attractive." To which her husband laughingly responded, "How a woman can spend so long before a mirror, just putting a tiny bit of lipstick on, is beyond me."[26] The message was that nudist women were not so different from other women; they might discard their clothes, but they did not abandon their feminine gender identity, with its attendant concern to look as attractive as possible. This emphasis on their attractiveness affirmed their femininity and respectability. Indeed, this strategy has been used in a variety of contexts involving women – from their entry into sport, to the paid workforce, and to military service during the Second World War – to assuage fears about a threat to femininity and the social order.[27]

One *Sunbathing for Health* reader questioned the wearing of makeup and nail polish by female models who were featured in the magazine, criticizing it as an attempt to improve on the natural body. In a moment of refreshing frankness, Mildred Harris responded,

> I am afraid that in going to a nudist club we do not cease to be artificial. We take most of the veneer of civilization with us, all our manners and customs, most of our thoughts about appearance are still with us, we simply remove our clothes and enjoy the freedom which we have without them in the sun and open air.[28]

What Harris did not say was that the importance of maintaining appearances weighed more heavily on women than on men. However, this was clearly conveyed in one of Bosc's columns, which quite cruelly played up any potential insecurities of female readers:

> The housewife and mother who writes in saying ... "I must do something right away to regain my figure, for lately I've noticed my husband's attention wandering to younger women"; or "He spends more time at the office with the secretary than he used to" ... does have a problem, and she should get busy right away working to make herself more attractive. It is so easy to get in a rut and neglect the little things that are so important. More than any other group, the housewife who spends her full day in the privacy of her own home has more opportunity and time for exercise. Therefore, there is no possible excuse that can be offered for her laxness in the attempt to correct any physical deficiency.[29]

This claim – that a wife who failed to make herself attractive had only herself to blame if her husband looked elsewhere – is ironic, coming as it did from a movement that advocated sexual intimacy based on emotional bonds rather than visual objectification.

## Gender Roles and the Decision to Try Nudism

In attempting to attract couples, *Sunbathing for Health* columnists cast men in the active role and women in the passive, in both their relationship and their decision to give nudism a try. Nudists believed that women were less likely to take the initiative to contact a club, to "take the plunge," without the leadership and prodding of their husbands, boyfriends, or fathers. Ray Connett advised male readers that the two main factors affecting a wife's receptiveness were her upbringing and her trust in her husband.[30] He wrote, "It is difficult to persuade the average single girl to try nudism. I would not advise this until you have been going with a girl for a long time. She must have complete confidence in you so that she trusts you to behave as a gentleman at all times. Even then I suggest that you start slowly."[31] Mildred Harris operated on the same assumption, that it was men who first became interested in nudism and who must coax their wives to try it: "I know from my correspondence this is so throughout the length and breadth of nudist America, just as it is in our own Sunny Trails club." She explained that her "big interest in life" was "to persuade others especially you scared, a bit stand-offish, or just plain bashful girls, to come to camp and try our life – *just once*!"[32] Harris's column was primarily addressed to the hesitant wives of male readers, offering advice to the husbands and encouragement to the women. She suggested that men adopt the strategy of leaving *Sunbathing for Health* lying around the house

> where the little woman can't help but see it ... Us gals are curious critters and if you haven't made her mad with arguments and cross words so that she picks it up and throws it in the fire, she will read it. And if she reads it, she'll have to admit that here and there even on my page of humble effort, there is a thread of honesty and sincerity, a gleam that indicates the clean moral and sane existence which is ours.[33]

She urged men, "You can win your wife with patience, tact, and perhaps a little nudge sometimes from one like me, who knows the silly fears and fancies of a woman's heart so well, who knows that nudism does sound awful to one who has never tried it."[34]

In some cases, men resorted to more than a little nudge. Lisa Stein declared herself initially opposed to the idea:

> When I first became a nudist, my husband has asked me a couple of years to come and see, and I said no way am I going there, I am not in my whole life am I going to take my clothes off in front of other people. Because in my mind it was some ... It was a no no. I wasn't brought up to think that way, even though I am a German, I wasn't a nudist in Germany ... Until one day he took me for a drive, and we went to a nudist club without my knowing, and before I knew where I was I was in a nudist club. And I found the people were very nice.[35]

Eric Jarvis offered a similar story. After emigrating from England to Canada in the 1950s, he decided to take his wife, June, to Sun Valley Gardens without her consent or forewarning. As he explained,

> I didn't tell my wife about what we were going to do, and we did have our eldest son as a child, at that time ... And so we went in and then of course I said, "Now we're, the campground we are doing is a nudist park." And she got all upset with that and immediately went down onto the floor of the backseat and hid her face, and she said, "I can't, I can't go in here." And I said, "Well, don't worry about it, it'll work out all right." And then I said, "Now we've just come to a sign." And she said, "What on earth does it say?" And I said, "It says, when in Rome, do as the Romans do." And she started cursing, "I don't care a damn about the Romans," and all the rest of it, and the next thing I knew we were at the prescribed campsite and we got out, and I said, "Well, we're here now," and after about an hour she felt quite comfortable.[36]

According to Jarvis, June eventually became "enthused" about nudism, and the couple went on to operate the Toronto Helios Society in the Newmarket area during the 1970s and early 1980s. Nevertheless, the coercive nature of her introduction to it speaks to broader social expectations that women subvert their own desires and defer to the wishes of their husbands – a phenomenon that Betty Friedan defined as "the forfeited self" in her landmark 1961 publication *The Feminine Mystique*. Accounts of women's first experiences with nudism can expose a tension between the liberation it purportedly offered women and the coercion that sometimes accompanied their initiation. In the 1970s, women would highlight this same tension in the sexual revolution, which left them "free to say yes (but not to say no)."[37]

In expressing an unwillingness to try nudism, some women may have cast themselves in the passive role to align with gendered expectations. Even though female nudists might be seen as subverting gender norms by rejecting the womanly virtue of modesty, their claims about their hesitancy followed by submission to a husband reaffirmed their identity as normal, respectable women. They often stressed their reluctance to join, their modesty and inhibition about being seen naked by men who were not their husbands, and doubts about how their children would react. They generally presented their path to nudism as an agreement to try it "just once," made solely to satisfy a husband. Marguerite Bosc described her conversion in this way:

> Years ago my husband asked if I would become a nudist with him. My answer was given in the positive because it was my place, as his loving wife, to do so ... When we agreed to share this happiness it meant that I would have to trust him implicitly, just as he would have to have complete trust in me.[38]

In another situation, Harris expressed surprise that a male reader had not convinced his wife to visit a club: "There must be something very wrong with the relationship between you, for rarely does one partner in a marriage object so strongly to the wishes of the other if they truly and sincerely love each other."[39] The gendering of the two "partners" was clear: if a wife dutifully acceded to the wishes of her husband, her irrational fears would be put to rest by his well-informed decision to investigate nudism. As Harris put it, "I suppose if we gals stopped to think of it, no man would risk losing his wife for one afternoon of ogling a few other wives without clothes if that were all there was to it."[40] In the oft repeated account, a woman's decision to try nudism for the sake of her husband was followed by a first-time experience that resolved all her doubts.

In part, stories were constructed in this manner to render nudist women relatable to women who might be interested in joining, assuaging their misgivings. As Harris frequently asserted, "I'm just another housewife who used to be scared too."[41] But depicting nudist women as "just like" all other women also seemed to reassure nudists of their own normalcy, demonstrating that though their practice might provide a degree of "body freedom," it did not disrupt gender roles. Responding to a reader's query about how nudist women would react to him as a single man, Connett advised, "Nudist girls are certainly not 'stand-offish,' but neither are they very forward. Let's say that they are 'natural.'"[42] Essentially, Connett's definition of a "natural" woman was a stereotypically feminine one.

During a 1962 CBC Radio program, reporter Fred Skelton interviewed a Calgary nudist named Betty, whose remarks display some mixed messaging which suggests that she shaped her story to fit with gendered expectations. When asked about how she became a nudist, she explained,

> We had been reading nudist books, especially my husband had been reading books, and I hoped this idea would pass and he'd forget it. It didn't pass, and he wanted to go to camp, so it was sort of a thing to keep peace in the family, well I'll go and I'll show, and you'll be proven wrong, that these people are sort of nuts, running around like this. But uh, my first hour in camp disproved my thoughts on it, because after the first hour I was sold on the idea, I had such a wonderful time.

Later, Skelton asked when she had removed her clothes during that visit. She replied, "I disrobed the first minute. And I think it was the easiest thing to do, to jump right into activities." Skelton pushed back, pointing out an apparent inconsistency with her initial account: "But you were mentioning that it was a bit of a problem to you, and you were hoping your husband would back down, but when you got out there you disrobed the first minute." Betty qualified her story: "It seemed to be the thing to do at the time ... I did so reluctantly. But it wasn't long, I was sold on the idea."[43] In her experiences with nudism, as well as in relating her story to a CBC reporter, Betty navigated cultural expectations of her as a woman – to be a dutiful wife and to exhibit modesty, even as she joined a nude mixed-sex recreational setting.

A story in *Sunbathing for Health* entitled "How Can Girls Model in the Nude?" also emphasized modesty where one might least expect to find it. Referring to a woman named Margery, the author, "A Naturist Photographer," stated that she was "one of the most photographed women in modern naturism in Britain, her photograph has now appeared in magazines all over the world ... How did all this come about? It is not because the model sought publicity – in fact Margery is a most retiring person, and is naturally reserved." Rather, it sprang from her willingness to aid the cause, summarized as, "I would rather not, but if it is going to help naturism, and particularly the club, then I will do it." In a perfect correlation to the attitude recommended to women whose husbands urged them to join a club, the author declared, "She has been asked to attempt every possible pose, some with danger to life and limb, and some impossible ones! She never refuses to try it out once." The article also stressed that Margery made many other contributions, including serving as club hostess and raising three children.[44]

### Masculinity

Unlike for women, nudist promotional material never entertained the possibility that modesty or bodily insecurity might impede men's participation. Nonetheless, some men privately expressed concerns. In 1949, Maritan Club leader Marcus Meed reported that two women were keen to join his club but their husbands were "simply bashful."[45] And male readers of *Sunbathing for Health* occasionally voiced fears that their physical appearance did not measure up to that of the models in the magazine.[46]

Whereas "false modesty" figured as the main obstacle to women's participation in social nudism, the most commonly cited hindrance for men was the fear of having an erection at a club. Time and again, male readers wrote to *Sunbathing for Health* for advice on how to avoid the situation or expressing curiosity about how clubs addressed it. One man voiced the typical concern that he would "be bothered by the presence of a nude female who is well proportioned ... I am doubtful whether it can be overcome enough for me to be an asset in a nudist colony or summer camp."[47] Male journalists who interviewed nudists also frequently raised the issue of sexual arousal and expressed surprise that it didn't occur.

Prospective male members were told that an erection was unacceptable at the club but were reassured that they could control the problem. When a male reader voiced apprehension about having a "physical reaction to nudity," Harris replied that his fear would be enough to guard against it. She concluded,

> I cannot tell you positively that there are not "some members whose thoughts must stray from the straight and narrow" because naturally no one can be sure what others are thinking. But I can say truthfully that I

have never seen the slightest indication of sexual excitement in all the years we have attended camp and I have never felt that any man held me in anything but the highest regard.[48]

In a more practical vein, Connett conceded to one letter-writer that though getting an erection "does not necessarily indicate sexual excitement," it would be interpreted as such and would be grounds for immediate expulsion. As he declared, "natural or not, an erection has no place in a nudist camp ... But believe me it will not happen if you decide in your own mind that it shall not happen. It is for you to decide, you can easily prevent it."[49] Recommended management strategies included staying physically active by performing jobs around the camp or engaging in recreational pursuits, keeping a towel at hand, and as a last resort, taking cover in the swimming pool or woods.

The work that nudism purported to perform was gendered. For women who suffered from bodily shame, it was held out as the path to self-confidence and acceptance of their bodies. For men, on the other hand, who were generally not seen as possessing inhibitions about shedding their clothes, it promised to satisfy "natural, normal curiosity" – "the desire to see a human body in its entirety" – and enable them to display a respectful and non-sexual regard for women's bodies.[50] To take the first step, both men and women needed to shake off conventional attitudes and begin to see and experience the body in a new light; this new sense of embodiment was to be reinforced through the practice itself.

In both cases, women's bodies were central to the project, and it was in this respect that nudism was most unorthodox: in its estimation, the act of looking at naked women was something that enhanced, rather than upset, men's self-control. In mainstream society, women were often castigated for dressing provocatively, an "attitude to female display" that, as Joanne Entwistle explains, "not only holds woman responsible for her own sexual behaviour, but for man's sexual behaviour too."[51] By contrast, nudism assigned responsibility for sexual arousal to the male viewer. This is precisely what nudists meant when they extolled their practice as offering "body freedom."[52] A *Sunbathing for Health* article asserted,

> Those who practice nudism have many advantages over those who do not. They have shaken off repression and suppression. They enjoy health, contentment, an active mind and a strong body – the inevitable results

> of living in the way that nature expected us to live. Most of all they enjoy freedom; freedom from the restraint of clothes; freedom from sexual inhibitions and perversions; freedom from physical ills and disabilities; freedom from nerves and other mental troubles brought about by the stress and strain of modern civilization.[53]

Nudism encouraged, not sexual licence but the freedom from being ruled by sexual passion and "perversions." This statement echoes Michael Hau's interpretation of what Weimar nudism contributed to masculine identity: "Body discipline and the adoption of a healthy life style was an important means for contemporaries to regain a sense of personal autonomy and re-create the illusion of an autonomous bourgeois subject that was in control of all aspects of life."[54]

It is notable that though a woman's entry into nudism was marked by the moment of initiation in which she first removed her clothes and cast aside the social taboo against nudity, a man's nudist identity was a work-in-progress, demanding constant self-discipline and subjecting him to ongoing scrutiny from fellow club members in a way that women were not. Historian Angus McLaren explains that "in the Victorian age there emerged a new sensitivity to male nudity that was carried on into the twentieth century." The legal and medical definition of exhibitionism as a specifically male crime and pathology "placed unprecedented restraints on the freedom of males to expose their bodies" and was a function of "new notions of civilized and restrained masculinity."[55] Nudism offered men the freedom to go nude without fear of legal trouble or questions about their mental state. It liberated the male body to be naked in a mixed-sex setting – an otherwise transgressive act – but this freedom was predicated on self-control and scrutiny from fellow members.

In interwar England, nudist Maurice Parmelee had claimed that nudism promoted gender equality and camaraderie. In postwar Canada, however, discussions of nudism's impact on gender relations were almost entirely confined to the marital relationship, reflecting its central social position. Ray Connett emphasized nudism's enhancement of emotional intimacy: "The feeling of sharing and of knowing each other is a beautiful lovely thing between nudist man and wife, something which inspires respect and confidence. This is something which is missing in so many non-nudist homes ... What confidence can exist between a man and wife whose very bodies stand between them?"[56] Others, however, saw nudism as a means of promoting marital well-being by enhancing women's beauty and femininity. In a rare acknowledgment of the scenario in which a wife might be more keen than her husband to attempt the nudist experiment, Van Tan Club member Carole Craig advised women, "You might point out that you will not lose your interest in dressing attractively nor will you detract from your innate femininity, which I am sure he cherishes, but rather you both will gain in health and a more relaxed personality which will accent your natural charms."[57] Craig and Connett agreed that nudism contributed to marital harmony, but their statements reveal differing perspectives on its ability to generate radically new ways of seeing the body – especially the female body.

Nudists were equally insistent that both men and women were integral to the movement and that sexuality was not. Ironically, while nudists fought to overcome female modesty and bodily insecurities in order to win women to the movement, they also highlighted nudist women's femininity and naturalized female beauty rituals in an effort to mitigate any perception of nudism as upsetting social norms. In a similar way, nudists rejected the exhibitionist label and redefined male nudity as respectable within carefully defined parameters. Clearly nudist men and women were not to shed their masculinity or femininity when they shed their clothes, and while sex might have no place in a nudist club, gender did.

# 5
# Raising Young Nudists

> Have you ever noticed how happy children are when they are allowed to play in the nude? This is because they are so much more closely attuned to nature than the adults who have grown away from that.
>
> – Karl Ruehle, "Where Are You Standing?"

> What we do is for the benefit of the young generation which we wish to grow up healthier and cleaner in mind and action ... They need nudism more than anyone else.
>
> – Karl Ruehle, *Sun Valley News*

THROUGHOUT THE TWENTIETH century the nudist movement adapted in response to social and cultural change. Its postwar form differed from its predecessor in two critical respects. First, concern over mental health – and its correlation with normative sexuality – became its main preoccupation. According to E.V. Miller, who wrote a health column for *Sunbathing for Health,*

> the standard of living in most civilized countries has risen phenomenally during recent years. We have better housing, purer food, and more leisure than our ancestors enjoyed. Great success has been achieved in preventing

> and curing disease and in providing more hygienic environmental conditions. Yet all this will go for nought if we cannot effect an improvement in the mental health of our people.[1]

Miller voiced a concern that many of his contemporaries shared, though he proposed an unconventional solution. Warning that "the need for relaxation is a desperate cry in this modern world," he stated, "There is no place more conducive to complete relaxation than a nudist camp ... [where] it is easy to forget the strain and tension of modern living, and to relax completely and utterly – at one with nature."[2]

The second major innovation of postwar nudism was that – in the midst of the baby boom – the nuclear family, and children in particular, became central to its rhetoric. Although clubs purportedly contributed to the psychological well-being of all, they argued that their greatest benefit would be to their youngest members. Early nudist parks had certainly welcomed families, but much of their appeal had been to independent men and women who joined gymnastics, hiking, or recreational groups, either same-sex or mixed. In the postwar period, nudists promoted their movement as the best means to raise a healthier new generation and hoped that, like suburban living, club membership would become part of the child-centred lifestyle that many Canadians embraced.[3]

Caroline Daley, Josie McLellan, and Brian Hoffman note that the postwar nudist movements in New Zealand, Germany, and the United States became increasingly "family-oriented," but these authors do not explore how prominently children figured in the rationalization of social nudity as "natural" and the degree to which they were used to cast it as a force for good.[4] In a 2008 photo essay by Marguerite Shaffer, "On the Environmental Nude," children are literally and figuratively erased from the frame in her analysis of four photographs she selected to chronicle the evolution of American nudism. Shaffer and the journal editors decided to crop a young girl out of a 1949 photo because of their concern over her full frontal nudity. The shot depicts a nudist family preparing a meal by a campfire at a Colorado nudist camp. Shaffer reads the image as representing "a post-World War II turn to outdoor recreation," and says nothing of children's participation and ideological significance in the nudist movement.[5] Though focused on the Canadian movement, this chapter rectifies the erasure of children's actual and symbolic position within postwar nudism both inside and outside Canadian borders.

As illustrated by the introductory quotes from Karl Ruehle, nudists drew on widely shared notions of childhood innocence and invoked the cultural authority of psychology to provide an ideological rationale and a functional purpose for their movement. Postwar nudists praised children as best exemplifying their movement's unashamed and carefree attitude toward nudity, and at the same time promoted children's involvement as a way to teach them to be self-regulating members of society. Underlying the relationship between children and nudism, therefore, was a dichotomy between the idealization of childhood as closely aligned with nature and the marketing of nudism as an effective way of disciplining children to conform with social norms. Even as children's bodies were used to naturalize nudity, nudists promoted their movement as a means of socializing them. Children figured prominently in nudist messaging and efforts to both level a cultural critique and secure respectability.

## Children as Natural Nudists

The principal manner in which Canadian nudists represented themselves was as a family movement. This was both a pragmatic decision to appeal to the large demographic of young families and a strategic means of underscoring the respectability of nudism, given that, as Brian Hoffman explains, "the public clung to the assumption that the family guarded against illicit forms of sexuality."[6] As previously described, clubs actively recruited nuclear families for membership, imposed gender ratios, and screened out undesirables. In the midst of growing social anxiety over "sex crimes" in Canada and the United States, nudists sought to establish a safe and comfortable place for their members, including children.[7] Ray Connett told *Sunbathing for Health* readers, "We would not willingly expose our children to the dangers which the presence of [deviant] individuals would entail."[8] Nudists derived a sense of security from their private member-only clubs, which they saw as providing a "physically and morally safe" environment for children. Mildred Harris catalogued the dangers that lurked in public: "When you read the papers, such incidents! Children in the public parks, on the way home from playgrounds, even going to the corner store – such things that happen, the beasts that prowl our city streets." By contrast, the nudist club was presented as a safe haven where parents could "bring the kiddies and almost forget about them. You never need to worry where they are, for all through the camp people are keeping a friendly eye on our children."[9]

Nudists commonly asserted that children were "nudists at heart" who naturally loved to be naked.[10] In a series of articles entitled "Our Sons and Daughters of Nature," *Sunbathing for Health* contributor Marguerite Bosc claimed, "Boys and girls playing outdoors with no clothing to hinder their play will have twice the amount of fun and happiness they normally would ... A child in this span of years loves to be without covering."[11] The promotion of nudism as a family-friendly activity hinged on the belief that children enjoyed it – that it was not foisted upon them, but that clubs simply provided the space and the freedom for them to play in their natural state. Moreover, prospective nudist parents were advised that their children might not even notice the lack of clothing at a club since many children "attach so little importance to clothes."[12]

Undergirding these remarks was a sentimentalization of both nature and childhood founded on a belief in the essential goodness of children and the natural world and the existence of an affinity between the two.[13] For the past two centuries, innocence has dominated perceptions of childhood in the West.[14] During the eighteenth and nineteenth centuries, the Christian belief that children were inherently sinful was gradually superseded by a view of children as innocence personified, "sinless, absent of sexual feelings, and oblivious to worldly concerns ... an uncorrupted element of nature."[15] Carolyn Steedman credits the Kindergarten movement with "propagat[ing] the idea of childhood as a garden, and the propriety of returning all children to their proper setting, which is also a Garden."[16] As industrialization gained steam and more and more people left the countryside for the city, nature was imbued with redemptive effects. In the twentieth century, the summer camp movement operated on the premise "that nature fostered an environment that kept sexual innocence intact. Purity of surroundings and purity of character were assumed to go hand in hand."[17] Nudists invoked children as symbols of both the innocence and connection to nature that they embraced.

Children's presence at nudist clubs helped combat popular misconceptions that clubs were hotbeds of sexuality. Ray Connett argued that children's presence "plac[ed] the purity and wholesomeness of the club activities beyond question."[18] Nudists invoked the innocence of children in proclaiming the respectability of the movement as a whole. But they also challenged the adult-child binary and used children to contest any simple equation of nudity with the erotic, begging a reconsideration of attitudes toward unclothed adult bodies as well. If nudity were natural for children, why not for adults too? And if children were nudists at heart, could their adult counterparts not be equally child-like in their attitude toward the body? Nudists cast themselves as "all true children of Nature, naked and as innocent of shame or lustful thinking as the newborn."[19]

Recounting their childhood experiences with parental attitudes regarding nudity, *Sunbathing for Health* readers displayed a desire to recapture the innocence of that time, either as they remembered it or wished it had been. A Winnipeg man described his struggle to overcome attitudes instilled in him as a child: "I was often told about the shame and impropriety of exposing one's naked body, not only to others, but also in seclusion."[20] One reader recalled being caught watching "nude Gypsies" as a child in Ireland and being severely punished.[21] An elderly Florida man who attributed his "inferiority complex" to his repressive childhood wished that he could relive life as a nudist.[22] Other readers praised their parents as open-minded and felt that they themselves had benefitted as a result. One man said his parents "believed in natural living" and that his mother, "doubtless considered eccentric," allowed the children to play outside in minimal clothing and in the nude indoors.[23] Karin Calvert observes that when childhood is conceptualized as a period of innocence – "the healthy natural state of freedom before the constraints of civilization" – "the inevitable loss of childhood ... [becomes] a kind of expulsion from the Garden of Eden."[24] Nudists argued that adults could, and should, go "back to the garden" and rediscover a sense of innocence and enjoyment of the "natural" state: "The man of today is a slave to the world of his own making, to its conventions and trivialities. He must return to nature and regain the freedom of spirit that were his in his youth."[25]

## Healthy Socialization

Even as nudists invoked children as evidence for the naturalness of nudity, they simultaneously promoted nudism as a way to successfully socialize children. Whereas children's innocence became an ideological pillar of the nudist movement, the promotion of normal socialization and the prevention of juvenile delinquency became its functional justification. In the postwar period, psychologists helped fuel public anxiety that mental illness, juvenile delinquency, and sexual deviance were critical problems. Mona Gleason characterizes the concerns over juvenile delinquency as a "moral panic" – fears that far exceed any actual threat. In part, these anxieties were generated by the way in which the term "juvenile delinquency" was deployed, encapsulating more than criminality and "conjur[ing] up a much broader set of qualities, combining truancy, anti-social behaviour, and habitual challenges to authority, which subverted the accepted paradigm of adult authority ... Psychologists portrayed juvenile delinquency as symptomatic of impaired psychological development."[26] Popular Canadian magazines such as *Maclean's* and *Saturday Night* regularly ran headlines that reflected, and played into, social and parental alarm, such as "Danger: Child Growing Up," "Will Your Youngster Turn to Crime?," "'Have' Delinquents: Why Do They Go Wrong?," and "Psychological Factors in Juvenile Crime."[27] Gleason explains that psychologists "often defined old problems in new ways ... [and] construct[ed] postwar problems as concerns best approached through psychological expertise."[28] During the interwar period, new child-rearing literature had emerged, authored by medical and psychological experts. Unlike the moral tone of nineteenth-century advice literature, the new manuals addressed the physical and, especially, mental "problems" of childhood and contributed to a "psychiatric culture" around children's health and happiness.[29] Shifting away from the eugenicist viewpoint in which "the 'malfunctions' of a child's psyche were seen primarily as inherited forms of developmental disorders," postwar psychologists emphasized the environmental influences on children's development.[30] Seeking to prevent the development of psychological problems, they increasingly directed advice to parents of "normal" children.

In response to this trend, nudist promoters invoked psychology to provide legitimacy to the movement. Ray Connett informed parents that the advice of child psychologists was consistent with the nudist philosophy and described how he and his wife began to practise nudism at home as parents of a young daughter:

> I obtained several books on child psychology and training from the local public library so that we might raise her according to the best modern principles. I was surprised to find in more than one of them advice which amounted to nudism in the home. These books advised parents to bathe with their children, dress and undress freely about the house and avoid any pretence of "modesty" or privacy about the body so that the children might grow up clean-minded and free of inhibitions or curiosity about the human body.[31]

Like her husband, Mildred Harris repeatedly appealed to the authority of psychology, claiming that "many modern child psychologists recommend a casual family type of nudity."[32]

Nudists echoed parenting advice in making children's psychological health a primary concern. A *Sunbathing for Health* article entitled "Create a Wholesome Atmosphere" warned readers,

> The responsibility for the emotional development of the child during infancy and early childhood rests with the parents, and great care should be exercised here because once a nervous or psychiatric disorder arises it is difficult to treat ... Many parents are not mature enough to exercise the self-discipline necessary to do the job right. Nervous disorders are becoming a serious problem.[33]

Sunny Trails members Hank and Virginia Moffat told CBC Radio reporter Bill Good that they valued the mental health benefits and the "atmosphere of moral correctness" that the club provided for their children.[34] Nudists held out their lifestyle as the best way to raised grounded, well-adjusted children and as something that any devoted parent should be willing to explore. Women who were reluctant to try nudism for their own benefit were urged to do so for the sake of their family's health and happiness. Harris exhorted her "Woman's Page" readers, "There is no good reason why you should deny your children, your husband and yourself, the joy and freedom, the helpful relaxation of our way of life."[35]

Though few, if any, North American child psychologists actually endorsed nudism, nudist rhetoric about parenting aligned with prevailing thinking on child development. Both nudists and child psychologists promoted the importance of sex education in the family, highlighted the impact of parental attitudes in determining children's feelings about the body, and believed that a positive body image was important to a child's sexual adjustment. The provision of sex education by schools and community organizations was a subject of public controversy, though growing consensus was emerging around the importance of sex education within the family. Nudists and psychologists agreed that it was an essential, though often neglected, parental responsibility. The most prominent psychological expert in Canada was Dr. William Blatz, director of the St. George's School for Child Study, a laboratory nursery school at the University of Toronto. He had come to public attention during the 1930s, as the educational consultant for the famous Dionne quintuplets. He also authored two child care manuals and dispensed advice through periodicals and radio programs. Blatz argued that "if parents were to spend only a portion of the time which they use in training their child to eat with a knife and fork in teaching him about sex, many of the problems of later life could be avoided."[36] In a similar vein, nudist Gerald Craig accused parents of failing to provide adequate sexual guidance to their children, concluding: "It is the home that is of paramount importance. Juvenile delinquency has increased at an alarming rate, and much of the blame rests with negligent, preoccupied and indifferent parents."[37]

Advice literature for parents generally agreed that they communicated their views about the body and sexuality to their children in all sorts of verbal and non-verbal ways. Samuel Laycock, well-known psychologist at the University of Saskatchewan, explained,

> All parents necessarily give sex education whether they want to or not. You see, sex education is far more than giving a child the so-called facts of life ... First of all there are the attitudes and feelings which a child develops towards his own body and his own body processes. Secondly there are the attitudes and ways of behaving towards those of the opposite sex. Thirdly there are the attitudes towards the husband-wife relationship and towards family living in the home.[38]

Nudists shared the conviction that children's attitudes were shaped by the outlook and behaviour of their parents. When a Mrs. M wrote angrily to *Sunbathing for Health,* objecting because her seventeen-year-old son had requested and received nudist literature in the mail, Harris sprang into action. In a scathing reply, she blamed the boy's curiosity on his mother's attitude toward the body and inadequate guidance. As Harris wrote,

> Any of our modern magazines for women *(Chatelaine, Ladies Home Journal, Cosmopolitan)* carry articles about children, juvenile delinquency, and sex education ... Well, Mrs. M., what have you told your boy? Nothing? Oh, yes you have. In a thousand little ways you have told him – with your eyes, your voice, hushed silences and locked doors – that his fine young body, and yours that gave him being, are filthy, obscene and loathsome beyond words.[39]

In general, both psychologists and nudists encouraged parents to demonstrate a positive attitude regarding the body and bodily functions. Blatz advised parents to use proper names, not nicknames, for all parts of the body, including genitals, and instructed them not to shame their child in any way while toilet training. He pointed out that children were naturally curious and warned parents against instilling in them a sense of embarrassment about their bodies. He explained, "Inadvisable methods of calling attention to special parts of the body, by some form of inhibition, will heighten his curiosity. Slapping a child's hands in the bath if he should touch his genitals increases the desire for further exploration."[40] Nudists were likewise concerned that children not be taught to see certain parts of the body as dirty. Harris lamented, "It is a shame and a pity, that we should replace childish innocence with these hideous attitudes of shame and obscenity."[41] Moreover, nudists concurred with psychologists that shaming merely reinforced undesired behaviour. As one nudist stated, "It is an established fact that where there are restrictions there is also a desire to break them ... Sex-curiosity is prevalent among the young. To a certain extent this curiosity is natural and healthy and the usual methods of adults in trying to repress or eradicate it are not only ridiculous but often harmful."[42]

## Juvenile Delinquency and Sex Education

Nudists contended that delinquency and deviance were rooted in harmful social attitudes about the naked body that promoted shame and inhibitions. Children were born with a "built-in attitude of morality and decency," but this changed as they were taught the taboos and inhibitions of adult society, inevitably with damaging psychological consequences.[43] It was mainstream society that exerted a corrupting influence on childhood innocence, for which nudism offered a remedy. As a flyer for Sun Valley Gardens declared:

> Nowadays' unhealthy attitude towards sex, created by the constant wearing of clothing and the exploitation of semi-nudity, does breed mental strain, nervous tensions and general unhappiness. If all people were allowed to bathe nude at the beaches, sex crimes and juvenile delinquency would drop to a minimum. Yes, *social nudity* is the only answer to this problem.[44]

Nudist literature frequently made the vague and unsubstantiated claim that not a single instance of juvenile delinquency could be found at a nudist club.[45] Nudists rejected the widespread notion that children must be shielded from the corrupting influence of nudity.[46] Instead, they believed that for children and adolescents, "association in the nude serve[d] as a safety valve for dispelling ignorance and pent-up curiosity regarding sex."[47]

Interestingly, the idea that mainstream attitudes regarding the body caused lasting psychological damage contradicted the seeming ease with which many adults took to nudism. Connett himself noted, "The way we are all raised it is remarkable that there aren't more 'bad ones.'"[48] Postwar psychologists understood deviant sexuality as a sign of immaturity.[49] From the nudist perspective, going naked enabled adults to satisfy their latent and natural juvenile curiosity about the body, thus progressing to normalcy and maturity. As Connett explained it,

> The desire to see a human body in its entirety is not a symptom of mental disorder. It would be more truly said that a lack of any such desire would indicate disorder. There is no such lack in any of us, but most of us have been taught to repress it throughout all our lives. At what cost in fear, mental turmoil, and perversion, perhaps no one will ever know.[50]

But nudists had no wish to imply that their clubs were treatment centres, and focusing on sexual adjustment with respect to children was far less problematic. In other words, nudism was proffered as preventative rather than cure. In an article entitled "Accepting the Unsuitable: Leon Gilbert Writes on a Controversial Subject," a British nudist grappled with the question of what nudism could provide to those who had "some misguided view of sexual matters." Gilbert argued that "logically it is part of our principles" to give consideration to "cripples" who initially presented themselves well and gained entrance to a club but eventually revealed "their true character." He observed,

> In effect we say to all non-naturists: "Your attitude to health, clothes, and the body are all wrong. We naturists have found some better ideas." Some become readily acceptable "converts"! Some we find have deliberate evil intentions, desires, or hopes. Quite rightly we say, "out" and no argument. Others are found to have not quite the right idea. *If* they can be helped,

"cured," and we can affect the change, it would seem logical to try to do so. Success proves the case for naturism.[51]

Gilbert's position was controversial, flying in the face of screening policies at Canadian clubs. Most clubs did not see themselves in the business of "curing" people – especially men – with "screwy" attitudes toward sex. Instead, they concentrated on the psychological benefits of nudism for children. As they contended, "many adults will never be changed ... The younger generation, however, should be taught to understand and conquer their fears, or phobias."[52] Sun Valley Gardens, for example, espoused the goal

> that our youth be given a better start into life by giving them a chance to know about the facts of life from the earliest possible age and in a clean and proper way without prudish shame and cowardly lies ... Today these demands represent the rightful desire of a minority; tomorrow they may represent the priceless heritage of a majority.[53]

Nudist leaders held out the hope that their members would be "the pioneers of a happier, healthier and cleaner generation."[54]

Nudists joined the ranks of social reformers, educators, and physicians going back to the nineteenth century who believed "that sexuality needed to be retrieved from privacy and rescued from the distortions of respectability."[55] Before the Industrial Revolution, children "were part of every aspect of adult life, and privy to it," including sexual activity. But by the Victorian period, it had become "especially important to preserve childhood sexual innocence as long as possible, including ignorance of the sexual functions of one's own body."[56] In the late nineteenth century, however, social purity campaigners began to argue that far from protecting children, silence on the subject of sexuality left them vulnerable to misguidance or exploitation. They promoted sex education as a means of resisting a sexual double standard and eradicating prostitution and venereal disease. The social hygiene movement of the early twentieth century also crusaded for sex education to combat the spread of venereal disease, though grounding its message in scientific rather than moral reasoning. By the postwar period, "family life education" became the dominant framework promoted by sex educators. "Said to be a modern, 'scientific' program, based on contemporary pedagogic principles," Mary Louise Adams explains, "it emphasized positive values, not fear or shame."[57]

Historical scholarship on the sex education movement reveals that the distinction between science and morality was not clear-cut and that nineteenth- and twentieth-century reformers were usually more concerned with promoting socially acceptable sexual behaviours than with providing information about physiology or the mechanics of sex. Courtney Shah states, "What could have been a revolutionary way of empowering people was more often used to reinforce power relations."[58] Postwar family life education conveyed a clear moral message that sexual activity must be confined to marriage, shied away from discussion of sexual acts in favour of conversations about family life, dating, and social relationships, and implied that "young people could learn about sex, but they were not to engage in it."[59] This attitude was consistent with traditional Christian morality but was promoted on the basis of psychological health, individual happiness, and the social good.

Postwar parenting experts admonished parents to accept children's "natural" urges but to direct them into socially acceptable channels. Around the turn of the twentieth century, sexologists and psychologists such as Havelock Ellis, Albert Moll, and G. Stanley Hall challenged the notion of children's sexual innocence but did not entirely displace it.[60] Freud's theories about sexuality were particularly influential. He identified natural sexual drives in young children and understood them as guided by the pleasure instinct. But with proper socialization, Freud believed, these drives would find realization in "normal" sexual relations. He distinguished between repression and sublimation: whereas the latter entailed a healthy expression of sexual energy in socially acceptable sexual and non-sexual ways, the former constituted an unhealthy denial of the natural instincts and a failure to find appropriate outlet for them. Repression would express itself in what Freud defined as neuroses. In contrast, the sublimation of sexual energy was productive, fuelling the progress of civilization.[61]

William Blatz espoused a similar view in offering psychological advice to Canadian parents and educators. With reference to six physiological appetites – hunger, thirst, elimination, rest, change, and sex – he identified "a 'conflict' between personal enjoyment and the necessity for social conformity." He contended that forcing children to conform would produce "inner turmoil" caused by "frustration and the lack of gratification," whereas leaving them entirely free to gratify their desires would result in "anti-social" behaviour and an inability "to live comfortably with others." For Blatz, the ideal was a middle path in which children learned to internalize expectations:

> A training method which affords the best results takes into consideration both the child's enjoyment and the necessity for conforming. If the teacher develops in the child a *want* – a wish – to conform and demonstrates that conformity does not necessarily deprive the child of *all* satisfaction but often enhances gratification, then the education may turn out satisfactorily both for society and for the individual.[62]

In contrast to the rigid behaviourist approach promoted by influential American psychologist John Watson during the interwar years, postwar parenting advice generally rejected "autocratic parent-child relationships" and "despotic discipline;" just as the western Allies rejected political totalitarianism the field of child psychology turned away from dictatorial parenting methods.[63] Rather, the goal was for "sympathetic adult[s]" to "help the child enjoy taking part in necessary conformity – which is kept to the minimum."[64] Peter Stearns argues that

> in many ways the permissiveness advocates (far more than their behaviorist predecessors) were urging on parents the ambitious goal not simply of making sure their children adhered to some rules but of ensuring their proper attitude – which, the experts now insisted, could not be accomplished through command and punishment ... Getting a child to think and feel right, as well as to do right, represented an escalation of parental responsibilities, not a retreat from standards.[65]

In extolling the innocence and freedom of childhood, nudists also enlisted the body as a tool of socialization, pursuing the same goal as parents, teachers, and psychologists – to produce children who could channel and express bodily functions and desires in acceptable ways. They encouraged children to internalize social norms and develop self-control. Dismantling the taboos around nudity, they hoped, would encourage greater self-regulation among children, not less, and would teach them how to manage their impulses and conform with behavioural norms. Nudists saw embodiment as central to the development of a child's self-identity and socialization: "Nudist parents, rich or poor, give their children the most precious gift civilized people have in their power to bestow – a fuller knowledge of themselves through understanding and appreciation of their bodies."[66] Mona Gleason characterizes "the normal child" imagined by postwar psychologists as "a unique individual who successfully mastered conformity."[67] Arguably, nudism was one means of achieving this paradoxical state.

## Domestic Life

Nudists believed that domestic and social nudism was the best means of fulfilling the advice of child psychologists. But despite alignment of the objectives of child psychology and nudism and their agreement on the importance of positive messaging about children's bodies and bodily functions, their viewpoints diverged with respect to parental (not to mention extrafamilial) nudity. Generally speaking, parenting literature advised that permitting young boys and girls to bathe or play together in the nude was healthy and educational. However, psychologists were much more reluctant to approve of parental nudity in the presence of children. Connett himself conceded this point in 1954, when he revisited the subject. He acknowledged that the child psychologists he had read did "not actually advocat[e] nudism" and that they encouraged parental nudity only if the nuclear family did not include children of both sexes.[68] This was the position taken by American pediatrician Dr. Benjamin Spock in the 1957 edition of his bestselling advice manual *The Common Sense Book of Baby and Child Care.* Noting a trend toward "complete nudity in quite a few homes," he commented that "today's casual attitude is a lot healthier" than the "excessive modesty of the Victorian period" and agreed that it was "wholesome" for children of both sexes to occasionally see each other in the nude. But he was not convinced that parental nudity should be endorsed. He wrote, "there's evidence that at least some young children get upset by regularly seeing their parents naked. The reason is that young children's feelings for their parents are so intense."[69] Spock's hesitancy was grounded in concern over the power imbalance between parents and children, and the attendant intensity with which such an encounter was imbued. His perspective was informed by Freud's theory of the Oedipus complex, in which parents figured as the first objects of sexual desire for their children.

The issue was also one of concern to prospective nudist parents, who frequently worried about whether it was appropriate for children to see adults in the nude, especially themselves. A reader of Harris's *Sunbathing for Health* column suggested that the sight of her and her husband "completely nude ... would have a bad effect on my child." A couple expressed similar uncertainty during their membership interview with the Toronto Gymnosophical Society.[70] And responding to a new Sun Valley Gardens member who feared that nudism would be damaging to his children, Karl Ruehle countered that, in fact, "it is outright harmful to create an artificial barrier between them and yourselves. Besides, what we do is for the benefit of the young generation which we wish to grow up healthier and cleaner in mind and action ... They need nudism more than anyone else."[71]

Unlike Spock, who felt that parental authority made family nudity a perilous proposition, nudists believed that domestic and social nudism could minimize the distance between parents and children. Mildred Harris told her "Woman's Page" readers that "sleeping without night clothes, taking baths with the children, dressing and undressing together where it is warm and comfortable and chummy, are all a part of modern life."[72] Such a practice was complementary with modern, democratic values and could only strengthen family ties. A well-known British naturist declared, "The family is still the basis of our civilization, and Naturism can be the best basis of the happy family life."[73] Moreover, every family member could enjoy it, and nudists contrasted it favourably with other leisure pursuits. One woman had this message for mothers who were contemplating nudism: "As time goes on, you will spend as much time as you can at the nudist camp because it is an inexpensive outing – the children love it – and it is something your whole family can take part in. No more husband going off fishing or golfing or something else, while you and the children stay home on Sundays."[74] A club newsletter suggested, "Don't send your children away to expensive summer camps – join a Nudist club and go along with them."[75] Parents were warned that "leaving the children home with friends, or with grandmother or grandfather while you spend the day at camp is one of the most selfish thoughts you could possess."[76] Clearly, nudism was a logical extension of the modern democratic family model and the postwar emphasis on "family togetherness." At a time when psychologists worried about the erosion of traditional sources of family stability – religious, legal, economic – the movement cast itself as a new "force of cohesion" that promoted shared leisure and emotional intimacy between family members.[77]

Nudists presented their movement as a form of natural sex education that familiarized children with their own bodies and those of others. Moreover, by breaking down barriers between parents and children, it opened the door to frank discussions about the body and sexuality. Going naked together, they suggested, contributed to a trusting parent-child relationship – there were "no secrets in a nudist home."[78] But little was said about exactly what information about sex would be provided to children and adolescents. Throughout the twentieth century, the content of sex education was even more controversial than the question of whether to provide it, and nudists carefully steered clear of this minefield.[79]

There is some indication that parents used nudism to avoid having "the talk" with their children. A common trope was that participating in nudism resolved children's questions about sex. For example, Lisa Stein, owner of the Four Seasons Nature Park, suggested that

> it's the most easiest thing to do, for parents to bring up children in the nude, or in a nudist club. I can say that because I brought a son up in the nudist way of life. When he became a teenager there was just nothing to explain, it was all there. There was no sneaking behind the bushes and looking what the opposite sex looks like ... He'd grown up with it, there were much less questions.[80]

Given that physical contact and the slightest hint of sexual arousal were expressly forbidden at clubs, it is difficult to believe that merely looking at the opposite sex would leave "nothing to explain" for curious children and adolescents. Stein's suggestion is evocative of the sex education method promoted by earlier social purists: the study of flora and fauna. Sethna describes this as a rather obscure way of providing "just enough knowledge to curb their curiosity about sexual physiology while simultaneously indoctrinating them in the wonders of monogamous marriage and child rearing."[81]

### Children as Club Members

Children's actual position at the club was more marginal and problematic than the nudist philosophy might suggest. Whereas nudists claimed that "the backbone to the nudist movement are children" and made a point of recruiting nuclear families, children seem generally to have been significantly outnumbered by adults.[82] In a 1953 CBC Radio interview on the occasion of the official opening of the Sunny Trails Club, Ray Connett told the reporter that only seven of its fifty-eight members were children, though he also estimated that fifty-eight children had attended that day's event.[83] Kurt

Grell, a Sunny Chinooks member who contributed to a history of the club published in 2003, examined historical membership figures in the club records and concluded that they sometimes "inflated" the number of children. He questioned the accuracy of a November 1971 club membership count that reported fifty-seven adults and seventy children. In actuality, his research indicated that during the 1970s and 1980s the average ratio at Sunny Chinooks was thirty to thirty-five children for every hundred adults.[84] Canadian clubs may have inflated children's attendance numbers in their effort to portray nudism as family friendly. That said, during the peak of the baby boom in the 1950s and 1960s, the ratio of children to adults may well have been higher at the clubs than it would eventually be at Sunny Chinooks during the 1970s and 1980s. The ratio also varied from club to club depending on how child friendly they were in both attitude and amenities (such as kiddie pools and playgrounds).

Clubs were billed as welcoming locales for children, places where "mothers [could] turn the youngsters loose": "everything we have is designed with the thought of safety and enjoyment for the children."[85] Yet club leaders not infrequently expressed frustration with "negligent parents" for failing to monitor "unruly children" who were a nuisance to other members.[86] The Toronto Sunglades Club adopted the general rule that parents "keep proper surveillance over their juniors and refrain [sic] them immediately when a member is being annoyed."[87] More than once, clubs found it necessary to "remind parents that their children's safety is solely their own responsibility" and to discourage them from leaving children unattended at the pool.[88] Using even stronger language, Karl Ruehle informed Sun Valley Gardens members that "parents who leave their children without supervision are on the way out."[89] His introduction of a Mother of the Year Award for "the mother who took outstanding care of her children, also judging the children's conduct while at the Park," demonstrated which parent would be held responsible for minding the children.[90]

Children who slipped up on their toilet training could also be problematic at the club. The manager at Meadowbrook Sun Club advised parents "to keep their children a bit more under control," complaining that "especially the morning after a party, [they] don't get fed, they run around the grounds, do big jobs on the floor of the clubhouse and some of our willing members have to clean up the mess. That just is not fair. If you have children, you have responsibilities."[91] At the Ottawa Silva Sun Club, one of the "Ten Camp Rules" was that parents "keep untrained children in diapers."[92] In a large social club, there were limits to the freedom that children (and their parents) could enjoy. These complaints underscore Patricia Holland's comments on the sometimes jarring disjuncture between an idealized vision of childhood and the reality:

> Children bear the burden of a nostalgia for a remembered, childish impulsive self – an ambivalent nostalgia which becomes clear in the recurring moral panics around the potential uncontrollability of real children ... Children introduce disorder and pollution into a comfortable everyday life, and this theme runs alongside the idyllic beauty of childhood. The bodies of young children are leaky; they do not respect established boundaries.[93]

Children's voices are largely absent from the nudist archive, not only because of the scarcity of records containing children's voices but also because occasionally adults actively sought to silence them. As nudists moved between the club and the outside world, many preferred to keep their club involvement secret. For parents of young children, this posed a potential problem – unaware of the need for discretion, a child might innocently disclose the family secret to friends and neighbours. Prospective nudist parents mentioned this scenario, and the clubs themselves addressed it. Interviewed on CBC Radio, a Calgary Sunny Chinook said, "It's a very simple thing to explain to your child that this is something that is done with Mommy and Daddy and our other friends at camp but it is something that is not done in public, and is not discussed among people who are not members of the group."[94] When a reader alerted *Sunbathing for Health* that her child had been teased after telling other children about nudism, Harris replied that "a child of another race or religion will usually be accepted by its playmates if it does not emphasize the difference between them. So too with nudist children. Briefly, they must not brag about nudism, or they may suffer."[95] A 1965 publication of the Eastern Canadian Sunbathing Association, *The Sunshine Family*, simply assured parents that "very very few families have been embarrassed by talkative children," implying that perceptive children would internalize social norms.[96] These messages flew in the face of the nudist philosophy of openness and its equation of privacy with shame but represented an accommodation of adults who wished to avoid awkward conversations and social stigma.

As children entered puberty and adolescence, many became less interested in going to the club. The benefits and attractions of nudism for children could be a selling point for their parents, but the sell was more difficult when adolescents were involved. According to the London Sun Club, "Our biggest problem at the camp is creating enough interest for the teenagers."[97] The Sun Valley Gardens newsletter acknowledged, "We all know the youngsters and teenagers of our members are neglected very much as much as activities for them are concerned. No wonder we are having troubles to keep them interested in camp life if no-one cares about them."[98] Clubs sometimes discussed ways of increasing adolescents' interest in nudism, but they often attributed the lack of engagement to external variables: namely, that teenagers tended to become self-conscious about their bodies and were more likely to spend their leisure time with friends than with their parents. Ray Connett saw the teenaged years as difficult ones, even for those who were raised as nudists: "They are so conscious of their body changes and may want to keep their clothes on. It's a battle they are fighting within themselves and we don't want to aggravate it by insisting they have to take their clothes off."[99] In reference to their own daughter, Harris commented, "Inevitably ... the chums win out, for now our daughter, and this happens in other nudist families too, feels more like going with a gang of youngsters her age, than coming to camp with us."[100] Harris and Connett subscribed to the view of adolescence promulgated by American psychologist G. Stanley Hall as a transitional period of "moral, sexual and psychological upheaval" associated with puberty.[101] In response, they suggested that parents be understanding and give space to teens during this difficult phase.

As the 1960s gave way to the 1970s, the baby boomers entered their teens and adulthood, birth rates declined, and the extreme emphasis on child rearing and domesticity gave way to the sexual revolution and second-wave feminism. In the midst of this demographic shift and climate of social ferment, the centrality of childhood waned in nudist discourse. They increasingly stressed the pleasurable aspects of going clothesless rather than nudism's ability to improve physical or mental health. In a 1974 CBC Radio report on the emergence of clothing-optional resorts, a couple commented on their children's reactions. The father observed, "It's strange enough that we feel very natural about nudity, but our children feel a little strange about it. And our younger boy, it took him two days before he took his clothes off, and our girl still isn't sure, and I think this is the effect of the school system."[102] Like many nudists before him, this man critiqued mainstream society for its detrimental impact on children's body image and self-identity. But noteworthy here is his suggestion that not all children took readily to nudism, in contrast to earlier rhetoric, and the acknowledgment that family participation was driven by the interests of the parents, not the children. It also indicates that the discourse about children as "nudists at heart" may have marginalized individual children's experiences with nudism and obscured the potential for them to be coerced into practices and settings with which they were uncomfortable. Nevertheless, the belief that nudism is both beneficial to and comfortable for children remains a cornerstone of the movements in Canada and the United States. For example, the website of the American Association for Nude Recreation enthuses that children "usually take to our clubs like ducks to water, joyfully running, playing, and splashing without a stitch on."[103]

During the postwar period, children came to occupy a central place in the ideological and practical arguments that rationalized the nudist movement, for a time becoming its raison d'être. In a 1956 column offering pointers for club leaders on public relations, Connett advised, "Always get into your story somewhere the cardinal principles of what we believe, why we believe them, what we do and so on. Emphasize the no liquor angle, the no juvenile delinquency angle and so on."[104] Though Connett and many nudists sincerely believed that their practice was beneficial to children, his comment reveals their awareness of their cultural context and their embrace of children's psychological well-being and sexual adjustment as goals shared inside and outside the movement. The pervasiveness of the normalcy discourse is well established by postwar historians. Significantly, the manner in which Canadian nudists redeployed psychological discourse to their own ends suggests its malleability, as well as its reach. While the postwar years established a discourse that persists in present-day nudism, with the advent of the 1970s the movement became increasingly likely to present nudism as an agreeable leisure pursuit and a modern lifestyle choice.

# PART 2
# Nudism on Display

# 6

# Photographs in *Sunbathing for Health* Magazine, 1947–59

> If we nudists wish to become an accepted part of the Canadian scene, if we hope to recruit more members, and above all, if we want the privilege of practicing nudism in our private clubs without fear of molestation by busy-bodies or snoopers, *we must cease to be strange.* There is only one way to do that. We must put ourselves in the public eye until the public eyebrow no longer raises in astonishment or shocked disapproval when they hear of us.
>
> – Ray Connett, Sunny Trails

During the postwar period, the Canadian nudist movement put itself "in the public eye" by using visual publicity designed to both attract interest and embody its philosophy. Such publicity took two forms: the photography published in *Sunbathing for Health* and the nudist pageant. A crucial component of their movement entailed teaching people to look at the body in a new light. During the nineteenth century, ideas about sight had changed: no longer perceived as a mechanical and objective process, it was now understood as corporeal and subjective. Nudists hoped that both would instill a new "way of seeing," while also winning converts.[1] The visual representations of nudism considered in this and the following chapter embodied both cultural critique and conformity. They were intended to upset conventional notions of nudity as obscene. At the same time, by tapping into the popularity of photography and pageants, and adhering to gender and sexual norms in doing so, nudists presented themselves as ordinary Canadians. Less intentionally, the representations highlighted some of the tensions and contradictions within the movement: they undermined the claim that nudism stripped away artifice and enabled people to relate to one another on a deeper, more meaningful level, and they cast doubt on the extent to which nudism rejected mainstream sexualization of the body – notably the female body – in favour of a more holistic attitude.

## *Sunbathing for Health*

*Sunbathing for Health* was a monthly magazine published in Toronto between 1947 and 1959. Regular features included nature and cooking columns, health and beauty series, reports on American and European clubs, testimonials from converts, and fictionalized accounts of first experiences with nudism. Each issue was about thirty-five pages long, approximately a third of which was devoted to full-page nude photos, with additional snapshots scattered throughout the text. Produced by American, British, and Canadian photographers, professional and amateur, nudist and non-nudist, their quality varied significantly. The photographs embedded in the text were typically taken by an amateur at a club, whereas the full-page format featured professional-quality work. The latter stood apart from the text and facilitated use of the magazine by consumers who were interested solely in the images. To avoid falling afoul of Canadian obscenity law, genitalia were retouched. Depending on local censorship and the decisions of individual vendors, the magazine could be difficult to acquire on newsstands in some parts of Canada, such as Quebec and Toronto, although subscriptions could be obtained by mail. As well as being distributed across Canada, *Sunbathing for Health* was widely distributed in the United States.[2]

The magazine was published by the Rex Book Company, a division of the Sinnott News Company based in Scarborough, Ontario, owned and operated by Thomas Harold Sinnott. Though seemingly sympathetic to the aims of the movement, Sinnott published the magazine for commercial rather than ideological reasons. In 1947, a single issue cost 35 cents and subscribers paid $3.75 per year; by 1959, this had risen to 50 cents per issue or $5.00 per year. Sinnott News was primarily a distribution company, and the mail-order service in the back of *Sunbathing for Health* was probably as profitable as the magazine itself.[3] Readers could order a wide range of literature through the publisher, including erotic fiction, advice books on health and sexuality, collections of nude photography, and nudist promotional material. Nudist readers, or those who declared themselves sympathetic to the philosophy, sometimes complained that the magazine was sold alongside "low-grade, girly, and exposé type of publications" and expressed displeasure with its mail-order advertisements.[4]

Nevertheless, *Sunbathing for Health* earned credibility by publishing articles and columns by bona fide nudists – including Canadian, American, British, and Australian ones – and particularly through the active involvement of Ray and Mildred Connett. Many columns came and went over the years, but their "Sunny Trails" and "Woman's Page" were mainstays for the entire publication run. Ray Connett edited the "Readers' Page" and corresponded with readers on behalf of the magazine. He also managed the "Directory of Nudist Clubs" and played a key role in the development of the Canadian movement by putting readers in touch with local organizers. It is unclear what kind of remuneration he received. What is clear is that his major concern was to put nudism "in the public eye" and to present it in an accurate, rational, and convincing manner.[5] The photos in *Sunbathing for Health* must therefore be read in the context of the Connetts' missionary zeal and the commercial interests of Sinnott News.

Far from being straightforward "illustrations" of nudism, as Connett implied, the *Sunbathing for Health* photographs drew on a variety of photographic genres and interacted with the text in complex and sometimes contradictory ways. Their messages were complicated by the competing interests of the movement and the magazine publisher: were the photos selling nudism or selling the magazine? Moreover, discussions of the images by columnists and readers reveal divergent understandings of the power and potential of photography to represent, and convert people to, the nudist way of seeing the body.

*Sunbathing for Health* emerged within an already established genre of nudist periodicals dating to the interwar period that included the American *Sunshine and Health,* the British *Health and Efficiency,* the *Australian Sunbather,* and the West German *Sonnenfreude* and *Helios.* Some, such as *Health and Efficiency* and *Sunbathing for Health,* were produced by commercial publishers, but others were produced by nudist organizations themselves. *Sunshine and Health,* for example, was the official publication of the American Sunbathing Association. In both cases, however, nude photos were a central component. They had two purposes – to provide documentation that offered non-nudists an insider's view of clubs, and to visually represent the philosophy that all parts of the body are wholesome.

The photographic content of the magazines evolved over time. In his analysis of *Sunshine and Health,* Brian Hoffman isolates the Second World War as an important transition point: "To support its struggling clubs and maintain its organization during the Second World War, [American] nudist leaders began to accentuate the erotic appeal of *S&H* by transforming the flagship nudist magazine to appeal to men of all sexualities."[6] Although erotic images of women entered mainstream advertising and periodicals early in the twentieth century, they proliferated during the Second World War. Pin-up photos were seen as morale boosters for soldiers and a respectable alternative to soliciting prostitutes or engaging in homosexuality.[7] Male physique photos also enjoyed a surge in popularity during the war, relying on the athletic alibi of bodybuilding to mask their homoerotic appeal. In keeping with these developments, nudist magazines combined "the avowedly asexual nudist tradition with more sexually suggestive motifs," printing photos that put attractive male and female models on display for visual consumption alongside more mundane pictures of nudist activities.[8] Despite their protestations to the contrary, nudist magazines participated in "the commodification of sexual images" that Joanne Meyerowitz suggests "partially supplanted the commodification of sexual acts" in the twentieth century.[9]

## Photographs of Women in *Sunbathing for Health*

A significant feature of *Sunbathing for Health* was the nude photographs of men, women, and children. Consistent with Canadian nudists' desire to establish themselves as a family movement, the mix of sexes in the magazine set it apart from such publications as *Strength and Health, Esquire,* and *Playboy,* which concentrated almost exclusively on either male or female bodies. But although photos of men and children appeared in *Sunbathing for Health,* women predominated. Each issue contained numerous full-page shots of them, most often alone but sometimes in groups of two or three (Figure 6.1). The front cover always featured a female model, with the back cover typically reserved for a male one.

The images of women ranged from a pictorial style – soft-focused and romantic in feel – to the slick, modern style of glamour photography. An image from the April 1952 issue combines elements of both, incorporating

**Figure 6.1** *Sunbathing for Health,* November 1947 | Courtesy of Naturist Education Foundation Research Library

a natural outdoor scene with a crisp close-up of an attractive model (Figure 6.2). She sits on a rock, leaning over the water, which reflects her arms and torso. Instead of looking into the lens, she glances down, smiling at her reflection. Her pose accentuates her breasts. The water shimmers in the sunlight, and tall reeds provide a contrasting background. Another image, appearing in the May–June 1952 issue, incorporates similar elements (Figure 6.3). Posing before a background of scrubby bushes, the model perches on a large rock, looking up and away from the camera, as if soaking up the sun. Her right arm is raised, elbow bent, and her hand touches her brow. This pose, together with the tucked-in abdomen and straight back, makes

**Figure 6.2** *Sunbathing for Health,* April 1952 | Courtesy of Naturist Education Foundation Research Library

**Figure 6.3** *Sunbathing for Health,* May–June 1952 | Courtesy of Naturist Education Foundation Research Library

her breasts the focal point of the shot. Her expression is blank, devoid of enjoyment, which may have been intended to convey an artistic, reflective tone that differentiated it from the pin-up genre. A large part of that genre's appeal was its depiction of women having a good time.

The full-page photos of female models were generally taken outdoors – on a beach, in a meadow or forest, on rocks, or by a stream – underscoring the naturalness of nudity and the cultural associations between women and nature. The models are almost never identified by name, essentializing them as ideals rather than individuals. They are usually highly posed, despite the apparent naturalness of the scene. Arms are often outstretched and toes pointed, signalling the appreciation of sun, air, or water. These positions also accentuate the curves of breasts, buttocks, hips, and legs. Despite the nudist emphasis on the wholesomeness of the entire body, breasts figure prominently in many shots. This was in keeping with the emphasis on full breasts in postwar fashions, as epitomized by Hollywood stars such as Marilyn Monroe and Jayne Mansfield. It confirms Anne Hollander's argument that "the perception and self-perception of nudity are dependent on a sense of clothing."[10] In other words, even unclothed there is no escaping culturally specific bodily ideals centred on the clothed state.

*Sunbathing for Health* appeared at a time when images of the female body were on regular display. Kenon Breazeale argues that *Esquire* magazine, launched in 1933, brought provocative images of the female body more firmly into the mainstream. In the midst of the Depression, astute marketing exploited gender anxiety derived from men's threatened breadwinner status to promote a new male identity organized around leisure, consumption, and desire.[11] *Playboy,* which debuted in 1953 – midway through the publication run of *Sunbathing for Health* – rejected domesticity and responsibility in favour of a hedonistic playboy culture. "Above all," Patricia Vettel-Becker observes, "the playboy consumes women."[12] Sexual representations of women reinforced gender difference and assuaged masculine anxieties arising out of the Depression and the Second World War. They performed this function for both the male consumer and photographer. In her study of postwar American photographic culture, Vettel-Becker traces the professionalization and masculinization of photography, and argues that "by objectifying women, male photographers subjectified themselves, not only as artists but as men."[13] Women were affected too. According to Joanne Meyerowitz, "cheesecake and borderline material [that successfully but narrowly avoided classification as pornography] arose in the confluence of rising consumerism, burgeoning mass production, and changing sexual mores. They comprised and reinforced a new taxonomy of sexual display that changed the ways that women were seen in public and perhaps also the ways that women saw themselves."[14] Visual representations both reflected and contributed to cultural change, including how masculine and feminine identities were portrayed and understood.

Normative gender roles also structured photographic practices at the time: most often, women posed in front of the camera and men stood behind it.[15] This held true for the shots in *Sunbathing for Health.* Columnist Marguerite Bosc suggested that many people purchased the magazine for its "numerous photographic expressions of beauty and nude loveliness," clearly referencing the images of women.[16] When a reader stated that a female was "naturally more photogenic than a male" and therefore an "ideal subject for photos," he voiced an assumption that was widespread inside and outside the nudist movement.[17] In one of her columns, Mildred Harris urged men to take nude photos of their wives and children. As to why

*Sunbathing for Health* did not contain "more genuine pictures of nudist activities," she blamed "bashful gals who say 'I haven't the figure' or even, but I hope not, 'Not me, I don't want *my* picture in a magazine.'"[18] Nowhere was a wife instructed to pick up a camera and aim it at her husband!

Blake McLachlan, photographic contributor to *Sunbathing for Health* and author of the column "Aids for the Amateur Photographer," underscored the gendered dynamic between male photographer and female subject. He mentioned that he frequently received wistful letters suggesting, "It must be wonderful to be in a position to call a selection of models, gather up camera and equipment and whiz out to some quiet sunlit haven, to spend the day, photographing beautiful girls." Attempting to inject a dose of reality into this fantasy, McLachlan described a recent day of shooting "where practically every conceivable difficulty arose."[19] In another instalment, he informed his readers that

> the American girl is world famous for a firm healthy body, perfect poise and delicate beauty. Your job is to capture and reproduce through the magic of the camera lens this fascinating figure of perfection. It often requires time and a great deal of patience to train the average girl into a competent subject for compositions of the nude. In most cases results achieved are well worth the effort.[20]

In this patronizing anecdote, McLachlan praised his models' bodies but placed particular emphasis on the masculine authority and competency required to capture a good photograph of them. Ironically, his own photographs often feature models who are awkwardly posed and have a lower-quality resolution than many others in the magazine.

Despite this interplay between male photographer and female model, nudists favourably contrasted their non-erotic, "natural," or aesthetic appreciation for the nude body with the sexualization of women's bodies that typified popular culture. McLachlan instructed would-be photographers,

> You must be able to look upon the body as it is, a masterpiece of sumptuous beauty to be photographically molded into a refined composition of line, form, mass and shadow. Any indication of a sensual or suggestive aspect should be forever omitted from your "nudes." You should have a deep down distaste for all things in the least obscene.

Driving the point home, he concluded, "pictures of the nude must inspire rather than excite."[21] Elsewhere in McLachlan's column, however, there is the suggestion that, even for him, the line between nude and pin-up was a fine one. He cautioned his readers that jewellery is

> absolutely taboo in outdoor work unless it is a distinct supporting factor to the general theme ... Otherwise, your composition may classify as a pin-up picture. If shoes are worn they should be the flat heel or sandal type; never the high heel type. Admittedly the wearing of a high heel shoe does lend an added appeal to the leg ... But we do not strive for this alone. Our interest is picturing the female nudist in a natural environment, engaging in athletic activity or basking in the health-providing rays of the sun.[22]

McLachlan suggested that having clothes "strewn about in the picture" or capturing a model's personality created an "undressed suggestion" that was antithetical to nude photography. He also advised that models should not look directly into the camera.[23]

His perspective on nude photography stands in contrast to the opinion expressed by renowned art historian Kenneth Clark in his 1956 publication *The Nude: A Study in Ideal Form.* Clark "claimed that any artistic nude, no matter how abstract, should be able to 'arouse in the spectator some vestige of erotic feeling.' If not, he argued, it is simply 'bad art.'"[24] Some photographic contributors to *Sunbathing for Health* demonstrated agreement with Clark rather than McLachlan. One such photographer was Ed Lange, a prominent American nudist photographer who had worked in fashion photography and was a frequent contributor to the magazine. He did not hesitate to pose his models in less rustic settings than those favoured by McLachlan, such as on the concrete pool decks of the many California nudist clubs that he frequented. Nor did he ban jewellery and "personality." To the contrary, he seemed to want to capture personality, and his subjects often meet the camera's gaze, drawing in the viewer. Figure 6.4 shows a typical Lange shot. The smiling model appears to be sunbathing at a club. She wears sunglasses and earrings, and is seated on a towel. Another image, with no identification of model or photographer, was very probably taken by Lange: it displays his crisp style and it too shows a woman enjoying herself at a club. She stands on the ladder of a swimming pool, presumably on her way into the water, with immaculately styled hair, heavily made-up

**Figure 6.4** Oakdale Ranch, California. Photo by Ed Lange. *Sunbathing for Health,* May 1957 | Courtesy of Naturist Education Foundation Research Library

**Figure 6.5** *Sunbathing for Health,* July 1956 | Courtesy of Naturist Education Foundation Research Library

face, and prominent earrings (Figure 6.5). Lange was a member of the American Sunbathing Association and active in the nudist movement when he took these photographs. But in 1958, a US Supreme Court ruling in *Sunshine Book Company v. Summerfield* found that the photographs of completely nude men, women, and children in *Sunshine and Health* were not obscene because they had "redeeming social importance." Emboldened by this development, Lange went on to create "a line of ultra-liberal nudist magazines" that portrayed more graphic, unapologetically erotic nudity, including some featuring young, adolescent models.[25] He also pushed the boundaries of orthodox nudism as founder of Elysium Fields in 1968, a clothing-optional "human growth centre." Elysium Fields permitted physical contact between members, offered massage therapy on site, and between 1970 and 1984 featured an infamous Meditation Room that had a mattress as its only furnishing and was available for use by individuals or couples for a maximum of 30 minutes.[26]

## Physique Photography

Whereas many shots of women in *Sunbathing for Health* were produced by nudist photographers, this was not true for those of male models, reflecting anxiety about the homoerotic overtones of men taking and viewing pictures of other men. The professional photos of men in *Sunbathing for Health* belonged to the physique genre of photography, which dated back to turn-of-the-nineteenth-century strongmen such as Eugen Sandow but which reached its heyday in the 1950s.[27] Montrealer Tony Lanza was a particularly prolific contributor of such photos to *Sunbathing for Health*. A self-portrait in the June 1949 issue identified him as a "professional wrestler and Judo expert."[28] Lanza ran advertisements in the magazine selling photographs of "America's and Canada's best built men," and he volunteered his services to potential models, suggesting, "If in Montreal have your photograph taken. It may appear in this magazine" (Figure 6.6). Among his subjects were winners of bodybuilding contests, such as Allan Paivio – Mr. Canada of 1948, the famous Steve Reeves – Mr. America of 1947, and Robert Roy – Mr. Montreal of 1949.[29] Lanza worked closely with Joe and Ben Weider. The Montreal-born brothers, sons of Jewish immigrants from Poland, founded the International Federation of Bodybuilders and share much of the credit for establishing bodybuilding as an international sport.[30] They created a publishing empire of bodybuilding magazines, and David Chapman describes Tony Lanza as "the best of a number of talented photographers who had worked for Joe Weider and his fledgling magazine *Your Physique*." Lanza's pictures were published in magazines around the world.[31]

The other physique photographer whose work frequently appeared in *Sunbathing for Health* was Earle Forbes, a New Yorker. Scholar Thomas Waugh describes Forbes as part of "the first gay generation of physique photographers in the contemporary sense of the word," who, during the 1930s, began to fashion careers devoted almost exclusively to the physique genre. Historically, photographs of naked men were suppressed because of their association with homosexuality, so they were "camouflaged" by the insertion of references to classical Greek art and bodybuilding in order to render the nude male "socially tolerable."[32] Waugh characterizes this "current of 'physique' eroticism that flourished in the postwar decades" as "one of the great achievements of gay culture" and even suggests that the intense repression of homosexuality during the fifties may have derived from this increased visibility.[33] Whereas physique photos evaded censorship in the 1950s so long

**Figure 6.6** Advertisement for Tony Lanza, "World Famous Physique Photographer," *Sunbathing for Health,* April 1951 | Courtesy of Naturist Education Foundation Research Library

**Figure 6.7** Ovila Asselin, Montreal. Photo by Lanza. *Sunbathing for Health,* September 1948 | Courtesy of Naturist Education Foundation Research Library

**Figure 6.8** James Vichiconti, New York City. Photo by Earle Forbes. *Sunbathing for Health,* April 1949 | Courtesy of Naturist Education Foundation Research Library

as genitals were concealed, they were nonetheless widely associated with homosexuality. In *Sunbathing for Health,* this link was mitigated by the fact that photos of naked men appeared alongside those of women and children, with women predominating. Just as women's presence was vital to the clubs, and seen as certifying the heterosexuality and respectability of their male members, mixing the photos of female and male models facilitated readers' visual access to the male body without arousing suspicion.

Photos of male models differed dramatically from those of female models in *Sunbathing for Health.* A Lanza shot of Montreal bodybuilder and wrestler Ovila Asselin that appeared in the September 1948 issue exhibits many characteristic elements of physique photography (Figure 6.7). It was taken in a studio against a simple black backdrop that contrasts with Asselin's paler skin tone. He stands erect, with his arms bent and fists resting against his sides, showing off his muscular arms and chest. He has a straight nose and a square jaw, and he gazes confidently to his right. While Lanza photographed his models in both indoor and outdoor environments, the Earle Forbes images in *Sunbathing for Health* were all shot in a studio, with a simple black background. His male subjects stand, kneel, or sit in poses that display their muscles to best advantage, often with oiled bodies and sometimes holding vaguely classical props such as spears or swords. A Forbes photo of James Vichiconti depicts a young man, well-oiled and muscular, who looks directly into the lens (Figure 6.8). His full lips and intense gaze give the image a more erotic feel than Lanza's photos. Unlike the female models in *Sunbathing for Health,* male models were frequently identified by name.

By the postwar period, nudism had abandoned its preoccupation with physical fitness, but this older emphasis remained evident in the photographs printed in *Sunbathing for Health.* In his study of the nude, Kenneth Clark concentrated on classical and Renaissance art, but he observed of photography, "Consciously, or unconsciously, photographers have usually recognized that in a photograph of the nude their real object is not to reproduce the naked body, but to imitate some artist's view of what the naked body should be like."[34] Blake McLachlan said much the same thing as he expounded on the differing strategies for composing nude studies of men and women. As he explained,

> The form of activity should ... be suited to the subject. If the study is of a male, the photo should express strength and activity. The sculptures of the ancient Greek athletes are splendid examples of how to portray

these essential characteristics ... With the female however, the exact opposite is the case. A female nude should portray lightness and delicacy in the curves of the body. There should never be any harsh lines or suggestion of heaviness.[35]

Both male and female models in *Sunbathing for Health* embodied a young, fit ideal. They were overwhelmingly white, with a few notable exceptions. The Asian American woman who appeared in the September 1953 issue was featured more than once in the magazine (Figure 6.9). She nonetheless adhered to the other criteria of being young, attractive, and feminine. The models represented distinct visions of idealized femininity and masculinity: men were muscular and athletic, women were slim and curvy. The photos were a reflection of racial and gender norms, as well as the genres of nude photography from which they derived.

Differences between the sexes were underscored even in the manner in which images were retouched. Unlike *Sunshine and Health*, which, by the

**Figure 6.9** *Sunbathing for Health*, September 1953 | Courtesy of Naturist Education Foundation Research Library

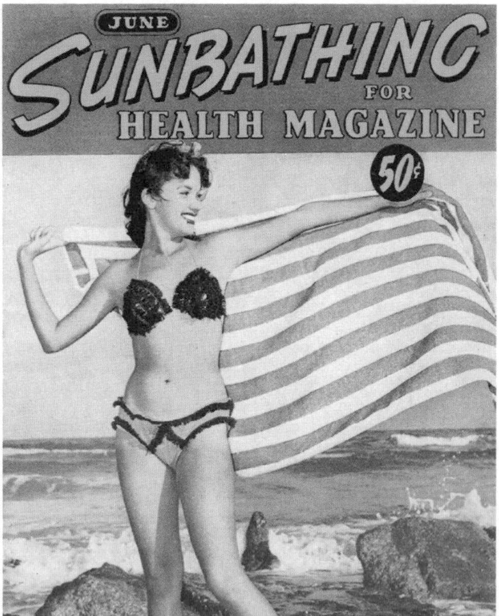


**Figure 6.10** *Sunbathing for Health*, June 1956 | Courtesy of Naturist Education Foundation Research Library

late 1950s, challenged American obscenity laws by publishing photos that included genitalia and pubic hair, the Canadian magazine carefully avoided legal trouble by retouching shots with full frontal nudity.[36] Depending on whether the subject were male or female, it employed different methods. The female pubic area was airbrushed away, sometimes quite inexpertly, but *Sunbathing for Health* shied away from castrating male models with the airbrush, instead covering their genitals with a bodybuilder's posing strap drawn in black ink. The manner of retouching worked to reassert sexual difference while simultaneously veiling it from sight. Symbolically, it furthered Victorian ideas that cast men as sexual and women as asexual. An interesting exception to this rule involved the cover photos: during the first half of the magazine's run, they featured nude women with exposed breasts, but in later years the models wore bathing suits in an effort to attain more widespread distribution (Figure 6.10). In March 1956, popular American pin-up model Bettie Page wore a bikini in her *Sunbathing for Health* cover shot, following closely on the heels of her January 1955 appearance as the *Playboy* centrefold.[37] Connett explained, "We feel it is better to reach the thousands more with this type of cover. The inside tells our story."[38]

## Children as Subjects and Consumers of *Sunbathing for Health*

In contrast to the full-page professional-quality photographs of adult models that filled the pages of *Sunbathing for Health*, the photos of children in the magazine were mainly amateur snapshots set within the text. The images were often candid and shot outdoors at a club. A photo from the April 1958 issue displays a group of children playing in the wading pool at Sunny Trails (Figure 6.11). It was not unusual for children to be photographed with animals, underscoring their connection to the natural world. The inclusion of their images testified to their participation in nudist activities and asserted the respectability of nudism as a family-friendly movement. Captions often delivered a clear message about how natural and comfortable nudism was for children. For example, a photo of a young boy on a swimming dock is captioned, "Children take to Naturism unconsciously, and the health benefits are very noticeable" (Figure 6.12).

These pictures relied on social tolerance for the nudity of young children to upset any simple equation of nude photography with the erotic or obscene. Emmanuel Cooper notes that "male and female childhood nudity was a perfectly acceptable subject in Victorian and Edwardian photography and

**Figure 6.11** The children's pool at Sunny Trails. Photo by Engler. *Sunbathing for Health,* April 1958 | Courtesy of Naturist Education Foundation Research Library

**Figure 6.12** *Sunbathing for Health,* October 1957 | Courtesy of Naturist Education Foundation Research Library

Children take to Naturism unconsciously, and the health benefits are very noticeable

the photographs exhibited with little fear of censorship."[39] In *Sunshine Book Company v. Summerfield*, a 1955 case involving *Sunshine and Health* magazine, an American lower court echoed this view. Judge Kirkland ruled that "the common acceptance of the American people" was that nude photographs of young children, even ones revealing their "diminutive and undeveloped genitalia," were not obscene "by virtue of their age of innocence" and that one would have to be "prudish" to consider them as such.[40] This seemed to be the case in Canada too; Canadian newspapers not uncommonly published pictures of children who had stripped down to cool off on hot summer days. In 1962, a Calgary Sunny Chinook noted that "every summer ... there's all kinds of pictures in the newspapers of little fellas that decide they want to get cool and they take off their sun suit."[41]

Kirkland suggested that the situation was more tenuous when photos depicted children who had entered puberty.[42] However, none of the images of children, of any age, in *Sunbathing for Health* aroused criticism from readers (unlike those of male and female models, as we shall see). This fact, combined with occasional queries as to why the magazine did not print more shots of children, could demonstrate an acceptance of the wholesomeness of the photos and their consistency with the nudist message. But it could also indicate a demand for nude photos of children by those who had a sexual interest in them. Growing cultural concern with pedophilia was beginning to raise occasional red flags about how photos of unclothed children might be viewed. A 1958 column by Mildred Harris suggests a degree of suspicion regarding the use of these photos. Encouraging readers to submit nude Christmas photos to the magazine, she advised, "Try some with the kiddies sitting around the tree opening presents. Just make sure they are holding something in their laps when you snap – yes, kiddies too, isn't it awful to think of those dirty minds trying to find fault with our way of life?"[43] Shots that revealed the genitals of children were airbrushed before publication. Notwithstanding Harris's remark, nude pictures of children raised far less concern during the postwar period than they do today.[44] It was not until 1993 that Canada first enacted legislation that dealt specifically with child pornography, when Section 163.1 was added to the Criminal Code, criminalizing the possession of child pornography and toughening the penalties for producing, distributing, and selling pornographic images of children.[45]

Just as parents who contemplated joining a club were primarily concerned with the impact of children seeing others in the nude, not vice versa, controversy surrounding nudist magazines centred on the dangers of children viewing the images, not on being photographed and viewed by adults. In 1951, a Protestant minister addressed a letter to *Sunbathing for Health* on behalf of the ministerial association in his town. At a recent meeting, the group had discussed the literature sold on local newsstands, including *Sunbathing for Health:*

> Reading through a recent copy we note the high tone of the several articles and the purposes as underlined therein. We may not agree with those ideas but we must record the sincerity of the writers and their intention of keeping to a high moral standard. However we deplore the use made of the nude pictures found therein.
>
> We know of at least one place where the teenagers sit down with these pictures and eat their snacks and feel that the way they discuss these pictures is not in accordance with your own principles of moral behaviour.
>
> We wonder therefore if you have ever thought about publishing your magazine without the pictures and still retain its good reading material. We would like your reaction to this idea.[46]

This comment reflected public anxiety about "indecent" literature such as pulp fiction, comic books, and "sexy magazines," and their potential harm to children and adolescents. Mary Louise Adams explains that a variety of organizations from church groups to labour unions raised the alarm about obscene material: "'Concerned citizens' claimed trashy books and magazines were powerful enough not just to threaten but to cancel the efforts of church, school, and home to educate young people about proper forms of sex and family living."[47] In England, a test for obscenity had been established in the 1868 case of *R. v. Hicklin* that was also applied by Canadian courts. It made children's perceived vulnerability as consumers of published material central to the legal prosecution of obscenity. In his *Hicklin* ruling, Chief Justice Alexander Cockburn declared, "I think the test of obscenity is this, whether the tendency of the matter charged as obscenity is to deprave and corrupt those whose minds are open to such immoral influences, and into whose hands a publication of this sort may fall."[48] The concerned minister who wrote to *Sunbathing for Health* did not suggest that its photos were obscene, but he did express uneasiness about their availability to, and impact on, impressionable youth. His comments underscore the cultural tension regarding images of the nude. His group did not take issue with the philosophy of nudism per se, but it did object to the photographs that appeared in the magazine.

Ray Connett featured the minister's letter and his own response in the March 1951 issue:

> While we deplore the misuse of our illustrations by curiosity seekers, we have long since resigned ourselves to this phase, for it is only a phase, in the education of readers. We receive many many letters from people who are now clean living nudists, some of them holding responsible positions in the movement, but who admit that in the beginning they were attracted to our magazines by the pictures and only turned to reading the articles later. The fact that they had their natural innate curiosity satisfied by pictures of people living and playing in natural, wholesome conditions and then had their minds turned by our texts toward a more moral outlook on life is sufficient justification for our continued use of pictures of our way of life to further its acceptance ...
>
> I am not being facetious when I suggest that the youth of your town, if deprived of our magazine illustrations, would turn again to that standby of an older generation, the ladies' section of the mail order catalogue ...
>
> If it is seriously considered that we should remove clean, wholesome nude pictures from the hands of our youngsters, pictures without a trace of suggestion or licentiousness, then we must not, dare not, stop there. We must, as a matter of course, go on to remove nudity from our art galleries, from our public statues, and from our great churches.[49]

Connett's response offers insight into nudist ideas about the role of photography: the pictures in *Sunbathing for Health* and other nudist publications were integral in presenting the nude body as natural and to be celebrated. They satisfied natural curiosity about the body in a non-prurient way – curiosity that was shared by many adults as well as youth, given the repressive social outlook on the body. Although Connett acknowledged that the images were open to different readings, or "misuse," he believed that, like nude bodies, they were not obscene. He also highlighted society's contradictory attitude toward depictions of the body and suggested that the photos in *Sunbathing for Health* were every bit as respectable as the art on display in galleries, city squares, and even churches. If people could find edification there, they could find it in *Sunbathing for Health* too.

**Figure 6.13** *Sunbathing for Health,* April 1958 | Courtesy of Naturist Education Foundation Research Library

## The Medium and the Message

Connett lamented that not enough good-quality photos of "genuine" Canadian nudists were submitted to the magazine. This was understandable given that CSA membership numbered only about five hundred in the mid-1950s, and many nudists wished to protect their privacy. But Connett also defended the selection of images: "Until we can fill our magazine with actual pictures of group activities we must content ourselves with our present works which at least have real artistic quality."[50] Though he preferred pictures that had a documentary purpose, showing "nudism as it is actually lived and enjoyed" (such as Figure 6.13), he defended the professional work in the magazine on the basis of its aesthetic merit. In his opinion, it functioned as a symbolic representation of the nudist philosophy by depicting people who appeared comfortable with their bodies and unashamed of their nudity.[51]

Connett also defended the use of the photographic medium itself:

> It is a simple fact that people have become accustomed to illustrations along with their texts. (Imagine a *Popular Mechanics* magazine without pictures!) ...
>
> When you consider that any nudist magazine will have as its prime consideration the winning of converts to our way of life, you will appreciate that we will naturally seek the most logical and effective way of doing so. This we have found ... can not be done without the use of illustrations. What we preach is, unfortunately, so difficult to believe that many doubt our motives even when countless pictures in our magazines speak openly and honestly of a way of life that is clean, wholesome and entirely moral. Without those pictures we simply would not have a chance of convincing doubters that our life without clothes is different from their filthy imaginings.[52]

Connett emphasized the centrality of the visual to modern life and the attendant need for nudism to participate in it. Photo magazines such as *Life* reached the height of their popularity between about 1945 and the late 1950s, when television became dominant.[53] The prominence of photography in *Sunbathing for Health* no doubt played a crucial role in driving sales, a fact of which Connett was aware, though he downplayed the particular appeal the nude photos may have held.

Photography was widely acknowledged as a favourite pastime among nudists, reflecting both their appreciation for the body and the general popularity of photography as a hobby. This prompted most clubs to adopt a standard set of rules governing the use of cameras. Only pre-approved members were permitted to take photographs, and they were required to obtain consent from their subjects, or, in the case of minors, from their parents. Some clubs restricted photography to a specific area. These regulations were intended to balance the interests of shutterbugs with the protection of privacy. Some clubs also formed camera clubs and solicited models from their membership.[54] Blake McLachlan's "Aids for the Amateur Photographer," which ran in *Sunbathing for Health* between 1949 and 1953, appealed to these budding photographers (Figure 6.14). Offering technical and artistic instruction, he devoted a large portion of his column to critiquing readers' submissions. Nude photography was becoming more widely practised outside the movement at this time. In 1950, McLachlan told his readers, "You, the amateur photographers of the outdoor nude, are pioneering a vast

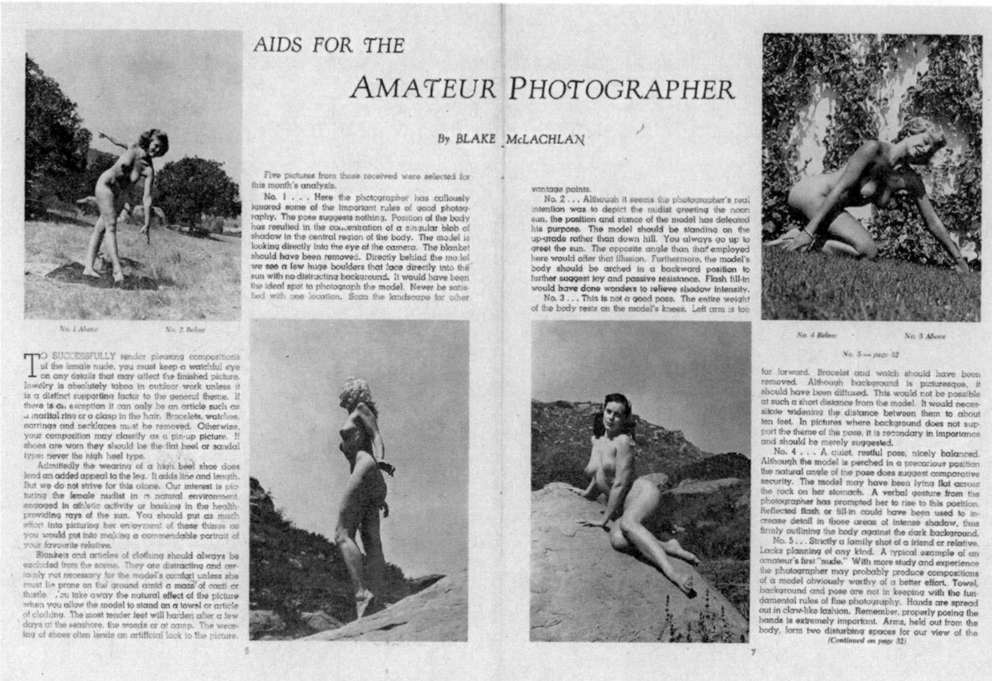

AIDS FOR THE AMATEUR PHOTOGRAPHER

By BLAKE McLACHLAN

No. 1 Above  No. 2 Below

TO SUCCESSFULLY render pleasing compositions of the female nude, you must keep a watchful eye on any details that may affect the finished picture. Jewelry is absolutely taboo in outdoor work unless it is a distinct supporting factor to the general theme. If there is an exception it can only be an article such as a marital ring or a clasp in the hair. Bracelets, watches, earrings and necklaces must be removed. Otherwise, your composition may classify as a pin-up picture. If shoes are worn they should be the flat heel or sandal type; never the high heel type.

Admittedly the wearing of a high heel shoe does lend an added appeal to the leg. It adds line and length. But we do not strive for this alone. Our interest is picturing the female nudist in a natural environment, engaged in athletic activity or basking in the health-providing rays of the sun. You should put as much effort into picturing her enjoyment of these things as you would put into making a commendable portrait of your favourite relative.

Blankets and articles of clothing should always be excluded from the scene. They are distracting and certainly not necessary for the model's comfort unless she must lie prone on the ground amid a mass of cacti or thistle. You take away the natural effect of the picture when you allow the model to stand on a towel or article of clothing. The most tender feet will harden after a few days at the seashore, the woods or at camp. The wearing of shoes often lends an artificial look to the picture.

Five pictures from those received were selected for this month's analysis.

No. 1 . . . Here the photographer has callously ignored some of the important rules of good photography. The pose suggests nothing. Position of the body has resulted in the concentration of a singular blob of shadow in the central region of the body. The model is looking directly into the eye of the camera. The blanket should have been removed. Directly behind the model we see a few huge boulders that face directly into the sun with no distracting background. It would have been the ideal spot to photograph the model. Never be satisfied with one location. Scan the landscape for other vantage points.

No. 2 . . . Although it seems the photographer's real intention was to depict the nudist greeting the noon sun, the position and stance of the model has defeated his purpose. The model should be standing on the up-grade rather than down hill. You always go up to greet the sun. The opposite angle than that employed here would offer that illusion. Furthermore, the model's body should be arched in a backward position to further suggest joy and passive resistance. Flash fill-in would have done wonders to relieve shadow intensity.

No. 3 . . . This is not a good pose. The entire weight of the body rests on the model's knees. Left arm is too far forward. Bracelet and watch should have been removed. Although background is picturesque, it should have been diffused. This would not be possible at such a short distance from the model. It would necessitate widening the distance between them to about ten feet. In pictures where background does not support the theme of the pose, it is secondary in importance and should be merely suggested.

No. 4 Below  No. 3 Above

No. 5 — page 32

No. 4 . . . A quiet, restful pose, nicely balanced. Although the model is perched in a precarious position the natural angle of the pose does suggest comparative security. The model may have been lying flat across the rock on her stomach. A verbal gesture from the photographer has prompted her to rise to this position. Reflected flash or fill-in could have been used to increase detail in those areas of intense shadow, thus firmly outlining the body against the dark background.

No. 5 . . . Strictly a family shot of a friend or relative. Lacks planning of any kind. A typical example of an amateur's first "nude." With more study and experience the photographer may probably produce compositions of a model obviously worthy of a better effort. Towel, background and pose are not in keeping with the fundamental rules of fine photography. Hands are spread out in claw-like fashion. Remember, properly posing the hands is extremely important. Arms, held out from the body, form two disturbing spaces for our view of the

(Continued on page 32)

**Figure 6.14** Blake McLachlan, Aids for the Amateur Photographer, *Sunbathing for Health,* April 1952 | Courtesy of Naturist Education Foundation Research Library

new field of unlimited possibilities in commercial illustration."[55] The launch of *Playboy* in 1953 confirmed the commercial value of nude photography.

Canadian nudists embraced photography for its popularity but also for its perceived power. McLachlan offered the following assessment of its importance:

> Pictures are the most powerful means of expression in our modern world. They replace the written word to a great extent in our magazines and newspapers. With a cosmopolitan population such as ours complete unity of thought would suffer considerably without proper pictorial illustration. Man may now appreciate to a far greater degree the absorbing events of the world about and beyond him through captioned story telling pictures than was possible not so many years ago. Without them our system of education would be retarded.[56]

McLachlan believed photographs told the story more accurately and convincingly than words, and would be read in the same way by everyone, thus promoting "unity of thought." Connett expressed a similar sentiment:

> If we wrote ten thousand words you might still come to camp prepared for a sexual thrill, but where, in all our pictures, do you see anything hinting at sexual activity? Nowhere! Then you come to our camp 'in the right frame of mind,' that is with a clean open heart, and prepared to act the part of a lady or gentleman.[57]

Scholar John Tagg argues that following the invention of photography in the nineteenth century, there occurred a "coupling of evidence and photography," a process in which the photograph became imbued with "evidential force" and was understood to reflect an objective reality.[58] This was reinforced during the postwar period. Vettel-Becker suggests that "never before had photography played such an authoritative role in everyday life," as it turned more toward science than to art and embraced the sense of being "grounded in reality and the quest for truth."[59] Adopting this perspective, nudists saw photography as a means to document camp life, thereby providing evidence to the public that nudism was all that it claimed to be – in the words of one *Sunbathing for Health* contributor, to "reveal truth, not a writer's imagination."[60] Connett believed that the photographs in *Sunbathing for Health* presented a "clean" and "wholesome" contrast to the public perception of nudism, suggesting that they would dispel people's "filthy imaginings." In a context in which "showing" took precedent over "telling," images offered "eyewitness" testimony rather than "hearsay."[61]

In the postwar culture of paranoia about communist espionage and closeted homosexuality, nudists increasingly opted to expose themselves to public view, rejecting strategies of concealment and secrecy that had been common during the 1930s and 1940s.[62] In the early days of organization, they had often resorted to placing discreetly worded ads in local newspapers, used only first names at the club, and avoided discussions about employment to protect their identities, even from one other. But during the 1950s, this began to change, and Connett played a leading role in promoting openness and transparency to public scrutiny. Photography, seen as offering a window onto reality, went hand in hand with this shifting attitude.

## Reader Responses

Despite their conviction that photographs displayed objective truth, readers often failed to see what *Sunbathing for Health* wanted them to see, to read the photos in a way that accorded with the nudist philosophy. Images of children and of club activities were accepted without criticism, suggesting that they were seen as consistent with the nudist philosophy conveyed in the text. But the numerous professional photos of men and women were more problematic to some readers, and writers such as Connett and Harris often defended their use and corrected associated misconceptions about nudism.

Confusion resulted from the airbrushing and retouching processes, as some readers were unaware that the photographs had been altered in this way. Some asked whether all nudist women shaved their pubic area and why the men were "covered up" with "a useless article which appears to be a bathing suit."[63] Others confessed that the images of attractive models heightened their insecurities about their own bodies. A female reader voiced concern about her breast size, having gained the impression from the photos that perhaps small-breasted women did not attend clubs but restricted themselves to sunbathing in private.[64] A well-meaning reader who practised nudism with his family sought advice regarding his wife's insecurity:

> My wife has got modesty again due to the photographs in your magazine showing other ladies with such beautiful bodies. My wife has had surgery and her stomach is large. I try to tell her that people just naturally take pictures of beautiful girls the same as they would anything else, such as a beautiful car or horse. And that there are other women in the same camp with the beautiful girls that have large, if not larger, stomachs than hers but she just can't believe it.[65]

Male readers expressed physical insecurities too. One man feared that his physique did not measure up to the standard of the male models.[66] A sixteen-year-old Vancouverite wondered "why all your photos are either of young 'cover girls' or 'muscle men'" and stated that he "would like to see some of your photo space given up to male nudists and to the majority of women who are not so perfect."[67] Another requested that the magazine "insert more group shots or [photos of] women of less charms and beauty" and offer more balanced representation of men and women to provide "a true cross section of nudist life."[68] Likewise, a man who had regularly purchased the magazine since 1944, including its previous incarnation as *Sunbathing and Health,* noted, "My only complaint is that it seems to be a 'house organ' for a photo-model association ... The emphasis seems to be more on beautiful American models than on a family basis."[69] From misunderstandings about the retouching process, to heightened physical insecurities, to suggestions that the photos were inconsistent with the textual message, readers questioned the use of images in *Sunbathing for Health.*

Connett, Harris, and other contributors continually reassured readers that nudists were no more attractive than the average person, that the good-looking members were simply more willing to have their pictures taken or were more in demand by photographers. Harris, in particular, felt herself to be working at cross-purposes with the images. She acknowledged that they merely heightened women's sense of intimidation about visiting a club and noted the top concern among female readers – that their bodies were inferior to those of the models.[70] She reflected, "Photographers naturally choose models who are the acme of physical perfection. Sometimes I wish they would aim their camera at some of the long and short, skinny and fat members, so that I would not have the task of reassuring people so often."[71] In a 1956 article titled "On Why the Editor May Reject," prominent English naturist and amateur photographer Leon Gilbert underlined the need "for pictures of a greater variety of 'types'" (Figure 6.15). He added, "it may well be that many naturists would rather see pictures of the girls of the moment rather than those of the typical girls and women in the clubs. I wonder which does the greater service for naturism, or do they both have their place in the scheme of things?" He concluded by issuing a challenge to photographers: "Almost anyone can make a picture of a blossoming-bosomed teen-ager on a swing, but who can make an attractive picture of her mother making tea for the club?"[72] Despite directing photographers to shoot a wider variety of "types," Gilbert accepted without question that their subjects would always be female.

When a male reader criticized the predominance of women and asked why it is "always the female form that is on display," Mildred Harris responded bluntly. The problem was men – "men readers who prefer pictures of women and men photographers who rarely point their camera at anything but women."[73] Another reader verified her remark:

# On Why the Editor May Reject

by Leon Gilbert

A correspondent sent several photographs to a naturist magazine. Some were rejected and some were kept. After several months none had been published. A politely strong letter went to the editor. The photos were all returned. The pictures came to me, with an indignant letter. Why, I am asked, were the photos rejected after such a long time?

I can only give the views of an experienced contributor. The standard of the studies was excellent. The poses were good. The subject was full figured, but had been taken to the best advantage. Incidentally the fuller figure does present publication problems.

Some of the studies did not seem quite suitable for publication, in my view. No doubt these were the first rejections. Here may be mentioned the indefinable quality of personal preference. Given two almost identical pictures some people, including editors, will prefer one and some the other. This cannot be argued and must be accepted.

Now what of the photos which all came back after the letter to the editor? I think that it is possible the contributor spoiled his hope of publication by impatience.

Good models, but the pose is stilted

A fine study of a full figure

Many contributors forget that a monthly magazine is in preparation many months in advance of publication. Special features and some regular items are planned, set up, and possibly with the printers (not forgetting time for engraving processes) only awaiting the fastest possible topical items. What seems a long wait to a contributor may be only a few issues to the editor.

It must be remembered that an editor invariably has a stock of material, like any other business man. He also receives unexpected news and this brings in the question of suitability. The editor thinks our friend's full figure studies have possibilities for future use. The photos would be added to stock. Next day an excellent article arrives for which these particular photos are just the right illustrations.

Such an opportunity may not occur for months, or it may not occur at all. This explains why an almost forgotten contribution is sometimes used, or something that is considered quite a poor effort. It happens to be the only suitable thing available (Continued on page 29)

26

**Figure 6.15** Leon Gilbert, "On Why the Editor May Reject," *Sunbathing for Health*, June 1956 | Courtesy of Naturist Education Foundation Research Library

> I have met hundreds of men in Vancouver, New Westminster, Victoria, Calgary, Lethbridge and Medicine Hat who, like me, have bought your magazine for years, not out of any interest whatsoever in nudism, but purely and simply for the vicarious thrill the pictures give them ... Every time we buy it at the news stands, the girl clerk gives us a knowing look.

His suggestion was that *Sunbathing for Health* commodified women's bodies for commercial gain, coupled with skepticism about the claim that its photos differed from mainstream erotic imagery. This reader's assertion is supported by the appearance of *Sunbathing for Health* alongside *Playboy* and *Penthouse* in men's magazine lots being sold on eBay in the present day.

Connett fired off a stinging rebuke: "What sort of men are you who derive a thrill from the clean wholesome pictures we portray?" He refuted Harris's claim that the overabundant photos of female models were commercially driven, motivated by the desires of a male readership:

> Let us make it clear right now that we do not "cater" to the men who buy our magazine. Not having ever made a survey of our reader audience, we are not even aware that we have a particular audience of men, though letters have revealed to us that it is usually the man who takes the lead in winning his wife and family to our way of life. We "cater" primarily to nudists. Naturally we point our text and pictures toward prospective nudists as well. Our job and our hope is to "sell" nudism.[74]

A central tenet of nudism was that "your body is what your mind makes it, obscene and shameful or fine and proud."[75] This belief makes sense of Connett's seemingly naive assertion that *Sunbathing for Health* contained not one "sexy" picture, "not one 'come hither' look," and "not one suggestive or suspicious-looking pose."[76] Individuals who condemned its photos or found them titillating were simply demonstrating the impurity of their own thoughts. Indeed, as a reader pointed out, "It is only people who have a corrupt mind who look upon the body with lust."[77] Nudists encouraged the self-regulation of sexual desire and believed that the mind could command the body, a claim that applied as much to examining nude photos as to actually visiting a club. In taking this stance, they declared that the mind of the viewer – not the images themselves – was the source of any sexual stimulation. Responding to the photos on an erotic level signalled one's immaturity and unsuitability for membership in a club, although Connett expressed optimism that such people could be re-educated. In this sense, viewing the photographs became more a test of conversion to the nudist way of thinking than an indisputable means of bringing it about. According to Joanne Meyerowitz, "The modern sexual code ... distinguished healthy cheesecake, attractive to normal men and women, from illicit pornography, appealing only to the abnormal." Defenders of "healthy cheesecake" contended that "women's bodies were lovely, bodily images were not shameful, and pictures only corrupted the abnormal mind."[78] The remarkable similarity between this and the views of Connett and other *Sunbathing for Health* contributors suggests that nudists were not in fact proposing to radically reframe the way in which people looked at images of the body, but were merely trying to move the bar so that nude photographs could qualify as healthy and harmless, not pornographic.

*Sunbathing for Health* ceased publication in 1959, after failing to make a profit for several months. That same year, Canada passed new legislation dealing with obscenity. Spurred on by revived social concern about "objectionable materials," the Senate Committee on Salacious and Indecent Literature had held public hearings in 1952 and 1953. Like the moral reformers of the late nineteenth and early twentieth centuries, those calling for tougher legislation were concerned about "the mass distribution of inexpensive materials that were easily accessible to a broad range of readers" and "the potential for moral corruption of vulnerable groups," especially the young.[79] In 1959, an amendment to the Criminal Code altered the definition of obscenity from material with "the tendency ... to deprave and corrupt those whose minds are open to such immoral influences" to "any publication a dominant characteristic of which is the undue exploitation of sex, or of sex and any one or more of the following subjects, namely, crime, horror, cruelty and violence."[80] Although intended to establish an objective standard for obscenity, that did not prove to be the case. When the courts began applying this legislation in *R. v. Brodie* (1962) and *R. v. Dominion News and Gifts* (1964), they threw out the Hicklin test and applied a "community-standards test," by which judges attempted to determine "a general average of community thinking and feeling" about what constituted an "undue exploitation of sex."[81] Under this test, the determining factor for obscenity was no longer whether the material might "corrupt" children but whether the average Canadian would tolerate others viewing it. Though the Hicklin era had seen a limited number of prosecutions, the community-standards test (which remained in place until overturned by *R. v. Butler* in 1992) demonstrated somewhat greater tolerance for sexual representations.[82] It reflected the changing cultural context and media landscape in Canada: magazines such as *Playboy,* with higher production values and more overtly erotic content than *Sunbathing for Health,* were becoming more widely available and more socially tolerable. *Playboy,* for example, reached peak circulation in 1972.

Throughout its existence, *Sunbathing for Health* contributors and readers engaged in an extended dialogue about the purpose, validity, and effectiveness of nude photographs in promoting their philosophy. The contributors argued that the images depicted the body as natural and wholesome, not erotic. But readers' comments and criticisms, and the responses they evoked, called this claim into question and suggested that issues of gender and sexuality were not as neatly addressed as nudists wished to believe. Read in terms of both its visual and textual messages, *Sunbathing for Health* was a site where nudists and non-nudists negotiated mainstream cultural values, contesting images of the naked body and its encoding. Whereas some nudists bemoaned the demise of the magazine, others believed that it had never been the best representation of their movement.

Over time, Connett confessed to mounting skepticism about the ability of photographs to upset mainstream associations between nudity and sexuality. In a 1957 issue, he wrote,

> Some nudists show their friends and relatives nude pictures taken at camp. Over the years however I have come to the conclusion that this is a risky business. Remember that if you show genuine, wholly natural nudist pictures to non-nudists you risk offending. It is too great a step for them, and even if they are prepared to accept nudism mentally, looking at a picture is not the same as seeing the completely natural, simple innocence of life at camp. To a degree I feel the same way about nudist magazines, particularly those which show natural unretouched close-ups.[83]

Increasingly, Connett turned his attention to other forms of public relations, such as open house events. He seemed to believe that they offered a more authentic experience of nudist life and were less open to criticism than the photographs in *Sunbathing for Health,* which had garnered so much attention. A feature of many open houses was the nudist pageant – another form of visual representation that, like the pictures in *Sunbathing for Health,* sought to change how Canadians saw the body and raised some of the same questions in the process.

# 7
# The Pageant Tradition and Miss Nude World

In the decades after the Second World War, Canadian nudist clubs and organizations regularly reported that a pageant to select a "Nudist Royal Family" – king, queen, and often, prince and princess – was a highlight of the summer season. They followed the lead of English and American nudists in incorporating pageants into their local and national gatherings.[1] The contests ranged in size from small local events, in which the king and queen were chosen by applause from the audience, to the elaborately staged Miss Nude World Contest. The latter was hosted by the Four Seasons Nature Park outside Hamilton, Ontario, during the early 1970s and was open to the public. The seemingly trivial beauty contest has become the subject of serious academic study. Scholars have highlighted the ways in which it has served as a platform for staging dominant cultural ideals and norms of femininity, race, and sexuality. But they have also demonstrated how the competitions, "by choosing an individual whose deportment, appearance, and style embodies the values and goals of a nation, locality, or group, expose these same values and goals to interpretation and challenge."[2] Postwar nudist clubs and organizations adapted the pageant to embody their philosophy and represent it to the public. In staging their own versions of the beauty contest, which reached its height of popularity during this period, they proclaimed both their distinctiveness from, and their likeness to, mainstream culture.[3] Nudist pageants attracted significant public attention by putting bodies, and nudism itself, on display. They laid bare the fact that the movement deviated from the mainstream in its attitude toward nudity, while simultaneously affirming sexual and gender norms.

## Royalty Pageants

The selection of a woman to embody an event, such as a May Queen, goes back at least to the Middle Ages, though appearance was not always the main criterion. In the second half of the nineteenth century, American fairs, circuses, and beach resorts began hosting beauty contests, selecting the winners on the basis of attractiveness. In Canada, they were slower to catch on, but they became increasingly popular and commonplace during the 1920s. The Miss America contest, launched in Atlantic City in 1920, helped bring pageants into the mainstream and provided a template for other pageants, including the incorporation of a swimsuit competition. According to Jane Nicholas, these competitions revealed the increasing importance of physical appearance in navigating the modern urban environment, as well as "a deeper class shift in commercial amusements with more working-class leisure opportunities (like movies) becoming part of a wider, cross-class popular culture, driven in particular by young women." Some vocal critics dismissed them as morally questionable, vain, or superficial, but they also enjoyed wide support and participation. As Nicholas notes, "In a few short years, beauty contests transformed from contentious public performances to widely accepted ones that reflected allegedly national standards for beauty."[4]

Pageants became a staple of the Canadian nudist movement early in its history. Shortly after the CSA was founded in 1947, its first king and queen were selected at its third annual convention, held in British Columbia in 1949.[5] Along with business meetings and a volleyball tournament, the pageant became a regular part of the annual summer conventions (Figure 7.1). The eastern and western Canadian regional conferences often chose royal families of their own, and Canadians who attended American Sunbathing Association conventions also frequently competed in their pageants. In addition, clubs from British Columbia to Quebec ran contests to bestow an array of titles on their members, including May Queen, Nudist Mother of the Year, and honorary club name bearers, such as Miss Sun Valley Gardens.[6] Although nudists tended not to take the pageants overly seriously, they were promoted as a visual representation of their philosophy that provided positive publicity and prompted Canadians to see the body in a new light. They were staged

8 THE VANCOUVER PROVINCE, Monday, July 18, 1955

**NUDIST MOTHER OF YEAR**, as chosen by members of Sunny Trails Nudist Club at North Vancouver, is Mrs. Phyllis Thomson, 25, of 4498 Marine, New Westminster. Holding mother's awards are John, 5, and Nancy, 6, who are also members of the club.

**Guests watch nudists select year's best undraped mother**

**Figure 7.1** The 1953 CSA royal family. *Sunshine and Health,* November 1953 | Courtesy of Naturist Education Foundation Research Library

**Figure 7.2** "Guests Watch Nudists Select Year's Best Undraped Mother," *Vancouver Province,* 18 July 1955

on club property and were generally not open to the public, but journalists were often invited to cover them and frequently did. Newspapers reported on the selection of "the Royal Family of Canadian Nudism" and the "Year's Best Undraped Mother" (Figure 7.2).[7] As a result, pageants became useful promotional tools, introducing the public to the movement.

Pageants were hypothetically based on standard criteria, which included "all-over tan," "general good health" or attractiveness, and personality and "contribution to nudism."[8] But because winners were generally chosen by applause from the audience, judging standards were admittedly flexible and relaxed. Connett, who had followed the American lead and helped to initiate pageants in Canada, noted that the selection "is based theoretically on best tan, physical fitness and personality. Often it is merely a matter of popularity."[9] Rather than acting as objective measures through which to pick a winner, the criteria underscored central tenets of the nudist philosophy.

An "all-over tan" was a badge of full-fledged membership, in contrast to the tan lines (sometimes teasingly referred to as "cottontails") that marked non-nudists (known as "textiles") and new members. It provided physical evidence of a contestant's commitment to nudism through exposure of the entire body to the sun and air. As one Canadian nudist wrote, it was "nature's mark of goodness and health" – physical *and* mental health, since fully exposing oneself to the sun at a club signalled a wholesome attitude regarding the body.[10]

In addition, the full body tan was aesthetically pleasing, and good looks were also a criterion in the assessment of entrants. This factor was variously described as "general good health," physical fitness, or attractiveness. Nudists were hardly exceptional in correlating beauty with physical health; in fact, Sander Gilman argues that "the equation of beauty with health and ugliness with illness is fundamental in the Western understanding of the body."[11] But the nudist philosophy affirmed aesthetic appreciation of the body in its own right. Nina Morris suggests that sensory perception – including the visual – held a prominent place in early nudist thought and practice.[12] Commenting on the pageant tradition, Connett noted, "We all enjoy a pretty face, a lovely tan, and a handsome figure, be it male or female."[13] The criterion of physical appearance embraced the visual pleasure to be derived from looking at the body, though it was pleasure that nudists defined as "natural" rather than sexual.

The third criterion was personality or personal contribution to nudism through service to the club or organization. This standard democratized the pageant to a certain extent, and local club contests particularly encouraged members of all ages, shapes, and sizes to compete. In the 1957 Miss/Mrs. Sun Valley Gardens contest, a young woman and her mother each received thirty-six votes from members. The newsletter reported that the title was awarded to the daughter after the mother declined it in favour of her.[14] Rose, a Sunny Chinook member who competed in a 1970s pageant, recalled, "The King and Queen had to be over eighteen, and often the queen had pretty saggy boobs and a flabby tummy. All contestants had to answer questions. I don't remember what the questions were, but often they had to do with the role that nudism played in their life."[15] Rose insisted that "the pageants were not beauty contests," echoing a sentiment commonly expressed by many pageant officials, even high profile ones such as Miss Canada and Miss America. As Patrizia Gentile explains, "This oft-repeated phrase sought to recast beauty contests as respectable and viable enterprises for women. Insisting that beauty contests were not really *beauty* contests became a crucial strategy in maintaining a hold on the values of chastity and virtue even as the last vestiges of the Victorian era disappeared."[16] Rose inferred that asking contestants about the role of nudism in their lives and their contributions to their club or the cause distinguished nudist pageants from their conventional counterparts by conveying that they were about more than appearance. It also flagged which participants would be the best ambassadors for nudism, as winners often became the focus of press coverage, especially the women who were chosen as queens.

Not everyone agreed that the pageants were more than superficial beauty contests, and they were not without controversy in Canadian nudist circles. Marcus Meed, an early CSA president and leader of the Maritans, expressed his philosophical opposition to pageants in his club newsletter. He noted approvingly that New Zealand did not stage them, referencing the editor of the *New Zealand Naturist* magazine, who reportedly stated that they "were inconsistent with New Zealand naturism's acceptance of all, irrespective of looks." To which Meed responded, "Well friends, some of us in Canada feel much the same way."[17] In 1956, the eastern division of the CSA declared that it was no longer in favour of the election of a royal family and returned the Bowman Trophy for CSA queen to the western division. Even so, it did not avoid contests altogether, replacing its royal pageant with the election of a Mr. and Miss/Mrs. Suntan.[18] The change was presumably intended to minimize a focus on physical attractiveness in favour of the more principled "all-over tan" criterion. Nonetheless, appearance evidently remained a factor. And the change seems to have been short-lived. By 1966, nudist royalty pageants were again a main feature of the ECSA convention.[19]

## Miss Nude World

Whereas nudists often downplayed the importance of beauty to their pageants, organizers of the Miss Nude World Contest, launched in 1970, placed even greater emphasis on physical attractiveness, in a competition featuring only female entrants.[20] According to Four Seasons owner and Miss Nude World producer Lisa Stein, "This is the most honest beauty contest there is. If you are beautiful in the nude then you are beautiful."[21] Her reasoning was consistent with the attitude expressed by California club owner Mel Hocker in a rant against conventional pageants:

> In my opinion there is only one way to hold a beauty contest. Require the contestants to appear in the nude, where they can naturally and normally display themselves with no girdle bathing suits, nor built-in foam rubber creations to deceive the onlookers. Many a doll would fall flat on her face without the archaic bathing suit to build her up ... An event which began with the selection of the gal with the most gorgeous figure, the Atlantic City Miss America Pageant, has deteriorated into a "talent" contest. Today's winners must be so diversified as to be able to make music on a tissue paper comb, play pattie-cake, operate a yo-yo, or compete in such mundane events as wearing formal gowns correctly. All this downgrades the contest into one which qualifies any misshapen miss who happens to have a good publicity agent.[22]

Not mincing any words, Hocker suggested that only a contest conducted in the nude, without a talent portion, would offer a "true" assessment of beauty. This is what the Miss Nude World Contest claimed to provide.

In a departure from the royalty pageants in which men, women, and children competed, the Miss Nude World Contest was open only to women, single or married, between the ages of eighteen and thirty, who were members of a nudist club. This final requirement was easily fulfilled: the 1974 Miss Nude World revealed to a CBC Radio interviewer that she had joined a club for the first time only the day before the pageant began.[23] The contest was not the first of its kind – between 1965 and 1969 clubs in California,

**Figure 7.3** "21-Year-Old Bookkeeper Is Nudist Queen," *Edmonton Journal*, 8 September 1970

Indiana, and Florida had hosted similar events – but it was a first for Canada. Although the promised international roster of entrants did not materialize in 1970, the competition quickly grew to become the pre-eminent "Miss Nude" event, to which winners of Miss Nude contests hosted by various Canadian and American clubs advanced.[24]

Unlike in the royalty pageants, where a round of applause selected the winner, Miss Nude World was judged by a panel of local community members and minor celebrities, including business owners, professional athletes, and members of the media (Figure 7.3). Media personality Gordon Sinclair was the most prominent among them, serving as a judge for the inaugural competition in 1970.[25] Contestants were privately interviewed by the judges and competed on stage in three events, progressively revealing more skin as they transitioned from evening gown, to bathing suit, to no clothes at all. They were not judged on talent. Pageant director Carl Alkerton explained that "even the simplest gesture in the nude could be misconstrued by the vice squad as ... of a suggestive or obscene nature."[26] But a talent portion would also have gone against the grain of what was intended to be "the ultimate in beauty contests."[27]

Contestants were appraised on their personality, poise, and appearance. Judges were supplied with a points system for scoring. Personality, which could garner a possible total of fifteen points, was subcategorized into character, conversation, and manner. It was primarily evaluated during a private interview with the judges and was intended to ensure that the winner would be a suitable representative for the pageant. Poise, also worth a total of fifteen points, was based on walk, posture, and composure. Appearance, worth twenty-five points, was broken down into five subdivisions: bathing suit, face and hair, hips and legs, bust, and "coloration" or tan. Each subdivision was judged on a scale from one to five, in which one was "poor," three was "average," and five was "superior." The 1976 Contest Rules informed competitors that they would "be judged on natural beauty. Natural make-up will be accepted. No breast surgery. No wigs. No shaved pubic area. No artificial means can be used to simulate a tan ... White high heel pumps or sandals are preferred."[28] Jewellery was optional. In other words, makeup was the only permitted artificial beauty aid, but it was to enhance "natural" beauty without being overly noticeable.

## Pageants, Publicity, and Profits

Both the Miss Nude World Contest and the royalty pageants were intended to provide publicity for the movement. In the early 1950s, CSA policy permitted all pageant entrants to have their pictures and names printed in nudist and mainstream publications.[29] The royalty pageants generally took place during an open house weekend or at a convention, events that were regularly covered by journalists, for whom the pageant was a favourite subject. In 1957, CBC reporter Bill Goode dubbed it "a beauty contest to end all beauty contests" and declared, "If there's a reporter ... who wouldn't like to watch a beauty contest at a nudist camp there's something the matter with that reporter."[30] The pageants became a gateway for media coverage of Canadian nudism more broadly, raising public awareness of the movement.

Lisa Stein conceived the Miss Nude World Contest as a source of publicity for her club. In a 1974 radio interview, she chronicled its origins:

> To get a new idea across you have to try and sell it. But how do you sell it? You sell any new product only with a gimmick! So we were thinking, what would the media pick up? What is a good gimmick for, for us to use? We had a new club, we had an indoor pool, we had certain facilities,

> and uh, we had no people. And we didn't want people from the other clubs, we wanted new people to become interested. So here it comes, the Miss Nude World Contest.[31]

The event provided publicity through both the spectators it attracted and the media coverage it garnered. Its attendance figures suggest that it succeeded in drawing a crowd. In 1971, approximately three thousand spectators attended, and it was reported that over five thousand people were turned away in 1972 after the venue reached capacity. Coverage of the event revealed that, "according to a police spokesman, the highway leading past the Four Seasons was backed up some four to six miles with traffic waiting to gain admission."[32] In the days leading up to the contest, organizers took competitors on a promotional circuit around southern Ontario that included press conferences and radio and television interviews. In 1970, entrants modelled in a fashion show at the opening of Hamilton's Queenston Mall and attended a blood donor clinic.[33] In addition, reporters descended annually on the Four Seasons for the weekend contest, and newspapers across the country regularly published its results (Figure 7.4). Director Carl Alkerton estimated that during its first three years, it had netted $500,000 worth of free publicity for the club and for nudism, although this claim is difficult to substantiate.[34] Lisa Stein boasted, "We had every media possible covering that contest, including Gordon Sinclair who was quite a personality in that time, Pierre Berton, and of course ... one Captain Andy, who was a friend of ours, who was, who had a television program in Hamilton, it was called The Captain Andy Show."[35] Regardless of the exact monetary value of the publicity, the Steins saw the contest as a public relations triumph, surpassing their expectations. They maintained that it "promoted more interest in the nudist movement in Canada and the United States than any other event."[36]

Whereas both the royalty pageants and the Miss Nude World Contest were devised as promotional measures, the latter was also a commercial enterprise. This was despite Lisa Stein's declaration that it was "a contest run in good taste ... with no exploitation of the girls, except to promote nudism."[37] The Four Seasons sold admission tickets as well as advertising space in its program. In 1975, the *Globe and Mail* reported that 6,500 people attended the pageant of that year, with the price of admission at $7.50.[38] Costs were kept down by relying on volunteer labour and soliciting prize donations from sponsors. The event also won new members, and thus more membership dues, for the Four Seasons. Stein gauged its success in monetary terms:

# Montreal Clerk Miss Nude World

FREELTON, Ont. (CP) — Rosemarie Hess, blue-eyed and blonde, stepped graciously forward Sunday night to accept her crown, clad in a simple, two-piece outfit—white shoes and a gold bracelet.

Mrs. Hess, 25, a Montreal department store clerk, was picked from among 17 contestants ranging in age between 16 and 31 to reign as Miss Nude World for 1971.

Her coronation took place before a crowd of 3,000 at the Four Seasons Nudist Resort in this community 15 miles north of Hamilton.

The French-speaking Swiss native who came to Canada with her husband four years ago was completely at ease before onlookers.

Displaying a lovely tan from top to toe of her five-foot-three-inch, 36-24-35 frame, Mrs. Hess said:

"After five minutes, it's no problem. There's nothing more to see after four minutes.

Of nudism, she said: "I love it."

She and her husband joined the clothesless cult in Europe five years ago.

Runner-up for the title, both single, were Ursula Lyond, 27, a Toronto book-keeper and Elsa Hambeck, an 18-year-old Austrian spending the summer in Toronto.

First prize was an eight-day trip to Florida. Other gifts included clothing, cosmetics, camping gear and a set of snow tires.

There were eight entrants from Ontario, eight from Quebec and one from Villa Park, Ill., in the pageant sponsored by the proprietors of the nature resort.

Winner and runner-up were chosen by a panel of 14—including two women—most of whom were journalists or broadcasters.



**MISS NUDE WORLD**

FREELTON, Ont.,—Rosemarie Hess, 25, of Montreal, wearing only a crown, high-heeled shoes and a thin sash, smiles for photographers after being named Miss Nude World 1971 in Freelton, Ont., Sunday.

(CP Journal Wirephoto)

**Figure 7.4** "Miss Nude World," *Ottawa Citizen*, 26 July 1971

"Our Miss Nude World Contest the first year was a big success, financially as well as member-wise, which is financially again. We were nine months in operation and we could afford to build an outdoor pool, we could afford to extend our facilities, our shower and toilet facilities." Due to the pageant, "We could afford to put here country club facilities, and compete with every country club in the southern Ontario area."[39] In her book about the ways in which Americans embraced nudity in their quest for a natural and authentic life, Sarah Schrank argues that, "though heralded as the key to freedom from modernity's worst excesses, naked living was, throughout the twentieth century, deeply susceptible to capitalism's commodification and objectification of the body."[40] In part, this was a function of social resistance to public nudity, which has effectively confined the nude lifestyle to private (and profit-seeking) spaces. Few Canadian clubs have made a profit, but the Miss Nude World Contest stands as an example of nudity being successfully marketed for financial gain within the nudist movement.

The publicity and commercial success of the Miss Nude format inspired other Canadian clubs to run similar contests, including some newly formed ventures in Quebec. Nearly twenty years after the raid on the Montreal Quetans Club had quashed early organizing in that province, the movement re-emerged, with ten clubs established during the 1970s.[41] According to James Woycke, pageants in the vein of the Miss Nude World Contest provided significant publicity for these clubs. Founded in 1972, the Club Naturiste Adam et Eve attracted thousands of spectators and extensive media coverage for its Miss Nude Quebec contest, and the World Queen of Nudism contest hosted by Paradis Terrestre also helped that club to quickly acquire more than a thousand members.[42]

However, the commercialism of the Miss Nude World Contest was distasteful to other club owners. Contest Director Carl Alkerton himself acknowledged that from the outset many regarded the contest "with a lot of suspicion as it was felt that a promotion of this nature would have harmful repercussions on the Nudist Recreation Movement."[43] Nearby Sun Valley Gardens owner Karl Ruehle clearly had the Four Seasons in mind when he complained that "there are some camps which compete with the others for the most facilities, and have a really country club atmosphere of commercialism, even to the point of exploitation, in some instances."[44] Even Summerset Nudist Resort owner Ted Lisiecki, in announcing that his club would host the first Miss Nude Ontario Contest in 1973, expressed mixed feelings about the idea. In his newsletter, he wrestled with the problem:

> I know that the biggest percentage of the attending public will be coming to the contest with the idea of looking over the pretty girls on the stage. From my point, I can visualize that some of these visitors will form a different outlook on social nudism, and won't form the idea in their minds that we are exploiting the nude body at all times. One may think that the financial aspect plays the main part to influence us in staging this contest. It is practically true, because like everyone else we need cash to operate the park. This seems to be the only way we can offer the serenity at other times.[45]

Lisiecki seemed barely convinced by his own rationalization for hosting the contest and uncertain about whether it would do more good than harm.

## Pageants, Bodily Display, and Cultural Change

The nudist royalty pageants and the Miss Nude World Contest generated publicity and profits to varying degrees, but in doing so, what philosophical messages did the pageants convey? Their most obvious feature, and the reason they captured the attention they did, was that they put naked bodies on display and encouraged viewers to look. Moreover, they did so in the context of a "family friendly" recreational setting, not a strip club or an adult film. The philosophy that nudity was natural and not erotic informed both the royalty pageants and the Miss Nude World Contest.

And yet, the contests exploited the much criticized taboo against nudity by displaying the body for the sake of publicity. In doing so, nudists often showed a naïveté or wilful blindness to the possibility that it might be viewed in an erotic way. An American nudist described nudist pageants as follows: "To the many witnessing for the first time a contest unhampered with bathing attire, will come the revelation that here, indeed, is a presentation having none of the erotic implications so evident where a portion of the body remains concealed. And to them, future contests, considered 'acceptable by society,' will be viewed with considerable cynicism."[46] These comments echo similar arguments about the non-erotic appreciation of nudist photography.

In the case of Miss Nude World, the public ticket sales, the non-nudist judging panel, the presence of clothed audience members, and the staging of the naked body as the culminating moment turned nudity into a spectacle. Appraising certain parts of a contestant's physique – bust, hips, legs – was at odds with the philosophical emphasis on bodily integrity. In a 1974 episode of the CBC Radio program *Identities,* about the Miss Nude World pageant, Lisa Stein can be heard at the competition introducing each competitor by her name and measurements – bust, waist, and hips. Media coverage of the contest also reported these. Although organizers protested that what they offered was "clean" and "in good taste," "that the burlesque and erotic have no part in nudism," the message that nudity was natural was easily lost in the mix.[47] In a moment of candour, Stein admitted that her contest "goes against the whole philosophy of nudism, we agree to that. But it has done a job, it has shown people who know nothing about nudism a nudist club, and what kind of people go to a nudist club, and that was the whole idea behind it."[48] The hope was that as they gazed at the contestants, audience members would also take note of the club setting and all that it had to offer.

Like the Miss Nude World Contest, the royalty pageants made a display of the unclothed body to stimulate public interest in the movement. But they differed in a significant respect – the nudist audience – which enabled them to more successfully convey the nudist message. Significantly, the bodies of contestants and spectators worked together to perform this task, and the latter were integral to the consistency and effectiveness of the message, especially as it was transmitted to visiting journalists. As fellow nudists, audience members naturalized the nakedness of competitors, mitigating the potential for it to be interpreted as exhibitionist. They also embodied the nudist philosophy by displaying appreciation for the entrants, on the one hand, and no signs of sexual arousal, on the other. In doing so, they signalled their conversion to the nudist gaze, demonstrating that their practice could disrupt socialized ways of looking and re-educate people to see the body in a new light.

Whereas all these contests pushed the bounds of social tolerance for nudity, they also worked to affirm the normalcy of nudists, in particular by adhering to sexual and gender norms. At a fundamental level, the royalty pageants were about gender. The selection of a male king and a female queen reflected the mixed-sex composition of the clubs and underscored the embrace of normative heterosexuality. But just as photos of women in *Sunbathing for Health* far outnumbered those of men, the pageant queen received the most attention from nudists and non-nudists alike, even though a king was elected too (and often a prince and princess). In their differing ways, these pageants and the Miss Nude World Contest accepted the culturally dominant treatment of women as visual objects, or what Laura Mulvey terms their "to-be-looked-at-ness."[49]

The Miss Nude World Contest was overt in making a spectacle of women's bodies. Although the royalty pageants were less so, the CSA queen was the only member of her royal family to be awarded a trophy, and she was subject to the greatest media scrutiny. When CBC reporter Bill Goode dubbed the nudist pageant "a beauty contest to end all beauty contests" and claimed that there was "something the matter" with any reporter who was uninterested in it, the gendering of the reporter as male and the contestant as female was clear. Nudists encouraged female winners to take the media spotlight. Mildred Harris described the reaction of reporters who covered the 1954 CSA convention at the Sunny Trails Club upon being introduced to the past CSA queen:

> Our Queen of last year, Arleigh, had an amusing experience on Sunday when reporters and photographers were present from almost every paper, including the press services such as Canadian Press and British United Press. When they found she was last year's Queen they pestered her for some good pictures, in the nude of course. And one particularly aggressive photographer was kidding her about being backward so she said, "O.K., if you'll join me you can have my picture." And he did![50]

As hoped, Arleigh became the pretty face of nudism in the campaign to promote it to the public. Like the many corporations that have used women's bodies to sell commodities, nudist clubs used women's bodies to market their movement.[51]

The attention given to the female contestants also served another function. Patrizia Gentile argues that workplace beauty contests mitigated social fears about a loss of femininity that attended women's increased workforce presence during the mid-twentieth century.[52] Her observation translates well into the context of nudist pageants, as nudists were anxious to demonstrate that their practice did not entail women's rejection of gender norms. Female pageant entrants demonstrated that despite exchanging their clothes for the "natural state," nudist women still subscribed to normative beauty standards and retained their feminine identity.

Why did women enter these competitions? There were prizes at stake, some valuable and others bizarre. The Miss Nude World grand prize was typically a trip to Florida or the Caribbean, courtesy of a travel agency, but local businesses also donated an assortment of others, including a fur coat, a diamond and emerald ring, a bikini, a bicycle, a TV, a radio, and a pet monkey.[53] It is useful to distinguish between entrants who were long-time nudists and those who joined a club solely to participate in the competition. Committed nudist women who entered the royalty pageants or the Miss Nude World Contest often told reporters they did so simply for fun or at the urging of family and friends, underscoring their modesty. The *Acton Free Press,* reporting on the third-place finish of local resident Barbara Uuldricks in the inaugural Miss Nude World Contest, noted that she entered after "her friends at the [Four Seasons] camp talked her into it. She had never been in a beauty contest before but they were sure she could win and her husband was all in favour."[54] Miss Nude World entrants who had not previously participated in nudism often had practical motivations. Several mentioned aspirations to become a model or actress, hoping that the publicity generated by the contest would raise their profile and perhaps provide the necessary break to launch a career. Jane Nicholas observes that beauty contests enabled women to perform as modern women, to embody "a new type of modern femininity ... based on the characteristics of pleasure, self-promotion, heterosexual desire, and the deliberate solicitation of attention."[55] To be a modern woman meant being judged on the basis of physical appearance; entering a beauty contest was a means for a woman to do so in a public forum and on her own initiative. These contests held out the possibility of economic gain, or simply the validation that came from social approval.

At the same time, promises of "social and cultural power for appearing beautiful" could prove a fiction.[56] A *Globe and Mail* article about the 1974 Miss Nude World, Judi Walden, reported that winning the contest brought her "exposure. Too much of it." After her California club gave out her contact information, Walden was hounded by letters and phone calls requesting that she pose for nude photographs, causing her to move three times in an effort to recover her privacy. According to Walden, "she was told last year when she captured the Miss Nude World title that she must let anyone who wanted to photograph her do so." But she did not want her photos to be published in magazines and claimed that she had not been paid for the ones that were, despite the assurances of organizers that she would receive 10 percent of the proceeds. In addition, some of the promised prizes had never materialized, including a barbeque and a television. Walden had turned down several modelling job offers "because they wanted me to pose nude." All in all, she said of the Miss Nude World Contest, "I'd never do it again."[57] Although her negative experience may have been partially due to the fact that she lived in California, the centre of the pornography industry, comments by the 1978 Miss Nude World, a nineteen-year-old Florida woman named Judy Portinga, suggest that it was not unique. While noting that she hoped to model but also planned to study business administration, Portinga made a point of telling reporters that she was not interested in posing nude, "because most nude modelling represents sexual activities, and that's not what nudism is all about."[58]

The experiences of these two winners speak to the challenge of disassociating nudity from sexuality. The Miss Nude World Contest was launched amidst significant changes in Canadian society, including more openness about sexuality and more overt sexual objectification of women.[59] The large number of spectators who attended the contest in the early 1970s is indicative of a tolerance and appetite for this type of spectacle, at least among a segment of the public. At the same time, the contest should be understood as a conservative reaction against the rise of second-wave feminism. By 1970, feminists around the world had become vocal in highlighting sexual inequality, demanding equal rights and equal pay, and criticizing the subjugation and objectification of women. In 1968, a feminist group staged a protest at the Miss America pageant in Atlantic City, thus making many North Americans aware of feminism for the first time. The protesters were labelled "bra burners" in the media, despite no actual bra burning. However, they did place "instruments of torture to women" – including bras, high-heeled shoes, and dishcloths – in a "freedom trashcan." They also crowned a live sheep Miss America, "to parody the way the contestants ... are appraised and judged like animals at a county fair."[60] In Canada, the Simon Fraser University Student Society entered a protest candidate, Janiel Jolley, in the 1970 Miss Canadian University Pageant, which was held annually at Waterloo Lutheran University (now Wilfrid Laurier University). In a letter to her fellow competitors, Jolley outlined her intention not to insult them but to "raise issues of sexual exploitation of women, point out that women participate in beauty contests because this society provides us with so few arenas in which we can appear, and to expose the nature of an educational system that perpetuates the objectification and dehumanization of women."[61] The protest received widespread media coverage and contributed to the cancellation of the Miss Canadian University Pageant later that year.

Despite bringing important issues to public attention, anti-pageant protests – and second-wave feminism more broadly – met with significant ridicule and backlash. It was in this context that the Four Seasons launched the Miss Nude World Contest. In doing so, its organizers implicitly affirmed the objectification of women, defended pageants for their entertainment and commercial value, and dismissed critics as uptight radicals. Coverage of the first Miss Nude World Contest in the *Edmonton Journal* explored the issue of feminism in reporting on the winner, Rhonda Stallan: "Rejecting any connection with the women's liberation movement, Miss Stallan told newsmen that she still enjoys being treated as a woman."[62]

Pageant contestants served an important function by underscoring that nudist women retained their femininity and that nudists themselves were not radicals. The contests communicated that their movement was not a fanatical cult but a pleasurable leisure activity pursued by ordinary Canadians. As Carl Alkerton explained it, Miss Nude World Contest organizers hoped to show "that people who belong are just like their next-door neighbours."[63] Whereas the royalty pageants stressed the family-friendly respectability of nudism, the Miss Nude World Contest offered an updated take on the movement as "not a health thing anymore ... just another form of recreation."[64] Pageants demonstrated that nudism was "good fun" and that nudists did not take themselves too seriously – like other Canadians, they sought pleasure and relaxation in their free time. One nudist explained, "A nudist club does not consist solely of deadly serious people, their minds directed exclusively to the job of improving their health, figures and skin pigmentation. They have fun too, and it is this enjoyment, reflected in their faces, freed from obsessions and confusion, which provide them with an outlook on life which many envy."[65] Nudist pageants offered a good time, something that the Miss Nude World organizers viewed as a productive end in itself. As a result, they remained popular through the 1970s, for their entertainment and commercial value.[66]

Belgian historian Evert Peeters observes, "The power and mystery of the natural experience ... influenced the way in which ideals of life reform were communicated to others. If this ecstatic sensation could be shared but not explained, it was the theatricality of the behavior itself that became the major means of propaganda. Nudists did not primarily try to convince but to involve."[67] The photographs in *Sunbathing for Health* and the pageants both featured performances of unashamed attitudes toward the body and were means of involving the broader public in nudism. Nudists argued that the models featured in *Sunbathing for Health* and the women who entered pageants exemplified the wholesome, unashamed attitude toward the body that their philosophy promoted. In moments of frankness, however, some acknowledged that rather than upsetting mainstream ways of seeing, the photographs and pageants served merely to attract people who might not have known about or considered joining a club. This public appeal depended on an exploitation of the taboo nature of nudity and made a spectacle of nude bodies – women's in particular. In doing so, the photos and pageants undermined some of the very foundations of nudism and were as revealing of the tensions and contradictions within it as they were of the bodies on display. They conveyed that nudists were not so different from everyone else, although perhaps not for the reasons that they would have chosen to highlight.

# PART 3

# Nudism, the Natural Environment, and the Regulation of Space

# 8

# Cultivating Nature and Protecting Privacy at the Club

The preceding chapters have devoted significant attention to how nudists rhetorically framed their practice of social nudity. In this section, I concentrate on how the environment – both built and natural – framed nude bodies. Historian Caroline Daley argues that "the history of nudism is a history of space and place as well as a history of bodies."[1] To illuminate this interrelationship, the present chapter discusses the nudist club setting, and the subsequent one turns to Vancouver's Wreck Beach, which became Canada's most popular clothing-optional beach during the 1970s. Here, I build on the work of historical geographers and environmental historians who approach space as constitutive, "rather than geography being simply a fixed spatial background over which historical processes play."[2] In examining the controversy regarding three nude paintings that were displayed at the 1927 Canadian National Exhibition in Toronto, Jane Nicholas demonstrates that public attitudes toward the nude were not uniform, but were shaped by the space in which it was displayed, as well as its content and audience. She argues that "space is never neutral"; in other words, views of nudity are situational and situated.[3] The chapters that follow approach clubs and beaches as both socially constructed spaces and natural environments. Members of the nudist movement and users of Wreck Beach all defined nakedness as natural. But they differed in their approaches to nature and in their attitudes regarding the body and sexuality. The private location of nudist clubs, in contrast to the public location of Wreck Beach, also had significant ramifications for boundary making, both physical and symbolic. For clarity's sake, I use the term "nudists" to refer exclusively to club members, despite the fact that the press and the public often applied it to bathers at Wreck Beach as well.

Though choosing to shed their clothes in a social context, members of the Canadian nudist movement had little in common with other social groups who have done so, such as anti-modern romantics, back-to-the-landers, or hippies. Rather, they were mostly urban and suburban-dwelling people whose social critique was limited. They may have challenged the social taboo against nudity, but they presented it as a recreational pastime that was complementary to modern values. They also accepted the dominant modernist outlook in their ideas about the natural world, even as they invoked nature as justification for their practice. Sean Kheraj characterizes modernism as the belief "that nature, society, and the self could be tamed by the application of instrumental reason and sound expertise."[4] In developing club properties and dissociating nudity and sexuality – in taming nature and human nature – nudists adopted a modernist approach, at its height in the fifties and sixties, which viewed nature as imperfect and in need of improvement through human intervention. At the same time, they recognized that not all Canadians shared their view of nudity and derived security and legitimacy from confining their activities to private property. In the 1970s a small number of nudists began to align themselves with the emergent environmentalism of the period and helped shift the Canadian movement toward self-identifying as "naturist" rather than "nudist," but they remained in the minority, and the rhetorical shift constituted a reassertion of traditional nudist values in the face of cultural change more than a new approach to the natural world.

## Attitudes toward Nature

The natural setting was crucial in defining and justifying nudity at the clubs. Nudity was seen as "a natural way of living" and as promoting a sense of connection with the natural world: having "free[d] your body of its traditional allegiance to clothes, you will realize that your clothes have been a barrier to true harmony with nature. Nude, you are a part of nature ... The communion with nature refreshes and cleanses the mind and stimulates the body."[5] In turn, the club setting naturalized the nudity that occurred there. Nudists acknowledged that the practice was unnatural in many modern contexts, but argued that it offered the best way to enjoy the outdoors and should be embraced in a recreational setting. "Because it is natural for men and women to go about their daily routine fully clothed, does that mean that it is unnatural for them to shed their clothes under special circumstances and for strictly moral purposes?" asked *Sunbathing for Health* rhetorically. "It is natural to bathe in the nude. It seems natural to swim the same way."[6] In photography, the outdoor locale rationalized the model's nudity, and it performed the same function for club members. Karl Ruehle asserted, "The sun-tanned body in the natural setting does not look naked or bare, it just looks natural."[7]

The ideal club lay within easy reach of the city but was distant enough to provide an escape from "civilization" and access to "nature." Lakesun, situated on a small lake outside of Kingston, Ontario, featured "acres of fine camping sites available for those who enjoy really getting away from the trappings of modern civilization and enjoying the great outdoors, and where else could it be more enjoyable than in the great Canadian forests?"[8] Perched on the slopes of Grouse Mountain in North Vancouver, the Van Tan Club extolled its mountain and ocean views. In promotional material, many clubs boasted about their beautiful settings and outdoor recreational opportunities. While tapping into the popularity of camping and recreation, descriptions of the geographical features of the clubs also reinforced the philosophy of nudity as natural through an emphasis on the natural environment in which it took place.

If clubs were natural spaces, they were not, however, undeveloped ones. In fact, they frequently defined their progress in terms of taming wild spaces and constructing amenities such as playgrounds, volleyball courts, swimming holes, and pools.[9] Many were not located on bodies of water that were suitable for swimming. Finding affordable property within easy reach of a city was challenging, and many clubs settled for properties with a stream or creek that could be enlarged. This was the case with Glen Echo, established in the Newmarket area north of Toronto on a wooded site that had formerly been a lumber camp. It created a swimming hole by bulldozing a riverbed and damming a stream.[10] Sunny Trails tackled a similar project, excavating a lake that offered members a place to cool off and play in the water on hot summer days – an essential amenity for a successful club. The Lakesun Club, as its name suggests, did rejoice in a lakeside location, but it did not include the naturally sandy beach that owner Hans Behrmann desired. Thus, he extended the beach by laying down sand, a move he repeated after the lake washed it away.[11]

Throughout the postwar period, Canadian nudists kept busy cutting down trees, digging pools, and building clubhouses to create appealing campgrounds and to make a variety of recreational activities available. In the early years, most clubs were co-operatively run, and members were required to help landscape and develop facilities. Other clubs offered reduced membership rates in exchange for work hours. As time went on, the largest clubs became proprietary, including Sun Valley Gardens, Glen Echo, and the Four Seasons, and owners found that members would rather pay higher rates than perform manual labour on their weekends or holidays. Karl Ruehle positively distinguished the experience of attending a proprietary club (such as Sun Valley Gardens) from that of joining a co-operatively run one: "At a co-op club you are part owner. That's why you have the privilege to clean culverts and toilets, besides many other unpleasant things. At SVG you are expected only to enjoy yourself. That's why you pay a fee only and are not bothered with 'Working Parties.'"[12]

Higher fees also translated into more elaborate amenities. Lisa Stein explained the rationale behind the opening of the Four Seasons Nature Park in 1969:

> We could see that times were changing and that people just wouldn't be satisfied with a mountain stream and no facilities. And outhouses and this kind of thing wouldn't go over anymore. So we decided we would go up to country club standards ... We were going to please the majority of the people and we would open a year-round resort with what people wanted: bar facilities, dining room facilities, entertainment.[13]

In its 1969 brochure, Four Seasons advertised the following enticements: "Color T.V., a snack bar, showers, heated indoor pool, sauna baths, ping pong and billiard tables, flush toilets – in fact, urban living in a country setting for utter comfort."[14] Practically speaking, indoor conveniences such as pools, saunas, and clubhouses enabled clubs to offer events year-round and to stay connected with their members, reducing the chances of losing them from one summer to the next. Proprietary clubs were also the most aggressive in membership recruitment, seeking greater revenue to finance their improvements and believing that, in turn, better facilities would translate into more members. Reporting on plans for a new building to house washrooms, sauna, and dormitory, Ruehle told Sun Valley members,

> Of course, a lot will depend on ... new membership influx. If we are going to offer commercial accommodation and facilities, we will have to operate commercial to a certain extent. A little lame club with 20 or 30 families can never dream of such installations as we have to look forward to ... Be assured that the fees you pay are invested again for your enjoyment and convenience. Some is used – of course – to pay us a living.[15]

The development of club property was informed by a particular understanding of nature. In 1952, Ray Connett first visited the property that subsequently housed the Sunny Trails Club. He was enchanted by what he saw – "truly a natural park, where vines and small brush had been slashed and burned, the ground raked laboriously and grass seed planted. The effect was nature as we dream it should be, whereas nature in the raw is often ugly and cruel."[16] In evoking "nature as we dream it should be," Connett defined it as something that required cultivation, not antithetical to culture but enhanced by it. He and many of his fellow nudists saw nature as imperfect and improved by human intervention; in fact, human labour was necessary to produce ideal landscapes. Nature at its best was actively created not passively encountered.[17] In 1973, Lakesun owner Hans Behrmann expressed satisfaction that "our landscaping program has turned our grounds into a garden."[18]

Carolyn Merchant traces the roots of this modernist orientation toward nature:

> Beginning in the seventeenth century and proceeding to the present, New World colonists have undertaken a massive effort to reinvent the whole earth in the image of the Garden of Eden. Aided by the Christian doctrine of redemption and the inventions of science, technology, and capitalism, the long-term goal of the recovery project has been to turn the earth itself into a vast cultivated garden.

The task of taming nature was connected to the taming of human nature: "The civilizing process not only removed wild beasts from the pastoral lands of the garden; it suppressed the wild animal in men."[19] In a similar way, the cultivation of club property paralleled that of mind and body. Nudists sought to dissociate nudity and sexuality by taming and channelling bodily impulses and desires. The two tasks were directly linked in Ray

Connett's advice on how to avoid getting an erection at the club: "If a man goes to a nudist club and sits about day-dreaming and ogling, he is asking for trouble, and he will get it. If he goes to camp and swings into a round of work and play he will be admired and respected."[20] Male sexuality remained an ongoing concern for clubs, and men were advised to redirect it to stereotypically masculine physical tasks such as manual labour or athletic activities. Thus, the self-disciplinary project reflected, and at times contributed to, the cultivation of club property. David Matless argues that a similar relationship was promoted in reconstruction-era Britain: "Both citizen and country were to be improved. Environmental and social visions were necessarily combined ... as part of a cultural movement seeking a design for modern life."[21]

While investing significant time and resources in the development of their properties and facilities, a few club owners identified nature conservation as a driving motivation. When asked why he purchased property on which to found a club in 1959, Sunny Glades owner Stan Wortner explained, "Well I wasn't so interested in a club ... I was always interested in conservation." Wortner noted that the sole source of conflict with local residents was his disapproval of hunting, not his nudism: some locals were in the habit of using his property as "their private hunting reserve" in the fall, and "Since I was opposed to hunting, we ran into some problems that way."[22] Likewise, Lakesun owner Hans Behrmann informed members, "From the beginning our plan was to disturb as little as possible for fear of scaring away wildlife ... Naturists have always been conservation minded. We are sure you all agree." In the same breath, he equated his club's progress with "building facilities and conveniences for ourselves as humans."[23] But Behrmann was willing to make some sacrifices to protect nature. He had fallen in love with waterskiing while visiting the Norhaven Club in the 1950s, and after opening Lakesun he purchased a speedboat to provide waterskiing there. By 1973, however, the club had discontinued its use of the boat. Behrmann had become concerned that it was disturbing the loons on the lake, and with the end to power-boating the birds returned.[24] Not all wildlife was equally valuable to Behrmann, however. In the spring 1975 newsletter, he told club members, "To preserve our good bass fishing we all must pull out more sunfish ... We have no intention to have our delicious tasting bass be crowded out by sunfish." He also mentioned that the club was expanding its parking areas to better accommodate the large number of trailers that members brought with them.[25]

## The Emergence of Modern Environmentalism and Naturism in Canada

As Canada entered a period of dramatic social and cultural changes in the second half of the 1960s, the nudist movement rethought some of its policies and practices. Previous chapters have discussed its reactions to social drinking, the sexual revolution, and second-wave feminism. Another significant development was the rise of the environmental movement, and some nudist individuals and clubs found a new purpose through re-emphasizing the connection between nudity and nature, adopting the term "naturist" to describe themselves.

French, German, and British nudists had long referred to themselves as naturists, and when the word was employed in Canada during the 1950s and 1960s it was typically by European immigrants. Though often used interchangeably with "nudist," "naturist" could also evoke the wider physical health emphasis of the early German movement. For example, in 1958 German immigrant Karl Ruehle explained the distinction: "Nudism is part of Naturism. Naturism covers every possible aspect of healthful living while nudism is more or less the sunbathing angle and is neglecting gymnastics, food control, etc. which are important if one wants to maintain best possible health and well-being. Naturists also strive for habit control and cut down smoking and drinking to moderate uses."[26] Well into the 1970s, "naturism" suggested an association with Europe, whereas "nudism" was common to Canada and the United States. When the Fédération québécoise de naturisme/Quebec Federation of Naturism (FQN) was established in 1977, it had difficulties in convincing Quebec clubs to affiliate, due to suspicions that it represented "European style naturism" and might try "to impose naturism on the clubs by banning beer, meat, and smoking."[27]

Increasingly, however, naturists did not advocate a return to lifestyle habits such as teetotalling or vegetarianism, and instead distinguished themselves from nudists in two key ways: rejecting what they saw as the commercialization and exploitation of nudity (in society generally and at some clubs), and placing renewed importance on nudity as offering a deeper connection to, and respect for, nature. La Pommerie, established by French immigrant Jean-Marcel Boucher in the Montreal area in 1976, advocated for naturism: offering "more than a suntan, tennis, and Molson's," it embraced the principles of ecology.[28] Many of its members co-founded the FQN in 1977. The FQN called on Quebec clubs to provide "a recreational setting as much as possible compatible with the naturist ideal" through "exclusion or control of ordinary nuisances: noise, pollution, commercial promotions, sexist manifestations."[29] Among other things, the FQN pushed for the banning of Miss Nude and royalty pageants, and for the protection of a peaceful camp environment. In 2011, Michael Vaïs, an early member of La Pommerie and a key proponent of the naturist movement in Canada, distinguished between the types of clubs that operated in Quebec during the 1970s:

> Some of them called themselves nudists and others naturists. Some of them were really only concerned with having people nude, you know, and uh, continued to drink their beer as they did elsewhere, and have that loud music near the lake or near the swimming pool and so on ... Among them you had some people who were not really any different, you know, than ordinary campers except that they were naked, you see? But I will tell you a minority were more concerned with nature, and this is especially the case at La Pommerie. So at the Federation [FQN], of course, we were very concerned with ecology, with environmental issues, and with nature. I mean, we, we, we fought for the word, for the concept of naturism, for the definition of naturism which is accepted by the International Naturist Federation.[30]

In 1985, a new nation-wide umbrella organization, the Federation of Canadian Naturists (FCN), followed the Quebec body in taking on the naturist identity. It advocated respect for self, others, and the natural world, and sought to represent non-landed clubs – that rented local facilities, travelled to other clubs, or used clothing-optional beaches rather than possessing property – as well as traditional land-owning clubs. Though the FCN tapped into growing environmental concern, in many ways its philosophy of body acceptance and emphasis on the naturalness of nudity constituted a reassertion of 1950s nudist values and a rejection of the more experimental innovations of some clubs in the early 1970s, rather than a groundbreaking new form of nudism.

The extensive property development at many clubs and their use of car camping, trailers, and amenities stand in contrast to the more "hands-off" approach to nature advocated by nude sunbathers at Wreck Beach, as discussed in the next chapter. Despite their differing approaches, however, nudists, naturists, and Wreck Beach users "appeal[ed] to nature for moral authority." William Cronon explains the power of this invocation: "The great attraction of nature for those who wish to ground their moral vision in external reality is ... its capacity to take disputed values and make them seem innate, essential, eternal, non-negotiable." He suggests that in the post-Enlightenment age, "Nature has become a secular deity."[31] Despite the difficulty of determining what constituted a natural environment, and the nuances entailed in defining nudity as natural in some settings but not in others, nudists consistently rationalized their recreational nudity through this powerful association.

## Private versus Public Property

Nudist clubs were located on private property, though many prominent nudists looked forward to the day when their philosophy would so influence mainstream society that nudity would be accepted in public spaces such as parks and beaches. Throughout its publication run, a stated purpose of *Sunbathing for Health* was "to eventually persuade local authorities to supply facilities so that the full benefit of our regime can be realized."[32] Questioned about the future of the nudist movement in Canada, CSA national secretary Peggy Parkes told a CBC Radio reporter,

> The idea that we hope to put across is to get it accepted to such an extent that we can have nude beaches, the way they have in Europe. In Denmark, for instance, and in some places in Germany, there are public beaches where anybody can just walk on there and take off their clothes and sunbathe and swim, and there is no, no trouble whatsoever about this.[33]

Sun Valley Gardens owner Karl Ruehle similarly defined the "ultimate goal of nudism" as "social nudity anyplace in the country for relaxation and pleasure."[34]

Despite such professions of hope, Canadian nudists typically did little more than pay lip service to this objective. In a 1962 issue of *Sun Valley News,* Karl Ruehle attacked them for their complacency:

> [Sixty] years of constant fighting lay behind the Nudist Movement, with the ground-work done mainly by nudists in Germany, France, Great Britain and the USA. In Canada we have come a long way, too, however, and in contrast to European Nudism, most members here have the notion

> that holding a membership card is already enough done to promote the Nudist Movement in Canada ... With becoming a member of a nudist club, you subscribe and pledge to further the Nudist Movement in any way possible. Although nothing much is said or written about this, every thinking member should realize that his first and foremost aim is to strengthen the idea of nudism, that his own membership is secured, that his children may have the same privilege too, that nudism no longer is frowned upon and confused with strip-tease, and that nudity once again shall reign on the beaches as the unmistakable sign that the people of this nation have regained a high moral standard – and this shall be your and mine – OUR – aim.[35]

Yet even individuals such as Ruehle rarely looked beyond the limited strategy of membership recruitment. Ray Connett suggested that the movement lacked the strength and resources to successfully challenge laws against public nudity and conceded that most nudists were "content if we may have nudity and the freedom of body and movement in the sun and open air within the confines of our private clubs."[36]

Why were nudists so half-hearted about promoting the acceptance of nudity? American sociologist Ellen Woodall critiques American clubs for being complicit with the capitalist system and so motivated by profit as to pursue nudism almost entirely within the private setting.[37] This claim does not ring true for the postwar Canadian movement. Whether run by a co-operative or a proprietor, clubs were hardly a profitable enterprise. Looking back on the early years of their development, Sunny Glades owner Stan Wortner observed,

> In hindsight, a lot of the attempts were, ended up as failures, only because, probably because they were undercapitalized. Now we're back in the 1950s, when probably the average wage, if you made $50 a week you made more than the average wage, say $200 a month or something like that. So property, you know, was still cheap but you still had to make that hurdle of buying and then developing it. And a lot of the people who bought property weren't funded well enough to expand.[38]

Developing a club from the ground up was hard work, and clubs did well to stay afloat financially. A steady stream of new members was required to replace departing ones. Membership dues went to operating costs, and profits were often reinvested to finance improvements to the grounds and facilities. It took years for most Canadian clubs to purchase land and develop amenities that could rival public recreational sites. Furthermore, the clubs frequently lay a considerable distance from urban centres because property prices closer to town were prohibitively expensive for them.

There were other reasons, then, why Canadian nudists generally looked no farther than club property lines in their pursuit of social nudism. In essence, they substituted the protections derived from private property rights for the protection of clothing or the homes that they had temporarily abandoned. The private nature of their clubs afforded them a legal footing. In his *Sunbathing for Health* column, Ray Connett routinely explained the Criminal Code prohibition against public nudity and emphasized the importance of adhering to it. In his opinion, failure to comply would have potentially disastrous repercussions for the movement. In 1957, he commented on a Vancouver newspaper account that fifteen nude sunbathers had been spotted in Stanley Park and reported to police. He denounced "secret sunbathers in public parks, beaches, etc." as "a menace to organized nudism. Every time such an incident on public property shocks the non-nudist public the legal right of nudists to sunbathe on secluded private property is jeopardized."[39] In return for obeying the law, nudists earned legal protection. On the most basic level, they were safeguarded from legal prosecution by confining their activities to screened private property. They could also seek police assistance if their property rights were violated. Some clubs maintained regular communication with local law enforcement, even issuing an open invitation to police to patrol the property. In the summer of 1957, Sun Valley Gardens reported two occasions on which police were called in to deal with trespassers. Karl Ruehle noted that "immediate attention by the police made it possible to arrest in one time 12 and at another time 7 youngsters while invading the camp site ... This news went all over Canada by air [radio broadcast] or papers."[40] This sort of incident cast nudists as the wronged party whose property and privacy rights had been transgressed and affirmed their self-image as respectable, law-abiding citizens.[41] Situating clubs on private property afforded legal standing and, just as significantly, moral high ground in making their case for nudism.

## The Regulation of Space

The use of private property also enabled nudists to regulate the space itself: to decide whom to admit and to dictate standards of behaviour. In other words, they could control their environment in a way that was not possible at public sites. One consequence of this was that clubs could offer a less crowded and purportedly more relaxing experience than might be enjoyed elsewhere. One *Sunbathing for Health* contributor complained that

> the most common place for having a sunbath, namely the beach, is certainly not ideal for the purpose ... When the bathing place is situated near a big city people are lying so close that they can hardly do anything beyond lying still for hours on the same spot, becoming completely inactive and indolent. This is meant to be a relaxation, a sort of counterpoise to the nervous hurry of everyday life. I wonder whether it really amounts to this.[42]

This observation references the crowding that occurred at many public recreational areas such as beaches and campgrounds during the decades after the Second World War.[43] For this writer, the nudist club was the preferable alternative. Likewise, a brochure for Ontario's Summerset Nudist Resort advertised, "There is ample room here at Summerset Nudist Resort. No waiting for admission. No crowded beaches. No parking problems." The message was designed to appeal to those "who want to get away from the hustle and bustle of every day life," and the place to do it, they were told, was at a private nudist club.[44] As Canadians flocked to national and provincial parks, campgrounds, and beaches, the clubs offered an escape from the crowds. Davis and Lorenzkowski suggest that the desire for psychological and physical space after enduring crowded wartime conditions on public transportation prompted many Canadians to reject public transit in favour of personal vehicles when the war ended.[45] They expressed their desire for privacy in other ways: by exchanging urban apartments for houses in the suburbs and sometimes by favouring more secluded private recreational sites over public ones.

Beyond simply limiting their numbers of people, the clubs offered "cultural privacy," which Tabor Stone defines as the "need and desire of individuals to be among other persons who share their values, norms, beliefs, and standards of behaviour, and to exclude from their presence individuals with other norms and standards."[46] The clubs could determine whom to admit and could demand that they comply with the rules. The main objective of their screening practices was to ensure a balance between the sexes and to create a family atmosphere. But screening could also exclude anyone who was seen as socially undesirable. As a result, nudists bragged that club membership was of "the very highest calibre," and this, combined with clear standards of conduct, contributed to a better environment than a public setting could offer. A Sunny Chinook named Betty told a CBC reporter, "The standards at camp are far, far higher than you'd ever see on a public beach."[47] Sunny Trails member Larry elaborated on this point:

> There are lots of times at the beach where you will see a couple lying together on a blanket or something like that, even underneath a blanket which is far worse than walking around like we are, natural in the nude ... The people wouldn't be allowed to do that here and they wouldn't want to either because there are too many other interesting things to do and we don't get that type of people, because they are carefully screened and considered before they are allowed to come here. It is worth a lot to come to a place where you are free of those demoralizing influences.[48]

In the late 1960s and early 1970s, Lakesun owner Hans Behrmann took aim at the counterculture and used his property rights to exclude men whose appearance signalled alignment with it. Affirming that "the 'new' or 'contemporary' morality will not be tolerated in our park," he barred long-haired men from admission for "hygienic and sanitary reasons" (though offering no rationale for why long-haired women did not pose the same potential hygiene risk). He told his members, "We put our ideals above money to give you members the kind of company and decent atmosphere you enjoy at Lakesun, free from disturbing and bad influence."[49] Underlying these claims about safety and moral uprightness were concerns about postwar society. Given this, the private club was integral to the experience of social nudism for many people; membership screening and behavioural policies conveyed a sense of security, which contrasted favourably with the disorder of public spaces.

This sense of security was also based on the belief that all members shared the same perspective on nudity. In letters of introduction and in interviews, prospective members were asked to describe their attitude toward it. Anyone who bungled this part of the test by failing to express views consistent with the nudist philosophy would probably not be invited to visit a club. Ray Connett explained why clubs were not open to the public:

> Nudists are entitled to their privacy as much as non-nudists ... We would soon lose many of our members, particularly our lady members if we set about putting on a peep show for every moron who, rather than apply in the normal manner for membership in a club, chose to skulk through the adjoining bushes like some hungry animal or malevolent spirit. We would not willingly expose our children to the dangers which the presence of such individuals would entail.[50]

Connett cast club property as a civilized space, safe from untamed, "animal"-like sexual deviants.

Because clubs stressed that nudity was a natural, not primarily sexual, state, and they expected members to conduct themselves in a manner consistent with this philosophy. This included no obvious staring, no physical contact, and no signs of sexual arousal. Anyone who failed to conform faced expulsion. Furthermore, the expectation that all members would go nude when comfortable – a requirement in the swimming pool, which carried much less leniency for men than for women – had an equalizing effect and minimized the potential for anyone to feel violated by the gaze of a fellow member. Both factors conveyed the feeling that social nudity at the club did not entail "mak[ing] a public display of ourselves."[51] Although being curious about the naked body was perfectly normal, making people uncomfortable was not permitted. Karl Ruehle informed Sun Valley members that

> a real nudist does not mind by whom he or she is seen, because to a real nudist the entire body is pure and wholesome ... Of course, if some fellow ... should make improper advances, obviously stare at you, and shows otherwise that he does not control himself, we [the Ruehles] will be the first ones to hear about it.[52]

Club property lines established a space in which nudity was defined on the movement's terms and afforded protection from the prurient view of individuals who might interpret it as erotic or transgressive. Nudity became the new normal within the boundaries of the club.

Finally, the private property location protected members from public criticism. Clubs and promoters worked to educate the public about the legality of nudist activities at the club and to offer reassurance that nudists had no desire to cause offence. As Marlies Ruehle, co-owner of Sun Valley

Gardens, declared to CBC journalist June Callwood, "We don't want to offend anybody, that's why we are staying in our own place. We wouldn't think of going out on the street like that [naked], or downtown."[53] Nudists espoused a "live and let live" attitude, taking pains to convey their respect for those who did not share their view of nudity.[54] They hoped that this approach would be reciprocated in tolerance for their clubs. "We must respect the rights of other people who through the years and generations of prudery do not believe as we do," Ray Connett asserted. "We have a democratic right to practice nudism, but our fellow men have an equal right not to be offended by the sight of our nude activities which may be contrary to their belief."[55] Harris reflected, "We are not out to convert the world to nudism, or as they often say, to get everyone out of their clothes. No indeed! If we can merely obtain a degree of tolerance which will permit us to go to camp unmolested, and be known in our own neighbourhoods as nudists without social ostracism, that will suffice."[56] Her comment indicates that the club context offered protection to both nudists and non-nudists by containing nude bodies within a clearly demarcated, carefully tended, and privately owned space. In the world of nudism, good fences made for good neighbours.

The naturalistic setting and private property location of their clubs were both essential to the postwar Canadian nudist experience. However much it may have been manipulated, the natural environment provided philosophical justification for recreational nudity, and the private property location afforded nudists practical protection. Clearly defined property boundaries separated them from disapproving eyes and enabled them to regulate club space. It safeguarded member privacy, shielded the public from offence, and provided a legal and moral basis for social nudity. Secluded and private club locations also minimized nudists' sense of transgression and contributed to their self-identity as neighbourly, respectable, and liberal-minded citizens who were not so different from anyone else.

# 9

# Defending Nature and Public Nudity at Wreck Beach, 1969–79

In 1978, the first annual report of the Wreck Beach Area Advisory Committee noted, "These are the late 1970's, and among the total population are a significant number of people who crave a much more natural environment when they go to partake of the benefits of sun, sand and sea."[1] For this group, a "natural" beach environment included the freedom to go nude. Wreck Beach had no formal affiliation with the nudist movement and was not an officially sanctioned clothing-optional site. But beginning in 1970 this isolated strip of land skirting Vancouver's Point Grey peninsula rapidly transformed into Canada's most infamous spot for skinny-dipping. This development, and the brief comment in the 1978 report of the Wreck Beach Committee, underscores some important societal shifts underway at this time. But the explanation for the rise to prominence of nudity on Wreck Beach also drew on established nudist discourse that depicted the practice of recreational, social nudity as a logical extension of the natural environment. In favouring such an environment, the advisory committee reflected the growing appeal of ecology and an increasing tendency to "equat[e] human intervention with environmental destruction."[2] Unlike nudist clubs, with their marked emphasis on property development, Wreck Beach users rallied against development projects throughout the 1970s, including a proposed marina, access road, and interventions to stabilize the cliffs above. In addition, Wreck Beach was a less regulated space and a more ambiguous context for nudity than the managed environment of the nudist club. As a consequence, nudity at Wreck Beach was more appealing for some, and more threatening for others, than nudity in the club setting.

Prior to 1969, Wreck Beach was a little-known site off the beaten path. It sits beneath steep, 250-foot cliffs that drop away from the University of British Columbia (UBC) above and is accessible only by foot or by boat. In 1930, the City of Vancouver leased the Point Grey foreshore from the Province of British Columbia for a ninety-nine-year period, and the area came under the jurisdiction of the Vancouver Park Board.[3] Initially, Wreck Beach was used mainly by UBC staff, students, and nearby residents. It was a choice spot for skinny-dipping, but this was not widely advertised.[4] Its transformation into a popular nude bathing locale began in 1969, and visitors soon numbered in the thousands on peak summer days. As a result, this secluded and previously little-known spot became contested terrain. Debate centred on whether nude bathing should be permitted and on how best to manage the delicate environment of beach and cliffs. These issues were intricately entwined and complicated by the number of interested parties, which included the Vancouver Park Board and City Council, the University of British Columbia, beachgoers, nearby property owners, and the general public. Another interested party was the Musqueam First Nation. Point Grey was part of its traditional territory, which, like most of British Columbia, has never been ceded. In 1976, the nation issued the Musqueam Declaration, in which it asserted its rights to the area.[5] Nonetheless, its rights were ignored by beach users, UBC, and the park board alike. However much it was contested as a space for nude bathing, Wreck Beach remained uncontested as settler space through the 1970s and beyond.

## The Beach Environment and Environmental Activism

In the modern West, beaches have been sought out as places of both healthful rejuvenation and carnivalesque pleasure.[6] In the nineteenth century, the middle-class "obsession with health" provided the primary rationale for going to the seashore, but by about 1900 beaches were becoming more heterogeneous, increasingly accessible and attractive to the working classes for a day of escape and recreation. Places such as England's Blackpool, New York's Coney Island, and on a more modest scale, Canada's Toronto Island and Winnipeg Beach, drew crowds by combining a pleasant beach setting and commercial entertainment. But even less elaborate seaside settings, as Dale

Barbour points out, attained allure as "a boundary point between culture and nature."[7]

In light of the social mixing and sensuality of sunbathing and swimming, beaches fuelled moral concerns about bodily exposure and prompted efforts to regulate bathing practices. Nude bathing remained the norm in the first half of the nineteenth century, though generally "unclothed bodies [were shielded] from public view." By the late nineteenth century, however, swimsuits became mandatory as men and women, working and middle class, mingled in growing numbers on the beach. During the 1920s and 1930s, neck-to-knee bathing costume requirements rapidly gave way as "burgeoning consumerism propagated a new culture of pleasure and a new tolerance of the revealed body."[8] The beach was a unique space where men and women could exhibit more of their bodies than they could in everyday life. But shrinking bathing suits did not liberate the body. Instead, modern advertising reinforced and promoted an idealized body, one shaped by self-disciplinary techniques of diet and exercise. Individuals were pressured to comply with bodily norms through the scrutinizing gaze of the public.[9] Although the amount of visible skin changed, bodily display has been an integral aspect of beach-going since the nineteenth century. Caroline Daley observes of New Zealand beaches that "even in the days of neck-to-knee costumes, voyeurs flocked to the seaside."[10] It is no coincidence that beauty contests such as the Miss America Pageant provided a stage for "bathing beauties" and were initially held on or near a beach.[11] The history of modern beaches shows that bathing bodies, and the beaches they frequented, have been ongoing sites of "struggle between pleasure and discipline."[12]

During the late 1960s, "nude scenes" emerged on the coasts of England, Australia, and most prevalently, in California, as hundreds, sometimes thousands, of people flocked to isolated beaches where most of them doffed their clothes.[13] Wreck Beach joined this "free beach" movement, which was connected to the countercultural currents of the sixties. Nudity in this context symbolized a rejection of materialism and a liberation from repressive social values and uptight attitudes toward the body and its functions, what Marguerite Shaffer describes as "a kind of personalized political performance."[14] The event that put Wreck Beach on the map, a Nude-In of late August 1970, articulated a connection to countercultural "happenings," such as the Human Be-Ins held in San Francisco in early 1967 and in New York and Vancouver later that spring. The Wreck Beach Nude-In was promoted by the *Georgia Straight,* an alternative newspaper, and one of the organizers was Korky Day, a war resister from California.[15] *Vancouver Sun* coverage of the event painted an evocative picture: "Although Sunday was a hot day, the atmosphere on the beach can best be described as 'cool.' Both the nudists and the other people spent the afternoon in harmony. As the people soaked in the sun, several impromptu bands of bongos, conga drums, flutes, guitars, and maracas provided music."[16] It is not a coincidence that Canada's first free beach emerged in Vancouver, not far from Kitsilano, which, together with Toronto's Yorkville, was the epicentre for Canadian youthful rebellion during this period.[17]

Historian Lawrence Aronsen suggests that "the counterculture nudity movement found an ideal location at Wreck Beach," which was only later "co-opted by the mainstream."[18] It should be noted, however, that from the earliest reporting, journalists highlighted the diversity of people at the beach – both "long-hairs" and "straight."[19] Beachgoers and visiting journalists depicted the people who used the site much as nudists described their membership. One local informed *Vancouver Sun* readers, "These are simply Vancouverites and visitors, made up of as broad a cross-section of society as you would encounter anywhere (perhaps a little top-heavy with UBC PhDs), but otherwise a peaceful assortment of young and old, singles and groups."[20] Journalist Larry Emrick declared the beach "a haven for hundreds ... teachers, students, secretaries, lawyers, laborers, craftsmen, journalists, moms, dads, kids and dogs. In fact it's just like [nearby] Spanish Banks or English Bay except they wear a little less."[21] Whereas the rise of nudity on Wreck Beach had clear connections to hip culture, the number and range of people who frequented it suggest that it was also related to deeper structural changes in society. The sexual revolution and the growing emphasis on individual rights and freedoms – personified by the new Prime Minister, Pierre Elliott Trudeau – form an important backdrop to the growing popularity of nude bathing at Wreck Beach.[22]

The history of nude bathing at Wreck Beach is also intimately connected with the efforts of beach users to block changes to the Point Grey beaches and the cliffs above. Between 1969 and 1970, two issues propelled the beach into the public spotlight. In early 1969, the Vancouver Park Board authorized construction of a $500,000 road linking Wreck Beach with the popular Spanish Banks area to the east. The board believed that the road would address the ongoing erosion of the cliffs and would enable greater public access to Wreck Beach.[23] Long-term plans for the site included a marina and rowing course. A student-led protest, supported by some university faculty, conservationists, and local residents, blocked construction and convinced the park board to reconsider, arguing that the road would not control erosion and would compromise "a beach of unsurpassed beauty and peace ... the last of its kind in Vancouver."[24] The plan was scrapped, but this was only the first of several confrontations between the board and UBC, on the one side, and Wreck Beach users and environmental activists, on the other, regarding development and erosion control.

An incident the following year did even more to spark public interest in Wreck Beach. On 11 August 1970, the RCMP arrested thirteen nude bathers at the beach, nine men and four women ranging in age from eighteen to fifty-five.[25] They were charged with committing an indecent act under section 158 of the Criminal Code. The charges came midway through a summer that witnessed a surge in the popularity of nude bathing at the beach. An RCMP officer reported, "We've been getting complaints all year from residents of the area that they can't use the beach because the nudists have taken over."[26] The thirteen arrested individuals were allegedly only a few "among 'hundreds' who on fine days enjoy the delights of the seashore in the nude."[27] Twenty-six-year-old Sheila Beaupre was the third of the thirteen to appear in court. Like the two tried before her, she was convicted and sentenced to a fifty-dollar fine or ten days in jail. Provincial Court Judge M.E. Ferguson ruled that nudity in a public place such as Wreck Beach was offensive to the public, despite the testimony of RCMP Constable Steven Leach that although many people were present, "There had been no specific complaints about nude sunbathing that day and that 85 per cent of the people on the beach were nude."[28] Beaupre appealed her case to the British Columbia Supreme Court, which quashed her conviction. According to Supreme Court Justice J.G. Gould, she had been charged under the wrong section of the Criminal Code. He determined that the section 158 charge of "'willfully do[ing] an indecent act in a public place in the presence of one or more persons' ... connotes something more active, with greater moral turpitude than the mere state of being nude in a public place." Merely being undressed in a public place "without lawful excuse" was covered under section 159, which should have been applied in her case.[29] Being charged under section 159, however, required the prior consent of the attorney general. In the aftermath of the Supreme Court ruling, consent to charge nude bathers at Wreck Beach was not forthcoming. The year 1970 marked the last time that anyone was prosecuted for going nude at Wreck Beach, although the beach did not receive its official "clothing-optional" designation until 1991.[30]

SKINNY-DIPPERS AT WRECK BEACH . . . "we don't hurt anybody"

'FREEDOM FROM PROSECUTION'

Nudists seek beach rights

**Figure 9.1** "Nudists Seek Beach Rights," *Vancouver Sun,* 14 August 1970 | Material republished with the express permission of *Vancouver Sun,* a division of Postmedia Network Inc.

The August 1970 arrests fixed the media spotlight on Wreck Beach. In addition to reporting on the legal action, local journalists visited the beach for themselves. Within days, a story appeared on the front page of the *Vancouver Sun,* complete with a photo, shot from behind, of a nude man, woman, and child walking hand in hand along the beach (Figure 9.1). The article declared that "Wreck Beach nudists" wanted "freedom from clothes and freedom from prosecution."[31] The public response was dramatic. According to one beach regular, 1,500 people turned up on the following day alone. Less than two weeks later, the Nude-In was staged. Intended as a show of support for the arrested thirteen, it drew an estimated two to three thousand people, approximately three hundred of whom went nude, and made the front page of the city's two major newspapers. The *Vancouver Province* reported,

> Hundreds of cars clogged Marine Drive as people, many of whom said they didn't even know where Wreck Beach was, left their cars on the road and clambered down steep cliffs near the University of B.C.'s Totem Park to look or take part in the nude-in. It was no easy beach to reach. The curious and converted had to scramble down the cliff and hike a mile over log booms and mud up to their knees to reach the beach where most of Sunday's nudists looked like they've spent most of their summer. Many of the unclothed lay around, played guitar, read and swam, apparently oblivious to the throng of onlookers who walked up and down the beach taking in the sights.[32]

Wreck Beach was now on the public radar and had become synonymous with nudity.

The following summer, the *Vancouver Sun* noted "the revival of nudism at Wreck Beach" by hundreds of people, to which the attorney general's office was "turning a friendly blind eye."[33] Over the next five years, nude bathing persisted at the beach without criminal prosecution and with little public objection. However, during this period a new effort to reduce erosion of the cliffs rekindled conflict on the environmental front. In 1973, the park board, with the support of UBC and $350,000 in provincial funding, announced plans to build up a three-thousand-foot stretch of Wreck Beach by adding gravel and sand. The scheme was intended to stabilize the cliffs by reducing erosion from wave action. Critics questioned the motivation of the board and the university, as well as the effectiveness of the plan. They feared it was a step toward greater beach development, akin to the 1969 park board road proposal, and highlighted the university's self-interest in preserving the cliffs at the expense of the beach: "They own all the land at the top, land which is receding year-by-year."[34] In particular, the planned Museum of Man (now the Museum of Anthropology), constructed between 1974 and 1976, was to be located in a spectacular setting near the edge of the cliff. Regarding the proposal itself, a Vancouver geologist outlined the major objections: the rate and causes of cliff erosion had not been sufficiently researched; alternative courses of action had not been considered; and in all likelihood, the newly deposited sand would quickly be swept away, leaving only the gravel underlay.[35]

Despite these concerns, the board forged ahead. In March 1974, around two hundred protesters blocked bulldozers at the beach and delayed the project for more than a month. One carried a sign that read, "Museum of

**Figure 9.2** Protesters and bulldozers on Wreck Beach, March 1974. | Image 41.1/54-1, University of British Columbia Archives

Man or Natural Man?" questioning whether the new museum should take precedence over the beach below (Figure 9.2). Although the board met with some of the demonstrators – identified in the newspaper as "members of a committee to preserve the beach in its natural state" – the two sides could not reach consensus. The board secured a court injunction prohibiting interference, and the work proceeded.[36] In the aftermath, the park board and the UBC Alumni Association felt it necessary to ameliorate public relations and placed an advertisement in the *Vancouver Province* declaring "We're Building a Beach for You." Explaining the project and the rationale behind it, the ad appealed to the public for its "support and enthusiasm for this project which will provide you with new and natural recreational beachland."[37]

Unfortunately, critics of the project were proven right. Only one year later, most of the sand fill was gone, washed away by ocean waves.[38] Not only did the project fail to address the erosion, it also worsened the tension surrounding use of the beach. Korky Day, an outspoken beach advocate, explained, "Just as the environmentalist and nudist critics of this plan predicted, it has left the beach covered with rocks and pebbles, causing nudists to move to the east."[39] This brought nude bathers closer to the west end of Spanish Banks, a popular Vancouver beach, which sparked a second round of publicity, and the greatest debate, about nudity at Wreck Beach. In the summer of 1977, Pentecostal minister and Vancouver alderman Bernice Gerard, together with Citizens for Integrity, a group whose purpose was to uphold "the moral values of the Judeo-Christian tradition," expressed anxiety about nudity "spilling over" from Wreck Beach onto Spanish Banks West.[40] To bring the issue to public attention, and in the hopes of convincing the attorney general to enforce the law, they held a walk from Spanish Banks to Wreck Beach on Sunday, 10 July. Gerard was lampooned by the press, but she did bring attention to her cause: for the remainder of the summer, the park board, city council, and the local papers were flooded with letters both for and against nude bathing at Wreck Beach.

Although beach users and their allies had not managed to thwart the park board fill project of 1974, they did influence the board's approach to the area. In this regard, the blockades and lobbying fit within a larger story of anti-development activism in Vancouver during this period. In the 1960s, concerned citizens began forming groups to contest a number of development projects planned for Greater Vancouver. These included the Four Seasons project to construct a major high-rise development at Coal Harbour, at the entrance to Stanley Park, and plans for a freeway that would have cut through the Strathcona, Chinatown, and Gastown neighbourhoods. Through alliances of various stakeholders, including residents and business owners, environmental activists, planners, and politicians, both projects were ultimately shelved, despite support from pro-development mayor Tom Campbell (1967–72) and the Non-Partisan Association (NPA), which held a majority on Vancouver City Council throughout most of the 1960s and early 1970s.[41]

In the 1972 municipal election, The Electors' Action Movement (TEAM) won the majority of council seats, and its leader, Art Phillips, replaced Campbell as mayor. TEAM had formed in 1968 as a centrist alternative to the conservative NPA and the left-leaning Coalition of Progressive Electors.

With Phillips at the helm, public consultation became central to decision making about urban development. Back in 1969, the park board had developed its beach road plan without consulting the public. In 1977, however, when it hoped to install portable washrooms on or near the beach and to upgrade the trails, it took a cautious approach that respected the concerns of beachgoers. Chairman Ian Bain stressed that both projects would retain "the natural beauty of the area."[42] More importantly, in February 1977 the board struck a committee – the Wreck Beach Area Advisory Committee – whose purpose was to "represent the needs, interest and preferences of all beach users." It was mandated to meet throughout a one-year period and report back to the board with recommendations regarding the protection of the foreshore.[43] The vision and approach of the board had changed in response to the activism of dedicated beach users and reflected broader political developments in Vancouver as a whole.

The new committee included a variety of people, such as Korky Day and teacher Judy Williams, who were devoted to protecting both the beach itself and the practice of nude bathing there. Although initially envisioned as a temporary committee, it carried on under the leadership of Williams to become the official voice of Wreck Beach users and continues today as the Wreck Beach Preservation Society. It sought to ensure that the beach "be retained in as natural a state as possible." This task was complicated by the fact that the sand on the beach was deposited by the erosion of the cliffs above; in other words, the retention of a natural sandy beach was "incompatible" with the protection of the cliffs (Figure 9.3).[44] Additionally, as a 1975 report stated, "The increasing utilization of Wreck Beach by people who want no change has caused change" – notably, foot traffic on the paths down to the beach had contributed to erosion.[45] Eventually conceding that preserving cliff and beach "in as near a natural state as possible" was the best that could be hoped for, the committee hired its own consultant and in 1979 prepared its "Alternative Proposal by the Wreck Beach Committee for the Cliff Erosion Task Force Committee of the University of British Columbia." This led to the construction of an erosion control berm in 1981 based on a compromise design worked out between the committee and UBC, each with advice from its own consultants and engineers. The committee newsletter declared, "Beach People's Persistence Pays Off" and expressed pleasure that the project "supplants the 1979 $12 million master plan proposal to deforest and contour a longer part of the bluffs and put larger rock on the beach."[46]

**Figure 9.3** An aerial view of the Point Grey Cliffs, showing Wreck Beach, the Museum of Anthropology (top right), and a Second World War searchlight tower, July 1983. | Image 1.1/16555-5, University of British Columbia Archives

## Wreck Beach as Public Space

For many regulars, the natural environment was essential to the experience of nude bathing at Wreck Beach. As one beach user explained, going nude was "genuinely beautiful in the large-scale primitive surroundings of Wreck Beach, against a background of great trees, logs, huge rocks and vast space."[47] Another reflected, "I go to Wreck Beach once in a while ... because I enjoy the sense of freedom in removing all my clothes in a natural setting. It helps to reawaken in me the knowledge that I am part of, not apart from, nature. I do not wish to disrobe at any other beach."[48] These individuals praised the fact that the Point Grey foreshore was "largely undisturbed by man's attempts to improve on nature." Although a public space, Wreck Beach was unique for its privacy and isolation, factors that many Vancouverites treasured and defended. Contrasting its pristine state with the extensive facilities and services – the "Coney Island" atmosphere – at other local beaches, activists sought to preserve it as a "haven."[49] In addition to fighting off large-scale development projects, they looked after the beach in smaller ways, carrying out their garbage for many years so that even trash cans need not be installed.

Other Vancouver residents agreed that the Wreck Beach area was "one of the last in the Lower Mainland that remains in a wilderness state," "a natural paradise" that constituted a unique asset to the city.[50] But not all agreed that nudity was a logical extension of the natural surroundings, and some complained that nude bathers defiled what was otherwise a beautiful place.[51] In their opinion, nudity at Wreck Beach was no more acceptable than nudity "in Stanley Park, on Granville Mall and other public places."[52] As Mrs. J. Oswald complained to Mayor Jack Volrich and city council, "You can be sure I would not be allowed to walk the streets of Vancouver in the nude. So why is nudity allowed at Wreck Beach?"[53] In fact, some feared that if authorities failed to act, it would soon spread to public parks and city streets.[54]

The central point of contention was that the beach was public property. In 1977, spurred on by the example of Bernice Gerard and what they perceived as the park board's tacit approval for nude bathing through its planned provision of toilets and garbage cans, more than forty-five Vancouverites wrote to the board and Mayor Volrich to voice their concerns.[55] Some objected on legal grounds, referring to the Criminal Code prohibition against public nudity and calling for its enforcement. Others offered practical objections – that tax dollars should not be spent on maintaining an area from which a section of the public felt alienated. Whatever their justification, the overriding sentiment was that "the beaches belong to all of us and yet the vast majority of us are unable to enjoy the area because of the very small minority whose moral and social conscience permits them to spend their recreational time in a public place in the nude."[56] Whereas the park board and the university focused on "the constant denuding of beach and bank of valuable sand by the action of surf and sea," some Vancouverites expressed greater anxiety about the "moral landslide" epitomized by nude bathing at Wreck Beach.[57]

Conveying the very attitudes that the Canadian nudist movement had fought against for three decades, opponents labelled nude bathing "obscene" and "indecent," decidedly "not innocent or wholesome."[58] One man declared "nudity on a beach ... just as obscene" as pornography on newsstands, and another suggested that "the sleazy patrons of the porno shops may have a look at the real thing" if they paid a visit to Wreck Beach.[59] More than one writer called on the mayor to stand up for public morality: "You do the

Canadian people and people everywhere an injustice; you sell our young people short in values by allowing this degeneration to continue and by appearing to sanction it."[60] A local woman declared, "I, and many other mothers in Vancouver, would not relish the thoughts of our children growing up with the idea that this is the acceptable norm for our society today. We can teach them at home ... but the fact is that they *are* influenced by society and it's up to us to see that good moral standards prevail in our City."[61] She was not alone in believing that nude bathing at Wreck Beach created an atmosphere unsuitable for children.

Although moral concerns were most frequently mentioned in these letters, others expressed embarrassment at the idea, or experience, of a face to face encounter with a naked person. They felt that no one should be "made uncomfortable" in this way at a public beach: "If I cannot go to any public beach with or without my children for fear of embarrassment, then it is certainly not a respectable area and should definitely not be classified as a public beach."[62] Some correspondents indicated that their embarrassment would be heightened if children were present, an interesting admission that reveals how arguments about children's well-being could be tied to adult self-interest, as well as ongoing concern regarding children's exposure to nude bodies.

Despite rejecting key tenets of nudism, many letters pointed to private nudist clubs as a more acceptable alternative. In a letter to the mayor and council, Elizabeth Marocchi stated, "I believe people have every right to be nude if they are willing to form clubs and pay for private resorts as was done previously. In no way is it right to detract from the freedom of average citizens by displaying their bodies on city beaches."[63] For these writers, confining nudity to private property was a workable compromise, a stance that brought them into a strange alignment with organized nudism. Alderman Bernice Gerard declared,

> The nudist takeover alienates this natural paradise from the average citizen. Not simply Wreck Beach, secluded as it is, but a long stretch of easily accessible public space is being used as an unregulated nudist camp ... Those who see nudism as something to be practiced in the privacy of the home or in a licensed nudist camp had better speak now, or they will find themselves psychologically alienated from their own beaches and hiking grounds.[64]

Wreck Beach was a far less regulated space than the carefully controlled environment of the nudist club. On the most basic level, as one beachgoer pointed out, "There is no gate where one must seek the approbation of guards to be allowed entry, as at a nudist camp." Instead, it was accessible to anyone who could navigate the trail and was used by a wide variety of people: students, transients, singles, and families; regular and occasional visitors; those who went nude and those who did not. Beachgoers interpreted the public nature of the site as inclusive, open to anyone who wanted "to escape the noise, hassles and overcrowding of this city's other less attractive beaches, many having the desire to get an over-all tan by not wearing bathing suits."[65] One explained, "These beaches are used by people of every walk of life, of many races and cultures, including families with children and grandparents."[66] Supporters of nude bathing at Wreck Beach depicted themselves as average citizens, implying that nothing morally questionable was unfolding there.

Critics, however, saw the beach as providing a haven for the "permissive crowd."[67] The (clothed) city beaches of Kitsilano and Jericho were also popular gathering places for hippie youth.[68] Nevertheless, the association of the hippie counterculture with Wreck Beach persisted well into the 1970s. In 1975, Gordon Shrum, executive director of the Vancouver Museums and Planetarium Association, characterized Wreck Beach users as "a bunch of naked hippies."[69] Other critics concurred. In a letter to the mayor, Frances Fuller stated,

> I am sick and tired of this group who defy the law at every turn and are apparently allowed by police to do ... as they like. We were forced to walk over them and listen to their obseneties [sic] if we wished to walk along Granville Street to enter the Hudson Bay Store in the late sixties. Then they took over Stanley Park.[70]

Another resident wrote to Mayor Volrich in 1977, "Hopefully we are not going to let a few 'misfits' run our city – not many votes from the Wreck Beach group, Mr. Volrich – in fact, it is doubtful if they are even property owners."[71] These characterizations reveal that hippie stereotypes and a lack of tolerance for their presence persisted beyond the late 1960s and early 1970s, when conflict between Vancouver's property-owning elites and transient young people was at its height.[72] What was an inclusive space for some was a breeding ground of countercultural dissent for others, and despite users' assertions that a broad cross-section of society frequented the beach, its association with the counterculture persisted. The law-and-order rhetoric that had held sway with city council during Tom Campbell's tenure as mayor continued to find expression in 1977 as a basis for opposition to nude bathing at Wreck Beach by a small but vocal minority of Vancouver residents.

## Secluded but Unbounded

Underlying the polarized characterizations of Wreck Beach was the reality that its open access and lack of clear parameters – geographical and behavioural – created a more ambiguous context for nudity than what nudist clubs offered. Beachgoers were largely self-policing, occupying a place described by historical geographer Rhys Evans as "institutionally marginal."[73] The beach was not serviced by lifeguards, and although the Point Grey foreshore is policed by the RCMP, the lack of road access has meant that "the vast majority of the beach remains out of institutional surveillance the majority of the time."[74] As a consequence, the spectatorial gaze was less regulated and sexuality was less neatly divorced from nudity than at a nudist club, where owners and executive committees enforced regulations.

Clothes were optional at Wreck Beach, which meant that individuals could wear bathing suits if they chose, something strictly taboo at a nudist club. Media coverage of the beach during the 1970s often noted the presence of both dressed and undressed people, and journalists and interviewees estimated that from 50 to 85 percent of people at the beach on any given day were nude, with the remainder wearing bathing suits or some other form of clothing.[75] Whereas going naked at Wreck Beach signalled full participation in the "free beach" environment, nudity was not required, and regulars espoused the philosophy that all comers were welcome to dress as they pleased.[76]

The presence of clothed people raised the spectre of voyeurism, something that nudist clubs felt they mitigated by having everyone go nude, circumstances permitting. In fact, Wreck Beach regulars acknowledged that voyeurs were a given at the beach. In 1972, a male Wreck Beach user told CBC Radio reporter Jurgen Hesse that "voyeurs are sort of coming out of the closet. They now have a place where they can go and look." Hesse asked, "Do you personally mind if someone looks at you?" His interviewee responded,

> No, uh, there was one fellow who came along here earlier today, and it wasn't until he passed I was going to ask him if he'd lost something [Hesse laughs]. But I didn't think of that in time. But, you know, he was sort of going very obviously. I was down, further down the beach and people were having a chuckle. There was someone up on top of the cliff with binoculars and apparently he'd started a little small landslide or something, leaning over the edge, and everyone got a big laugh out of that. Uh, I don't think, you know, people are bothered ... I mean people in the nude aren't uptight, and I don't think people who wear clothes down here are uptight, you know, or made to feel out of place.[77]

As these comments indicate, beachgoers responded to staring in a variety of ways: by ignoring it, by confronting the gawker, or by laughing it off. Their attitude toward voyeurism was more nonchalant than that of the nudist clubs, accepting it to some degree as unavoidable. Moreover, some expressed the attitude that being stared at while naked was not necessarily more invasive than being scrutinized while clothed. When Hesse asked a female beachgoer if she felt "offended" when clothed men looked at her, she replied, "No, not really, because, you know, a lot of the clothes I wear don't cover up that much anyway." She made it clear that being stared at in public was a regular occurrence.[78]

The lack of clear boundaries created more space for sexuality on the beach than at a club, in some cases welcome, in others not. According to *Vancouver Sun* journalist Jamie Craig, some men interpreted female nudity at Wreck Beach as a sign of availability:

> Women say they are more hassled by the randy chauvinist male at Wreck Beach than at other beaches. The reason seems to be that this chap figures, in his single-minded way, that if a lady likes to lie in the sun nude she is therefore "liberated" and therefore prepared to go to bed with him. It's similar to the familiar downtown scene of businessmen stopping what they call "hippie girls" and confidently propositioning them, because they think the ladies practice free love. Their mistake is that they believe love is a one-dimensional concept, chiefly involving sexual intercourse.[79]

Though a visit to Wreck Beach may have involved unwanted attention, consensual sex also took place there. Some beach users embraced the "naturalness" of the location as an inviting setting not only for nudity but also for sexual contact. Although it was public property, its cliffs, trees, rocks, and logs offered some privacy for those who sought it and enough seclusion for an erotic encounter. Gordon Brent Ingram indicates that it was a gay cruising area that predated the 1970s and widespread nude bathing at Point Grey, concentrated around a swampy area marginal to the main beach itself.[80] One Point Grey resident complained of stumbling upon a heterosexual couple engaged in intercourse.[81] They probably represented just the tip of the iceberg: a study of a California free beach published in 1977 reported that a variety of sexual acts occurred there on a regular basis, including masturbation and intercourse, in the open and discreetly.[82]

Alderman Gerard drew attention to the existence of a "gay beach" at Point Grey, which no doubt fuelled her opposition to nudity at Wreck Beach.[83] She also expressed discomfort with male nudity in general: "I think the human body is great but, as an average woman, I find the sight of a naked man offensive – I'm just not comfortable in his presence."[84] By all accounts, men outnumbered women at Wreck Beach.[85] Critics emphasized this fact and expressed unease that the locale had become "the preserve of male nudes." One Vancouver woman complained to City officials about a disturbing experience with nude men on the Point Grey foreshore. She was sitting on the beach when a man with an erection came by and lay down not far away; when she got up to leave, she found her path "blocked by more nude men." She explained, "I think of myself as a liberal thinker, nevertheless, I did not feel comfortable (I felt threatened) at the beach in front of our house."[86] Such encounters were exactly what nudist clubs took such pains to avoid, along with the "threatening" association between nudity and sexuality. Art historian Lynda Nead defines "the obscene body" as "the body without borders or containment."[87] In this sense, the project of making nudism respectable was one of enclosing and containing nudity and sexuality. Whereas female sexuality and its containment had been a major interest of nude art since about 1800, as far as postwar social nudity was concerned, male sexuality was most anxiety producing. In this respect, nudist clubs were better positioned than places like Wreck Beach to manage the problem, subjecting men to regular surveillance even as they carved out space for male nudity.

Also significant about the run-in between the woman and the nude men on the beach was that she lived on the University Endowment Lands, and the incident took place just west of Spanish Banks West, an area that many saw as lying beyond the boundaries of Wreck Beach. The Wreck Beach Area Advisory Committee believed that "most of the critics of nudity, oddly enough, appear to have been persons who do not use Wreck Beach, and likely never would."[88] No doubt, there was truth to this statement – a report on Gerard's protest march noted that "most of the protesters interviewed said this was their first trip to Wreck Beach" – but the City also received a number of complaints from Vancouverites, especially Point Grey residents, who did use the foreshore.[89] They objected to what they perceived as the co-opting of the area by outsiders.[90] Many were prepared to tolerate nude bathing at Wreck Beach but complained that it had gotten out of bounds, spreading east toward Spanish Banks. They objected to the "brazenness" of this and to the fact that they no longer felt comfortable on beaches they had once frequented. The issue was a lack of clear geographical boundaries. Because Wreck Beach had not been officially designated as clothing-optional, the park board was unwilling to provide relevant signage. This was a problem because the Point Grey peninsula was edged by a long stretch of undifferentiated beachfront. Even the variety of names ascribed to its beaches indicated some confusion: the area west of Spanish Banks was variously called University Beach, Acadia Beach, and Foreshore Park, and there was no clear demarcation of where Wreck Beach began.

This was evident in the confusion surrounding Gerard's beach walk in July 1977. Newspapers declared it an attempt to "liberate Wreck Beach from the nudists," whereas Gerard insisted that she had never set foot on Wreck Beach itself: "No amount of telling on my part could convince the reporters that I had *not* gone to Wreck Beach, that far-off idyllic haven; my whole point was that the nudists were spilling westward to Spanish Banks."[91] She had initially raised the alarm about "the nudist take-over of the beaches from Spanish Banks west to the Fraser" – in other words, the entire Point Grey foreshore including Wreck Beach – and sought to convince the attorney general to prosecute all public nudity.[92] But in the aftermath of the march, she backed away from this position. Like area residents, she now concentrated on confining nudity to Wreck Beach proper.

The Wreck Beach Area Advisory Committee acknowledged that unclear boundaries and the extension of nude bathing eastward were problems. However, the committee believed that the issue "centred around a number of [nude] individuals, minimal in number who deliberately walked east of the main nudist area towards Spanish Banks Area with the intention of getting some sort of a reaction out of the bathers in that area." As a solution, the committee recommended "that those individuals who are exhibiting for the purposes of obtaining a reaction from the general public should be discouraged, warned and possibly charged if repeat offenders are identified," though it admitted that this measure "would be difficult to enforce."[93] For this particular group to suggest that establishing the boundaries of the beach might require law enforcement was a strange turn of events, but it was a reflection of the challenges posed by unregulated public access. After a naked man walked past his family's picnic at "a spot a little west of Spanish Banks," a Vancouver man who had previously been little concerned about Wreck Beach wrote, "I felt infringed upon and was downright angry. Angry at him and at the people who want this freedom and yet will abuse the responsibility that comes with it."[94] Whereas Gerard's morality campaign was not taken seriously by the press or the users of Wreck Beach, the problem of nudity spilling into other spaces had the potential to turn public sentiment.

Critics who objected to Wreck Beach on moral grounds pointed to the Criminal Code provision against public nudity as indicative of "the values of the Canadian people" and called on officials to uphold them.[95] In contrast, the BC Civil Liberties Association declared, "It is clear that this society is not prepared to accept general nudity, nor are we suggesting such a policy. However, nude bathing seems to very many people in our society to be an altogether natural and decent thing."[96] During the 1970s, Canadian jurisprudence came to side with this latter point of view. In the case of three men who were initially convicted of "appearing nude in a public place" while skinny-dipping in the South Saskatchewan River in 1975, Justice J. MacPherson of the Saskatchewan Court of Queen's Bench quashed their conviction on the grounds that "it cannot be an offence to swim in the nude at a lonely place in Canada in summer. That is part of the pleasure of summer in Canada, particularly to young males."[97] Dale Barbour's study of nude bathing in early-twentieth-century Toronto confirms that young men and boys made extensive use of swimming holes in the local rivers and that "contrary to the myth of a buttoned-up Victorian era where the nudity was to be expelled as a mark of shame or savagery," Torontonians tolerated and even romanticized it. However, whereas "the undressed boy remained chaste in memory ... the undressed [adult] male did not age well in the twentieth century," subjected to growing suspicion of sexual predation.[98]

Almost as suddenly as free beaches emerged around 1970, streaking became a fad in 1974, erupting on university campuses, at sports events, and even at the 1974 Academy Awards, and judges' responses to streakers echoed their attitude toward skinny-dippers. Justice McIntyre overturned a 1974 conviction of a man for streaking at a Canadian Football League game in Regina, ruling that "I am satisfied that there is no sexual deviation or exploitation in 'streaking,'" and that the public response to streaking was one of "amused tolerance."[99] These court cases differentiated between types of public nudity and refused to interpret the incidents of streaking as transgressions of the law.

In 1978, after years of silence from the BC Attorney General's Office regarding the situation at Wreck Beach, Attorney General Garde Gardom, who also happened to be the MLA for Vancouver Point Grey, expressed the opinion that "skinny-dipping in the moderate sense is something that has been a bit of a way of life in Canada ever since we became a country." Therefore, it would be prosecuted only "if it can be shown the accused had the intent to insult or offend others."[100] This sounded akin to Karl Ruehle's hope that Canadian law would eventually "differentiat[e] between the two states of nudity, sexual nudity and recreational nudity" – the latter, it seemed, constructed as a youthful, boyish, innocuous activity, the former, a threatening and predatory act of an aggressive, mature male.[101] However, because Canadian nudists had taken the conservative approach of sheltering behind their private property rights, Gardom's statement was prompted, not by their activism but by the example of nude sunbathers at Wreck Beach.

THE FORMALIZED ESTABLISHMENT of Wreck Beach as a clothing-optional public site was born out of dedicated activism by beachgoers who defended both their right to go nude and the pristine character of the area. Their environmentalism set them apart from rank-and-file nudist club members, but the Wreck Beach Area Advisory Committee was not alone in deploring the "Coney Island approach" of the Vancouver Park Board during the 1970s. Debates over the fate of Wreck Beach occurred during a crucial decade in Vancouver's history, and some of the development proposals for the beach, including a road and a marina, joined various other schemes that were scuttled as a result of organized efforts by local citizens.

Wreck Beach offered nude bathers less protection and the non-nudist public less insulation from naked bodies than was afforded at nudist clubs. Open to the public, it was used by a wide cross-section of society. Yet it was secluded and difficult to reach, requiring a steep descent down trails or stairs. It had little formal regulation, and its context for nudity was more ambiguous than the contained space of a club. Additionally, its boundaries were not defined, prompting some Vancouverites to fear that its nudity would leak into adjacent spaces. All of these distinctions meant that to some Vancouverites, including some nudists, nudity at Wreck Beach was uncontained and threatening.

For Canadians who were interested in experimenting with the nudist lifestyle, the clubs and Wreck Beach held differing appeals. A club offered privacy and the company of like-minded individuals. At the beach, however, people came and went as they pleased, engaged in sexual behaviour if they wished, and dropped their clothes without first acquiring a membership card. Beachgoers and nudists both extolled the freedom of going nude, but freedom meant different things to these two groups. For Wreck Beach regulars, it meant a simple pleasure – "to lie freely in the sun, unencumbered by clothes."[102] For nudists, "body freedom" meant overcoming "sexual inhibitions and perversions" to experience nudity in a pure form.[103] Only within carefully defined parameters could this freedom be experienced, since nudists believed that "nakedness not based on firm principles is in danger to [sic] become immoral."[104]

It would be a mistake to draw a straight line from the nudist movement to the nude beach movement, to see the history of social nudity as a progression from one to the other.[105] Free beaches did not replace nudist clubs, as some nudists feared they would. Instead, clubs continue to operate as private campgrounds and resorts, applying the "family friendly" principles that have been their mainstay for more than fifty years. Private companies have also capitalized on the expansion of nude tourism.[106] For its part, Wreck Beach remains a place on the edge, literally and figuratively. Although Hanlan's Point on Toronto Island became clothing-optional in 1999, the nude beach scene has hardly flourished in Canada as it has elsewhere, even if Wreck Beach does regularly feature on lists of top beaches in the world, attracting tens of thousands of visitors each year.[107] Instead, these sites represent alternative ways of thinking about the body, nudity, and sexuality, and the relationship of people to the non-human environment. They illustrate differing attempts to come to grips with the place of nudity in modern life and to resolve tensions and debates that persist today.

# Conclusion

Since nudism took root in Canada over seventy years ago, its practitioners have endeavoured to persuade the public that, though it may be unconventional, it promotes individual well-being and the social good. They advertised their clubs as family-oriented: enhancing marital stability, contributing to family togetherness, and furthering the emotional and sexual development of children. The emphasis on the family and the upholding of racial, gender, and sexual norms imbued nudism with innocence, distancing it from sexuality and signalling its respectability.

Although they criticized cultural attitudes toward the nude body, nudists did not reject mainstream values, and they employed popular psychological discourse to assert their normalcy. They adhered to normative masculine and feminine gender identities and affirmed their belief in the heterosexual marriage. They used photography and pageants to market their philosophy and to convey that they were ordinary people who respected the law – and more "prudish" Canadians – by confining their activities to private property.

Canadian nudism has evolved since its beginnings, as the cultural changes of the late 1960s and the 1970s prompted it to question its policies. Some believed that a once progressive movement had fallen behind the times. Clubs relaxed their rules against drinking and accepted separated and divorced members. Some even adopted a clothing-optional policy. Perhaps the most emblematic change was the launch of the Miss Nude World pageant in 1970, though many clubs disapproved of the exploitation of female nudity for publicity and profits. In general, Canadian nudists increasingly emphasized the pleasurable aspects of going nude rather than its contributions to physical or mental health. Even in the midst of this upheaval, however, the vast majority of clubs maintained their family focus. A Sunny Trails member informed a visiting reporter, "This is not a vice camp but a recreational haven for outdoor families."[1] The Meadowbrook Sun Club newsletter described nudists as "a lot of naked, happy people doing very 'straight' things."[2]

The Canadian nudist movement continued to change after 1980. Some of the largest clubs have folded, including Sun Valley Gardens and the Four Seasons. The number of members and their average age have fluctuated, with many clubs reporting a "greying" of their membership. They are more open to single males than in the past and have also opened their gates to gay and lesbian members.

At the same time, the movement continues to affirm the basic principles explored here. As the Federation of Canadian Naturists website states, "Naturism is founded on family participation. Children in naturist families learn to appreciate the body as part of their natural environment. They grow up with healthful attitudes and accept the physical nature of both sexes and all ages without fear or shame." In addition, "most clubs welcome singles" but "try to maintain a balance between the sexes." The site advises men on how to handle an erection and reassures hesitant women. A reposted document by American nudist "Cheri Donna," entitled "Social Nudity from a Women's [sic] Point of View," is directed to women whose "significant other" wants them to try nudism. Asserting that "all the vague worries and fears I fretted about proved groundless," Donna tells women not to worry about being less attractive than other women since nudism is made up of "a normal cross-section of the population." She urges them to "believe in your mate ... since it means a great deal to him." Tips on how to behave at a club include "Treat others as you would wish to be treated. Don't stare, don't ogle, don't touch. No sex jokes, no innuendos." This advice is qualified, however: "After you get to know folks, some rules can be relaxed."[3]

The strict self-regulation within the movement stands in sharp contrast to its philosophy that nudity is natural and freeing. As a result, it is tempting to focus on the contradictions: the limited critique that privacy equals shame but only when it comes to nudity, not to other physical functions; the desire for freedom from the constraint of clothes but not from constraining social norms. One might be tempted to entirely dismiss the idea that nudism offers any meaningful form of freedom. Over the years, journalists often accepted nudists' self-image as normal, respectable citizens, but they sometimes denied that the practice provided emancipation. After visiting the Sunny Trails Club in 1955, journalist Jean Howarth wrote, "Apart from having nothing on, they were entirely conventional. They might have escaped from body covering but their souls still wore corsets."[4]

Certainly, this book has echoed that assessment in many ways. But I do not wish to follow Howarth in presenting myself as an enlightened outsider for whom nudists appear backward or outdated. To focus solely on the tensions within nudism misses what it reveals about the society in which it is practised. The movement casts into relief the contradictions of a culture where the body and sexuality are seen as central components of individual identity yet are constructed and constrained by normative social values. Paradoxically, by taking off their clothes at a club, nudists believe that they render the body less visible – less subject to scrutiny – than it is in their everyday lives, and that by placing themselves within the boundaries and regulations of a club, they find the space to go free. Historically, the Canadian movement did not open that space to everyone and did not attempt to disrupt social norms that no doubt many Canadians found more restrictive than their clothes. But that need not preclude the recognition that thousands of Canadians embraced nudism as a temporary respite from the mundane and as a practice that enabled them to see and experience the body in a new way.

The postwar nudist movement did not propose to remake Canadian society, but it did engage with significant concerns about modern life, presenting itself as a means of addressing them. Examining the movement offers new perspectives on postwar Canada. This study reveals that German immigrants played a major role in establishing and growing nudist clubs, and that, on the whole, they found acceptance among the Canadian public despite their recent wartime designation as "enemy aliens." As sexual norms shifted, nudists negotiated the change, making a case for their practice as both liberating and respectable. During the 1950s and 1960s, when children and child rearing became so central to Canadian life, the movement marketed itself as an effective if unconventional means of socializing children. It capitalized on the popularity of photography and pageants, illustrating both the possibilities and the limitations of these modes of publicity. And when environmentalism and public nudity went hand in hand during the 1970s, the traditional nudist movement expressed just one of many attitudes toward nature and public space that coexisted at the time.

Ultimately, the nudist movement demonstrates how the body may serve as a site of both social regulation and resistance, sometimes simultaneously. The tensions in postwar nudism reflected larger tensions in society. This study contributes to scholarship challenging the notion that attitudes about the body have progressively relaxed since the "repressive" Victorian era. In their history of sexuality in America, John D'Emilio and Estelle B. Freedman reject "a linear model of historical progress from repression towards sexual liberation" and suggest instead that "the history of sexuality in the U.S. has been, and no doubt will continue to be, characterized by a tangle of power relations that constantly reconstruct sexual norms."[5] The early twentieth century, Peter Stearns argues, featured "tensions between a new insistence on self-restraint – sometimes according to the older rules, sometimes according to novel expectations – and a new delight in personal gratification. We live still with these tensions, sometimes seeking to tighten restrictions ... and sometimes urging greater relaxation in the interest of individual freedom and mental health."[6] Among other things, Stearns highlights escalating standards of body maintenance, encompassing everything from dental hygiene to body odour to weight, as well as greater intolerance for sexual harassment or the expression of anger. Scholars such as Jane Nicholas underscore the consequences of a culture that is increasingly fixated on physical appearance, turning the body into a project, especially for women, who are expected to devote significant time and resources in cultivating an attractive appearance only to be objectified and scrutinized when they do.[7] The nudist movement demonstrates some of the other ways that Canadians grappled with embodiment and endeavoured to resolve the challenges and contradictions surrounding the body's place in modern society. My hope is that this study can tell us all something about our own complex negotiations in reconciling our individual bodies, identities, and behaviours with broader social norms and values.

# Notes

## Introduction

1 Parkes, "I'm a Nudist Mother," 16.
2 Ibid., 17.
3 Williams, *Turning to Nature,* 2.
4 On the early German nudist movement, see Hau, *The Cult of Health;* Ross, *Naked Germany;* Toepfer, *Empire of Ecstasy;* Williams, *Turning to Nature;* Jeffries, "For a Genuine and Noble Nakedness?" 62–84; Kruger, "There Goes This Art of Manliness," 135–58; and Möhring, "The German Nudist Movement," 45–62.
5 There is debate over the size of the German nudist movement, partially because the various Lebensreform movements overlapped, which makes it difficult to single out nudists. Williams estimates that about eighty thousand Germans practised nudism by the early 1930s, whereas another study suggests that fifty thousand belonged to nudist organizations and at least as many practised casual nudism. Williams, *Turning to Nature,* 24; Kruger, Kruger, and Treptau, "Nudism in Nazi Germany," 35. Studies by Ross, Williams, and Hau reveal the diversity of German nudism: whereas Ross focuses on its right-wing, nationalist strand, Williams highlights socialist organizations, and Hau considers middle-class expressions, which were primarily individualistic. The Canadian movement had most in common with the latter branch. Ross, *Naked Germany;* Hau, *The Cult of Health.*
6 Ross, *Naked Germany,* 1.
7 Some excellent scholarship on the movement outside of Germany has appeared in the twenty-first century. On Britain, see Morris, "Naked in Nature," 283–308; and Bell and Holliday, "Naked as Nature Intended," 127–40. For Belgium, see Peeters, "Authenticity and Asceticism," 432–61. On the United States, see Schrank, *Free and Natural;* Hoffman, *Naked;* Shaffer, "On the Environmental Nude," 126–39; and Woodall, "The American Nudist Movement," 264–84. On Australia and New Zealand, see Daley, "From Bush to Beach," 149–67; and Daley, *Leisure and Pleasure.*
8 Four Seasons Nature Park owner and German immigrant Lisa Stein observed a strong European presence at Ontario clubs, counting German, Dutch, French, English, and Scottish

immigrants among their members. *Identities,* CBC Radio, 11 November 1974, CBC Radio Archives, CBC Broadcasting Centre, Toronto (CBC RA). Also see Woycke, *Au Naturel,* 8–9.

9 On postwar vacationing and recreation, see Rugh, *Are We There Yet?;* Aron, *Working at Play;* Campbell, *A Century of Parks Canada;* Stevens, "Cars and Cottages," 26–56; and Tillotson, *The Public at Play.*

10 Secretary's Report, American Sunbathing Association Annual Report, 1963, American Nudist Research Library, Kissimmee, Florida (ANRL). Due to spotty record keeping, as well as concern for members' privacy, it is difficult to arrive at precise membership figures. For an organizational history of Canadian nudism, see Woycke, *Au Naturel.*

11 Deschênes operates the Bare Oaks Nature Resort in Sharon, Ontario. Although the podcast is publicly available, its primary audience is fellow nudists.

12 Cronon, "Introduction: In Search of Nature," 25.

13 Barcan, *Nudity,* 9–10.

14 Elias, *The Civilizing Process.*

15 Barbour, "Undressed Toronto," 3.

16 Karl Ruehle, "Promoting Nudism," *Sunbathing for Health,* April 1956, 26–27.

17 The work of Jane Nicholas highlights popular fears that the exposure of youth and working-class men to nude paintings would have dangerous consequences. Nicholas, "'A Figure of a Nude Woman,'" 330–32. Mary Louise Adams details debates about the harm to children and adolescents who were exposed to "indecent" literature such as pulp fiction, comic books, and "sexy magazines." Adams, *The Trouble with Normal,* 136–65.

18 Peeters, "Authenticity and Asceticism," 435–36.

19 de Certeau, *The Practice of Everyday Life,* xiv.

20 Ray Connett, Sunny Trails: A Nudist Call to Canada, *Sunbathing for Health,* May–June 1952, 9.

21 Bell and Holliday, "Naked as Nature Intended," 137 (emphasis in original).

22 Not every nudist embraced this perspective: Adolf Koch, who ran popular nude gymnastics schools in Berlin during the Weimar period, advocated a more liberal sexual morality. But he appears to have been an exception to the rule. See McLellan, "State Socialist Bodies," 54.

23 Foucault, *The History of Sexuality,* 23.

24 Möhring, "The German Nudist Movement," 53 (emphasis in original).

25 Karl Ruehle, "Juvenile Delinquency," *Sunbathing for Health,* September 1958, 25.

26 Elias, *The Civilizing Process,* 115.

27 "A Positive Attitude to Nudism Given," *Saskatoon Star-Phoenix,* 22 July 1972.

28 This phrase is borrowed from pioneering German nudist Richard Ungewitter, as quoted in Möhring, "The German Nudist Movement," 54–56. On British nudism, see Parmelee, *Nudism in Modern Life,* 80.

29 Williams, *Turning to Nature,* 43.

30 Barcan, "'Regaining What Mankind Has Lost,'" 71; Woloshyn, *Soaking Up the Rays.*

31 Macdonald, *Strong, Beautiful and Modern,* 12–13. Also see Zweiniger-Bargielowska, *Managing the Body.*

32 Segel, *Body Ascendant,* 1. Also see Kasson, *Houdini, Tarzan, and the Perfect Man;* Putney, *Muscular Christianity;* Grover, *Fitness in American Culture;* Daley, *Leisure and Pleasure;* and Howell, *Blood, Sweat, and Cheers.* The turn to nature is explored by Matless, "'The Art of Right Living,'" 93–122; and Matless, *Landscape and Englishness.* Also see Jasen, *Wild Things;* and Châtelet, "A Breath of Fresh Air," 107–27. Children's summer camps as a manifestation of modern efforts to reconnect with nature and the values associated with it have received the attention of North American historians. See Van Slyck, *A Manufactured Wilderness;* Paris, *Children's Nature;* and Wall, *The Nurture of Nature.*

33 For more on the influence of psychology and the preoccupation with juvenile delinquency in postwar Canada, see Adams, *The Trouble with Normal;* Gleason, *Normalizing the Ideal;* Sangster, "Creating Social and Moral Citizens," 337–58; and Sangster, *Girl Trouble.*
34 Châtelet, "Open-Air School Movement."
35 Möhring, "The German Nudist Movement," 46.
36 In a 1974 CBC Radio interview, Karl Ruehle acknowledged and distanced himself from the eugenicist orientation of German nudism in the Nazi era – "everything for the furtherment of the German, the Germanic race and so on." *Identities,* CBC Radio, 11 November 1974, CBC RA.
37 See Strong-Boag, "Home Dreams," 471–504; Harris, *Creeping Conformity*; and Owram, *Born at the Right Time.*
38 Readers' Page, *Sunbathing for Health,* November 1948, 18.
39 Entwistle, *The Fashioned Body,* 116–17.
40 Kuffert, *A Great Duty,* 15.
41 Harris, *Creeping Conformity,* 7.
42 Owram, *Born at the Right Time;* Sangster, *Regulating Girls and Women,* 129.
43 Gleason, *Normalizing the Ideal,* 4; Adams, *The Trouble with Normal.*
44 Adams, *The Trouble with Normal,* 23. The consequences of deviating from sexual norms in particular are detailed in Chenier, *Strangers in Our Midst;* Kinsman and Gentile, *The Canadian War on Queers;* and Sangster, *Regulating Girls and Women.* Historians have also tempered depictions of postwar conformity. L.B. Kuffert reveals that it was a major concern of some social critics at the time, who castigated Canadians for their passivity. The perspective of these cultural commentators has informed historical understandings of the postwar years, and Kuffert takes them seriously while cautioning against accepting their criticisms at face value. Similarly, Joy Parr's study of consumer culture, *Domestic Goods,* upsets ready-made assumptions about this period. Parr argues that Canadian consumers were not passive and conformist in their spending, but actively sought to influence the products they purchased and demonstrated values and habits distinct from their more affluent American neighbours. See Kuffert, *A Great Duty;* and Parr, *Domestic Goods.*
45 Adams, *The Trouble with Normal,* 19.

### Chapter 1: Building a Movement

1 Merrill and Merrill, *Among the Nudists;* Merrill and Merrill, *Nudism Comes to America;* Parmelee, *Nudism in Modern Life;* Norwood, *Nudism in England;* Welby, *The Naked Truth.*
2 Woycke, *Au Naturel,* 19. The official publication of the American Sunbathing Association, *The Nudist* was renamed *Sunshine and Health* in 1936. Hoffman, "'A Certain Amount of Prudishness,'" 711.
3 Woycke, *Au Naturel,* 19.
4 Ibid., 43.
5 Iacovetta, *Gatekeepers,* 10.
6 Ibid., 27; Freund, "Troubling Memories," 135. Also see Maeder, "Germans into Europeans," 227–46.
7 Freund, "Contesting the Meanings of Migration," 2, 7.
8 Sugiman, "Unmaking a Transnational Community," 68, 53.
9 Razack, *Race, Space, and the Law,* 1–2 (emphasis in original).
10 Speech by William Lyon Mackenzie King in the House of Commons, 1 May 1947. King conveniently ignored the historical contributions of Japanese and Chinese immigrants to Canada. Pamela Sugiman notes that Japanese immigration to Canada dates back to 1877,

and Chinese immigrants began arriving as early as the eighteenth century. Sugiman, "Unmaking a Transnational Community," 52.

11 Iacovetta, *Gatekeepers*, 26–27.

12 *Identities*, CBC Radio, 11 November 1974, CBC RA.

13 Hoerder, "Local, Continental, Global Migration," 33.

14 Woycke, *Au Naturel*, 118.

15 Ibid., 117–25.

16 Ibid., 131 (emphasis in original).

17 "Nudist Issue Raised," *Edmonton Journal*, 24 June 1967.

18 Maeder, "Germans into Europeans," 238. It should be noted that German nudist club founders were probably not displaced persons, as most came to Canada in the early to mid-1950s, after Germany's economic recovery was under way. Dirk Hoerder notes a distinction between "Rucksack-Deutsche" (literally, "backpack Germans," who could carry all their belongings on their backs) and "container Germans," who came slightly later and brought enough belongings to require transport via shipping container. Hoerder, "Local, Continental, Global Migration," 32.

19 *Identities*, CBC Radio, 11 November 1974, CBC RA.

20 "Fifty Years at the Ponderosa Nature Resort," Episode 72, Naturist Living Show podcast, 3 December 2014.

21 Newsletter, Spring 1971, Lakesun file, Federation of Canadian Naturists, Toronto (FCN).

22 "Old Clubs and a Young Woman in an Old Trailer," Episode 11, Naturist Living Show podcast, 5 September 2009.

23 "Fifty Years at the Ponderosa Nature Resort," Episode 72, Naturist Living Show podcast, 3 December 2014.

24 *Identities*, CBC Radio, 11 November 1974, CBC RA.

25 "Lessons from Naturist History," Episode 16, Naturist Living Show podcast, 15 February 2010.

26 Because it contained nude photographs, some municipalities and individual vendors restricted its sale.

27 Formed in the early 1940s, the Sun-Air-Freedom Lovers consisted mainly of residents of southern Ontario. But the club had difficulty locating a permanent home due to the high property values in the region. It leased sites on Georgian Bay for a number of summers, finally found a permanent property outside North Bay in 1948, and adopted the name Norhaven a short time later. From that point on, it primarily attracted members from the surrounding area. It closed in 1963. Woycke, *Au Naturel*, 97–100.

28 Ray Connett, Sunny Trails: A Nudist Call to Canada, *Sunbathing for Health*, January 1959, quoted in Woycke, *Au Naturel*, 12.

29 The issue of compulsory education was the main point of contention between Doukhobors and the state, although a decision to draft them into Selective Service during the Second World War also brought conflict. The BC community went through a period of significant unrest in the 1940s, during which time Sons of Freedom activists used public nudity and arson to oppose materialism within the community. See McLaren, "The State, Child-Snatching, and the Law," 259–93.

30 McLaren, "The Law and Public Nudity," 309. Public nudity is now covered under Criminal Code Section 174.

31 Wortner also noted that the OPP officer had an English accent and was knowledgeable about nudism, "probably from the U.K. or European side of things." "Old Clubs and a Young Woman in an Old Trailer," Episode 11, Naturist Living Show podcast, 5 September 2009.

32 Draft Constitution, 11 April 1959, Toronto Gymnosophical Society (TGS) file, FCN.

33 Readers' Page, *Sunbathing for Health*, September 1948, 22.

34 McLaren, "The State, Child-Snatching, and the Law," 306–7.
35 Androsoff, "A Larger Frame," 82.
36 A.J. Desireau to Hazel McKague, CSA Secretary, 25 May 1951, CSA Correspondence, FCN.
37 Mildred Harris, Woman's Page, *Sunbathing for Health,* May 1957, 17.
38 Regarding the image of Doukhobor women in media coverage, Androsoff notes two tendencies: one portrayed them sympathetically as "sisters" to Canadian women; the other, more common, approach was to cast them as "strangers." Androsoff, "A Larger Frame," 85. Here Androsoff references Marlene Epp, Franca Iacovetta, and Frances Swyripa, eds., *Sisters or Strangers? Immigrant, Ethnic, and Racialized Women in Canadian History* (Toronto: University of Toronto Press, 2004).
39 "Naturism Comes to Montreal – Thanks to C.S.A.," *Sunbathing for Health,* April 1949, 29; Gaetan Couture, "Quetans Now Firmly Established," *Sunbathing for Health,* June 1949, 29.
40 Gaetan Couture, "Montreal Quetans: Busy at Camp since May 7th," *Sunbathing for Health,* September 1950, 13.
41 Ray Connett, Sunny Trails: A Nudist Call to Canada, *Sunbathing for Health,* December 1951, 8–10.
42 Woycke, *Au Naturel,* 144.
43 Ibid., 145. Couture later moved to Ottawa, where he was charged and convicted with selling obscene photos following a 1957 police raid on his home.
44 Woycke, *Au Naturel,* 142–72.
45 "Quebec Naturism," Episode 35, Naturist Living Show podcast, 30 September 2011.
46 For more on Quebec in the 1970s, see Chapters 7 and 8.
47 Ray Connett, Sunny Trails: A Nudist Call to Canada, *Sunbathing for Health,* December 1951, 8–10.
48 "Lessons from Naturist History," Episode 16, Naturist Living Show podcast, 15 February 2010.
49 Reg Nicholls to Bill Cameron, 17 March 1956, TGS file, FCN.
50 Woycke, *Au Naturel,* 113–15; Membership List, 27 May 1958, TGS file, FCN. Glen Echo operated as a nudist campground until 2009. After failing to find nudist buyers, the Todorowskys, by then in their eighties, sold the property to a private buyer. "Nudists Are Losing a Place to Hang Out," *Toronto Star,* 28 August 2009.
51 Woycke, *Au Naturel,* 22.
52 Jean Barman notes that the population growth of British Columbia even outpaced that of southwestern Ontario. Fuelled by immigration, migration from other provinces, and the baby boom, its population tripled between 1941 and 1981, reaching 2.7 million. In the same period, Canada's population doubled. In 1961, approximately 60 percent of British Columbians were of British descent, one-third were of Continental European descent, and the largest number of the remainder were of Asian descent. Barman, *The West beyond the West,* 313.
53 Minutes of 1959 Eastern Convention of the CSA, 11 July 1959, quoted in Woycke, *Au Naturel,* 225.
54 Glen Eden Sun Club is still in operation. The Connetts died at the club in 1997.
55 Woycke, *Au Naturel,* 50.
56 Meeker, *Contacts Desired,* 38–41.
57 Woycke, *Au Naturel,* 118.
58 *Close Up,* CBC Television, 5 November 1961, Canadian Broadcasting Corporation collection, V1 8203-0165, Library and Archives Canada, Ottawa (LAC).
59 *Sun Valley News,* February 1959, Sun Valley Gardens file, FCN.
60 "2,300 Sign Cards at Nudist Club," *Surrey Leader,* 20 August 1959.
61 *Sun Valley News,* March 1960, Sun Valley Gardens file, FCN.

62 "Old Clubs and a Young Woman in an Old Trailer," Episode 11, Naturist Living Show podcast, 5 September 2009.

63 TGS Secretary to B. Breen, 3 September 1958, TGS file, FCN.

64 *Close Up*, CBC Television, 5 November 1961, Canadian Broadcasting Corporation collection, V1 8203-0165, LAC.

65 *Sun Valley News*, March 1959, Sun Valley Gardens file, FCN.

66 Introductory letter, undated (1960s), Silva Sun Club file, FCN.

67 Ray Connett, Sunny Trails: A Nudist Call to Canada, *Sunbathing for Health*, September 1951, 8, and October 1947, 13 (emphasis in original).

68 *News Spotlight*, CKNW Radio, 16 July 1953, Sunny Trails Nudist Club Collection, T4201:0001, BC Archives, Victoria (BCA).

69 *Identities*, CBC Radio, 11 November 1974, CBC RA.

70 "My Naturist Experience," *Sunbathing for Health*, July 1949, 11.

71 Ray Connett, Sunny Trails: A Nudist Call to Canada, *Sunbathing for Health*, April 1954, 8.

**Chapter 2: Constructing Community at the Club**

1 Walsh and High, "Rethinking the Concept," 257. The notion of imagined reality derives from the work of Benedict Anderson, who characterizes nations as "imagined communities" composed of people who embrace a sense of political community despite their lack of personal knowledge of, or connection to, most of the other members of the nation. Anderson, *Imagined Communities*, 5–6.

2 Wayne Johnston, "Nudism Is a Social Need," *Sunbathing for Health*, January 1953, 19.

3 *Assignment*, CBC Radio, 18 September 1962, CBC RA.

4 *News Spotlight*, CKNW Radio, 19 July 1953, Sunny Trails Nudist Club collection, T4201:0001, BCA.

5 Karl Ruehle, "Promoting Nudism," *Sunbathing for Health*, May 1956, 12.

6 Introductory letter, undated, Silva Sun Club file, FCN.

7 Ray Connett, Sunny Trails: A Nudist Call to Canada, *Sunbathing for Health*, November 1954, 10; Sunglades Constitution, 1952–53, and TGS Constitution, 1959, TGS file, FCN; Brochure, undated, Meadowbrook Sun Club file, ANRL.

8 Mildred Harris, Woman's Page, *Sunbathing for Health*, February 1954, 17. An early contribution to English nudist literature was *Nudism in England*, written by the Reverend C.E. Norwood, an Anglican clergyman.

9 *Assignment*, CBC Radio, 2 August 1960, CBC RA.

10 Ibid., 18 September 1962.

11 Ilfeld and Lauer, *Social Nudism in America*, 47.

12 Ray Connett, Sunny Trails: A Nudist Call to Canada, *Sunbathing for Health*, November 1954, 10.

13 Backhouse, *Colour-Coded*, 13–14.

14 Photo, *Sunbathing for Health*, January 1958, 9.

15 *Maritan News*, Spring 1959, Maritan Club file, FCN.

16 *Assignment*, CBC Radio, 17 September 1962, CBC RA.

17 *Sun Valley News*, December 1959, Sun Valley Gardens file, FCN.

18 "The Border Tans" (clipping), 1957, Border Tans Club file, ANRL.

19 Ray Connett to Joachim Wertheim, 18 November 1955, CSA Correspondence, FCN.

20 "Fifty Years at the Ponderosa Nature Resort," Episode 72, Naturist Living Show podcast, 3 December 2014.

21 Johnson, *The Nudists*, 66–80; Ilfeld and Lauer, *Social Nudism in America*, 69–71; Hartman, Fithian, and Johnson, *Nudist Society*, 91–103.

22 Johnson, *The Nudists,* 73.

23 Kinsey, Pomeroy, and Martin, *Sexual Behavior in the Human Male,* 366–367, 581. Interestingly, in the second Kinsey Report, *Sexual Behavior in the Human Female,* published in 1953, the researchers made no mention of class or educational differences, and instead contrasted the attitudes toward nudity in women born prior to, and after, 1900. See Kinsey et al., *Sexual Behavior in the Human Female,* 365.

24 "Quetans Now Firmly Established" (clipping), undated, FCN.

25 Mildred Harris, Woman's Page, *Sunbathing for Health,* July 1951, 17.

26 "Lessons from Naturist History," Episode 16, Naturist Living Show podcast, 15 February 2010.

27 *News Spotlight,* CKNW Radio, undated [July 1953], Sunny Trails Nudist Club collection, T4201:0003, BCA.

28 *The Meadowlark,* 14 February 1977, Meadowbrook Sun Club file, ANRL.

29 Ross Sanford, "A Glance at Nudism," *Sunbathing for Health,* May 1955, 20.

30 Goffman, *The Presentation of Self,* 30, 34.

31 Ray Connett, Sunny Trails: A Nudist Call to Canada, *Sunbathing for Health,* April 1947, 8.

32 Ibid., February 1955, 10.

33 By-Laws, 1964, TGS file, FCN.

34 Ray Connett, Sunny Trails: A Nudist Call to Canada, *Sunbathing for Health,* February 1955, 10.

35 "History of Bare Oaks," Episode 24, Naturist Living Show podcast, 31 October 2010.

36 Ray Connett, Sunny Trails: A Nudist Call to Canada, *Sunbathing for Health,* June 1955, 8.

37 Hoffman, *Naked,* 89, 131.

38 Gaetan Couture, "Montreal Quetans: Busy at Camp since May 7th," *Sunbathing for Health,* September 1950, 13.

39 Ray Connett, Sunny Trails: A Nudist Call to Canada, *Sunbathing for Health,* July 1947, 10–11.

40 Ibid., August 1948, 11.

41 *Sun Valley News,* January 1962, Sun Valley Gardens file, FCN.

42 Reg Nicholls to Ray Connett, 30 November 1948, TGS file, FCN.

43 Ray Connett, Sunny Trails: A Nudist Call to Canada, *Sunbathing for Health,* August 1948, 11–12 (emphasis in original).

44 Ibid., February 1952, 9.

45 *Sun Valley News,* 1962 Year-End Special, Sun Valley Gardens file, FCN.

46 "Quetans Visit S.A.F.L.s," *Sunbathing for Health,* September 1949, 27.

47 *Assignment,* CBC Radio, 20 September 1962, CBC RA.

48 Ibid., 19 September 1962.

49 Questionnaire, 18 February 1952, TGS file, FCN.

50 Readers' Page, *Sunbathing for Health,* November 1953, 15.

51 Ray Connett, Sunny Trails: A Nudist Call to Canada, *Sunbathing for Health,* June 1947, 7.

52 Ibid., June 1949, 13.

53 Gaetan Couture to CSA members, 19 November 1949, CSA Correspondence, FCN.

54 Questionnaire, 18 February 1952; also Albert to Ray Connett, 30 June 1951, TGS file, FCN.

55 Reg Nicholls to Ray Connett, 20 July 1951, CSA Correspondence, FCN (emphasis in original).

56 Board Meeting Minutes, 24 March 1965, Silva Sun Club file, FCN.

57 Amendments to Silva Sun By-Laws, undated, Silva Sun Club file, FCN.

58 Ray Connett to CSA/ASA leadership, 3 May 1956, Eaton Case file, FCN.

59 Ibid.

60 Norval Packwood to CSA leadership, 10 May 1956, Eaton Case file, FCN.

61 Ray Connett to CSA/ASA leadership, 3 May 1956, Eaton Case file, FCN.

62 Ray Connett, Sunny Trails: A Nudist Call to Canada, *Sunbathing for Health,* October 1947, 11.

63 Freedman, "'Uncontrolled Desires,'" 204; Chenier, *Strangers in Our Midst.* On the historical correlation of "deviance" and "abnormal sexuality," see Kinsman, *The Regulation of Desire;* and Terry, *An American Obsession.*

64 "Ferry Deckhand Held in Murder of B.C. Girl, 8," *Globe and Mail,* 30 April 1956; "Killed Girl, 8, B.C. Man to Hang," *Globe and Mail,* 13 April 1957; "Child Killer Hangs; Confesses to Crime," *Vancouver Sun,* 16 July 1957; Jack Wasserman, "About Now," *Vancouver Sun,* 17 July 1957.

65 *The Meadowlark,* 14 February 1977, Meadowbrook Sun Club file, ANRL.

66 Marcus Meed to Ray Connett, 10 April 1956, CSA Correspondence, FCN.

67 *News Spotlight,* CKNW Radio, undated [July 1953], Sunny Trails Nudist Club collection, T4201:0003, BCA. It's unclear what Connett meant by "queer." Gary Kinsman indicates that in the 1950s "there was an uneven shift away from gender inversion as the queer problem – the effeminate man or butch woman – towards same-gender eroticism in general." Kinsman, "The Canadian Cold War on Queers," 117.

68 Ray Connett, Sunny Trails: A Nudist Call to Canada, *Sunbathing for Health,* February 1955, 10.

69 Ibid., May–June 1952, 9.

70 Mildred Harris, Woman's Page, *Sunbathing for Health,* September 1951, 21.

71 Ray Connett, Sunny Trails: A Nudist Call to Canada, *Sunbathing for Health,* February 1953, 10.

72 "Lessons from Naturist History," Episode 16, Naturist Living Show podcast, 15 February 2010.

73 *Sun Valley News,* March 1960, Sun Valley Gardens file, FCN.

74 *The Meadowlark,* January 1976, Meadowbrook Sun Club file, ANRL.

75 *The Meadowlark,* April 1977, Meadowbrook Sun Club file, ANRL.

**Chapter 3: Regulating Sexuality**

1 For example, the most famous interwar nudist was Hans Suren, whose book *Man and Sunlight,* originally published in German and translated into English, sold 250,000 copies in the year it was published (1924). Morris notes that although Suren was deeply concerned about the association of nudity with sexuality, he refused to speak directly to the issue. Morris, "Naked in Nature," 295.

2 Williams, *Turning to Nature,* 45.

3 As Evert Peeters explains, mental health was a growing concern among nudists in interwar Belgium, who were influenced by psychoanalytic thought, phrenology, and techniques of self-suggestion. Peeters, "Authenticity and Asceticism," 447–54. Williams notes the good relationship that existed between Berlin nudist Adolf Koch and sexologist Magnus Hirschfeld, as well as the popularity of lectures on sexuality held at the Koch Schools in the late Weimar period. He suggests that sexuality became a greater focus for socialist nudist organizations at this time and that "in keeping with the tenets of the sex reform movement, socialist nudists argued that nudism was a method of making the sexuality of industrial workers more rational." Williams, *Turning to Nature,* 43.

4 Welby, *The Naked Truth,* 15, 19.

5 Sunglades Constitution, 1952/53, and Constitution, 1959, TGS file, FCN; brochure, undated, Meadowbrook Sun Club file, ANRL.

6 Webb, *Eden Regained,* 36.

7 Ray Connett, Sunny Trails: A Nudist Call to Canada, *Sunbathing for Health*, June 1955, 8.
8 Ibid.
9 Gerald S. Craig, "Nudism and Human Nature," *Sunbathing for Health*, July 1954, 6.
10 Adams, *The Trouble with Normal*. For a discussion of homosexuality during the Second World War, see Jackson, *One of the Boys*.
11 Ray Connett, Sunny Trails: A Nudist Call to Canada, *Sunbathing for Health*, March 1954, 8–9.
12 Ibid.
13 Steele, *Fashion and Eroticism*, 13.
14 Barcan, "'Regaining What Mankind Has Lost,'" 66.
15 W.S. Douglas, "The Myth of Modesty," *Canadian Nudist Profile*, 1969, 1.
16 *Close Up*, CBC Television, 5 November 1961, Canadian Broadcasting Corporation collection, V1 8203-0165, LAC.
17 Mildred Harris, Woman's Page, *Sunbathing for Health*, July 1948, 17 (emphasis in original).
18 Ray Connett, Sunny Trails: A Nudist Call to Canada, *Sunbathing for Health*, June 1953, 10.
19 On dress reform, see Mitchinson, *The Nature of Their Bodies*, 66–71; Steele, *Fashion and Eroticism*; Bourke, "The Great Male Renunciation," 23–33; and Burman, "Better and Brighter Clothes," 275–90.
20 Steele, *Fashion and Eroticism*, 25, citing Flugel, *The Psychology of Clothes*, 20–22.
21 Flugel, *The Psychology of Clothes*, 237–38.
22 Readers' Page, *Sunbathing for Health*, February 1955, 14–15 (emphasis in original).
23 Wayne Johnston, "Nudism Is a Social Need," *Sunbathing for Health*, January 1953, 19.
24 This echoes the argument of Norbert Elias that society-wide changes in feelings (such as shame) followed changes in behaviour related to bodily functions (concealment) rather than dictating them.
25 Elias, *The Civilizing Process*.
26 Ray Connett, Sunny Trails: A Nudist Call to Canada, *Sunbathing for Health*, July 1951, 9.
27 Karl Ruehle, "The Natural State," *Sunbathing for Health*, October 1956, 13, 31.
28 Eric Hammond, "Develop a Sane Mind in a Sound Body," *Sunbathing for Health*, December 1948, 7.
29 Max Edvold, "Nudism Is Not a Half Truth," *Sun Valley News*, April 1960, Sun Valley Gardens file, FCN. This article was reprinted from *Sun and Health*, a Danish magazine. Its comment about promoting discipline evokes Foucault's thinking on disciplinary "technologies of the self." Foucault, "Technologies of the Self," 16–49.
30 Readers' Page, *Sunbathing for Health*, December 1955, 14.
31 Mildred Harris, Woman's Page, *Sunbathing for Health*, September 1948, 17, and June 1955, 27.
32 Ray Connett, Sunny Trails: A Nudist Call to Canada, *Sunbathing for Health*, March 1954, 10.
33 Davis, *More Perfect Unions*, 12. The Anglican Church was the first to officially approve contraception, at the Lambeth Conference – a global gathering of Anglicans – in England in 1930. It was followed by others such as the United Church of Canada in 1937.
34 Bailey, *From Front Porch to Back Seat*. Birth rates shot up during the baby boom that followed the Second World War, but their long-term decline resumed in the early 1960s. Arlene Skolnick underlines the degree to which the 1950s represented a break from the past (rather than epitomizing it) by characterizing it as "the deviant decade" for its drop in age at first marriage, high birth rate, and low divorce rate, accompanied by greater insistence on gender difference. Skolnick, *Embattled Paradise*, 51.
35 Skolnick, *Embattled Paradise*, 44–45.
36 Bailey, *From Front Porch to Back Seat*, 142; Skolnick, *Embattled Paradise*, 86.

37 Davis, *More Perfect Unions,* 8.
38 D'Emilio and Freedman, *Intimate Matters,* 239–74.
39 See Adams, *The Trouble with Normal;* Gleason, *Normalizing the Ideal;* and Christie, "Sacred Sex," 348–76.
40 Readers' Page, *Sunbathing for Health,* June 1953, 25.
41 Petigny, "Illegitimacy, Postwar Psychology," 71–72.
42 Wall, "'They're 'More Children than Adults,'" 51; Sethna, "The University of Toronto Health Service," 268; Korinek, "'We're the Girls of the Pansy Parade,'" 119; Gentile, "Capital Queers," 187–214.
43 Edvold, "Nudism Is Not a Half Truth."
44 Excerpt attributed to Libby Jones, *Sun Valley News,* February 1960, Sun Valley Gardens file, FCN.
45 Ray Connett to Reg Nicholls, undated [ca. 1948], CSA Correspondence, FCN.
46 *Assignment,* CBC Radio, 20 September 1962, CBC RA.
47 Gerald S. Craig, "Nudism and Human Nature," *Sunbathing for Health,* July 1954, 11.
48 Karl Ruehle, "Where Are You Standing?" *Sunbathing for Health,* July 1956, 31.
49 "Lessons from Naturist History," Episode 16, Naturist Living Show podcast, 15 February 2010.
50 British nudist Leon Gilbert spelled out this assumption. Leon Gilbert, "Accepting the Unsuitable," *Sunbathing for Health,* November 1955, 6.
51 Sunglades Constitution, 1952/53, TGS file, FCN.
52 Brochure, undated, Ponderosa Nature Resort file, ANRL. Ponderosa was founded in 1964.
53 "Old Clubs and a Young Woman in an Old Trailer," Episode 11, Naturist Living Show podcast, 5 September 2009.
54 Mildred Harris, Woman's Page, *Sunbathing for Health,* April 1949, 24–25; Ray Connett, Sunny Trails: A Nudist Call to Canada, *Sunbathing for Health,* September 1954, 9–10.
55 Brochure, 1957, Norhaven file, FCN; Draft Constitution, 11 April 1959, TGS file, FCN; *Silva Sun Bulletin,* January 1966, Silva Sun Club file, FCN; Ray Connett, Sunny Trails: A Nudist Call to Canada, *Sunbathing for Health,* April 1954, 9; *Close Up,* CBC Television, 5 November 1961, Canadian Broadcasting Corporation collection, V1 8203-0165, LAC.
56 "Lessons from Naturist History," Episode 16, Naturist Living Show podcast, 15 February 2010.
57 Ray Connett, Sunny Trails: A Nudist Call to Canada, *Sunbathing for Health,* October 1957, 9.
58 Ross, *Burlesque West.*
59 Ray Connett, Sunny Trails: A Nudist Call to Canada, *Sunbathing for Health,* October 1957, 9.
60 Readers' Page, *Sunbathing for Health,* October 1953, 14–15.
61 Jack Scott, "I Went to a Nudist Camp," *Maclean's,* 15 October 1949, 27–28.
62 Sunny Chinooks Association, *Warm Winds,* 45–46, Special Collections, Calgary Public Library; Woycke, *Au Naturel,* 55, 122.
63 Calgary Sunny Chinooks, Club Minutes, 27 March 1971, Beaches file, FCN.
64 Newsletters, Spring 1967 and Spring 1969, Lakesun file, FCN.
65 Newsletter, Spring 1975, Lakesun file, FCN.
66 Woycke, *Au Naturel,* 55.
67 Ibid., 119.
68 Ibid., 55.
69 Doug Beckett interviewed on "Lessons from Naturist History," Episode 16, Naturist Living Show podcast, 15 February 2010.
70 Draft Constitution, 11 April 1959; and Constitution, 9 May 1964, TGS file, FCN.
71 Woycke, *Au Naturel,* 119.
72 "Nudist Issue Raised," *Edmonton Journal,* 24 June 1967; "Family Nudism Must Stop, Says Judge," *Edmonton Journal,* 6 October 1967.

73 Sunny Chinooks Association, *Warm Winds,* 43, Special Collections, Calgary Public Library.
74 Standing Rules – Additions, 15 April 1973, Meadowbrook Sun Club file, ANRL.
75 The Silva Sun and Helios clubs ran advertisements in the Personals section of their local papers throughout the 1960s and 1970s that consistently conveyed this message. See, for example, *Ottawa Citizen,* 15 June 1963, 17 May 1966, 2 September 1966, and 14 June 1975; *Edmonton Journal,* 3 June 1967, 15 March 1968, 31 December 1969, 11 September 1973, and 30 June 1978.

### Chapter 4: Navigating Gender Norms

1 Vertinsky, "'Building the Body Beautiful,'" 518–19.
2 Hau, *The Cult of Health,* 59.
3 Williams, *Turning to Nature,* 47.
4 Möhring, "The German Nudist Movement," 46–47. Private, but not social, nudity was encouraged by Mollie Stack, founder and leader of the Women's League of Health and Beauty, which was established in 1930 to promote physical fitness for women. By 1939, it boasted 170,000 members in Britain and the Commonwealth. Matthews, "'They Had Such a Lot of Fun,'" 29.
5 Parmelee, *Nudism in Modern Life,* 91–96.
6 William Welby, "Sex and Nudism: The Subordination of Sex," *Sunbathing and Health,* June 1946, 38.
7 Woman's Page, *Sunbathing for Health,* October 1956, 6 (emphasis in original).
8 V. McLeod, "Naturism and Marriage," *Sunbathing for Health,* November 1953, 7.
9 "Fifty Years at the Ponderosa Nature Resort," Episode 72, Naturist Living Show podcast, 3 December 2014.
10 "History of Bare Oaks," Episode 24, Naturist Living Show podcast, 31 October 2010.
11 This quote from a statement by the American Sunbathing Association, "What We Believe," was affirmed by many Canadian clubs and appeared on membership cards and brochures. ASA membership card (expiry 1969), Manitoba Outdoor Club, ANRL; Brochure, undated, Meadowbrook Sun Club file, ANRL.
12 *The Meadowlark,* 14 February 1977, Meadowbrook Sun Club file, ANRL.
13 Laqueur, *Making Sex,* 11 (emphasis in original). Judith Butler also makes this argument in *Gender Trouble* and *Bodies That Matter.*
14 Ray Connett, Sunny Trails: A Nudist Call to Canada, *Sunbathing for Health,* March 1954, 9.
15 Ruth Kirk, "A Mother Speaks for Nudism," Woman's Page, *Sunbathing for Health,* February 1955, 20; Peggy Parkes, CSA national secretary, on *Assignment,* CBC Radio, 2 August 1960, CBC RA.
16 *Assignment,* CBC Radio, 15 September 1959, CBC RA.
17 Mildred Harris, Woman's Page, *Sunbathing for Health,* August 1948, 17; Ray Connett, Sunny Trails: A Nudist Call to Canada, *Sunbathing for Health,* May 1954, 8.
18 *Assignment,* CBC Radio, 2 August 1960, CBC RA.
19 Mildred Harris, Woman's Page, *Sunbathing for Health,* July 1956, 24. On men's bodily insecurity, see the discussion of readers' letters to *Sunbathing for Health* in Chapter 6.
20 Ruth Kirk, "A Mother Speaks for Nudism," Woman's Page, *Sunbathing for Health,* February 1955, 20 (emphasis in original).
21 "Sunshine News," *Sunbathing for Health,* September 1951, 13.
22 Geraldine de Gruchy, "Trailer Camp a la Nude," *Sunbathing for Health,* October–November 1951, 26.
23 Mildred Harris, Woman's Page, *Sunbathing for Health,* December 1948, 17.
24 Joan Jessop, The Fine Art of Being Lovely, *Sunbathing for Health,* November 1947.

25 Marguerite Bosc, 7–11 Morning Exercise Club, *Sunbathing for Health,* March 1954, 18–19, 29.
26 Geraldine de Gruchy, "Trailer Camp a la Nude," *Sunbathing for Health,* October–November 1951, 26.
27 See Gordon, "'Any Desired Length,'" 29; Pierson, *"They're Still Women After All";* and Gentile, "'Government Girls' and 'Ottawa Men,'" 131–41.
28 Mildred Harris, Woman's Page, *Sunbathing for Health,* January 1957, 15.
29 Marguerite Bosc, 7–11 Morning Exercise Club, *Sunbathing for Health,* October 1953, 18.
30 Ray Connett, Sunny Trails: A Nudist Call to Canada, *Sunbathing for Health,* September 1949, 13.
31 Readers' Page, *Sunbathing for Health,* March 1955, 15.
32 Mildred Harris, Woman's Page, *Sunbathing for Health,* August 1955, 17 (emphasis in original).
33 Ibid., May 1955, 17.
34 Ibid., August 1954, 17.
35 *Identities,* CBC Radio, 11 November 1974, CBC RA.
36 "History of Bare Oaks," Episode 24, Naturist Living Show podcast, 31 October 2010.
37 Jong, "The Hite Report."
38 Marguerite Bosc, 7–11 Morning Exercise Club, *Sunbathing for Health,* August 1954, 18.
39 Mildred Harris, The Woman's Page, *Sunbathing for Health,* May 1954, 23.
40 Ibid., December 1953, 28.
41 Ibid., July 1956, 24.
42 Readers' Page, *Sunbathing for Health,* November 1953, 32.
43 *Assignment,* CBC Radio, 20 September 1962, CBC RA.
44 "How Can Girls Model in the Nude?" *Sunbathing for Health,* September 1955, 26. For a detailed discussion of the photography in *Sunbathing for Health,* see Chapter 6.
45 Marcus Meed to Reg Nicholls, 15 October 1949, CSA Correspondence, FCN.
46 Readers' Page, *Sunbathing for Health,* September 1951, 26.
47 Ibid., May 1955, 33.
48 Mildred Harris, Woman's Page, *Sunbathing for Health,* April 1949, 24–25.
49 Ray Connett, Sunny Trails: A Nudist Call to Canada, *Sunbathing for Health,* September 1954, 10.
50 Ibid., February 1956, 10.
51 Entwistle, *The Fashioned Body,* 150.
52 The phrase "body freedom" invokes a German term for nudism, *Freikorperkultur,* or "free body culture." In present-day Germany, the movement is most commonly known by the acronym FKK.
53 W. Hogarth, "Crusade for Naturism," *Sunbathing for Health,* August 1954, 28.
54 Hau, *The Cult of Health,* 10.
55 McLaren, *Trials of Masculinity,* 183, 191.
56 Ray Connett, Sunny Trails: A Nudist Call to Canada, *Sunbathing for Health,* May 1954, 8.
57 Carole Craig, Woman's Page, *Sunbathing for Health,* August 1956, 17.

**Chapter 5: Raising Young Nudists**

1 E.V. Miller, "Our Number One Health Problem," *Sunbathing for Health,* May 1954, 12–13. "Mental health" replaced the term "mental hygiene," which had been commonly used in the interwar period.
2 E.V. Miller, "Relax and Enjoy Life," *Sunbathing for Health,* January 1954, 28, 32.
3 On the child-centred culture of the postwar period, see Strong-Boag, "Home Dreams," 471–504; Harris, *Creeping Conformity;* and Owram, *Born at the Right Time.*

4 Daley, *Leisure and Pleasure;* McLellan, "State Socialist Bodies," 55, 68; McLellan, *Love in the Time of Communism,* 161–62; Hoffman, *Naked,* 131–68.
5 Shaffer, "On the Environmental Nude," 133.
6 Hoffman, *Naked,* 134.
7 Freedman, "'Uncontrolled Desires,'" 199–225; Chenier, *Strangers in Our Midst.*
8 Readers' Page, *Sunbathing for Health,* June 1956, 15.
9 Mildred Harris, Woman's Page, *Sunbathing for Health,* July 1955, 17. Gerald Eaton's 1956 arrest for the sexual assault and murder of an eight-year-old girl and the revelation that he had previously been accused of abusing three nudist girls (ages unclear) seriously undermine this claim, though the abuse purportedly did not take place on club grounds (see Chapter 2). The limited evidence does not indicate that child abuse was prevalent at the clubs, but it calls into question their image as safe havens for children.
10 Readers' Page, *Sunbathing for Health,* January 1953, 28; Ruth Kirk, "A Mother Speaks for Nudism," Woman's Page, *Sunbathing for Health,* February 1955, 20; *Identities,* CBC Radio, 11 November 1974, CBC RA.
11 Marguerite Bosc, Our Sons and Daughters of Nature, *Sunbathing for Health,* July 1951, 15.
12 Ray Connett, Sunny Trails: A Nudist Call to Canada, *Sunbathing for Health,* July 1954, 9.
13 Smith, "'The Ego Ideal of the Good Camper,'" 70–101; Zelizer, *Pricing the Priceless Child;* Cronon, "The Trouble with Wilderness," 69–90.
14 Heins, *Not in Front of the Children;* Holland, *Picturing Childhood;* Kincaid, *Child-Loving.*
15 Bernstein, *Racial Innocence,* 4. Robin Bernstein convincingly argues that innocence in the American setting was a descriptor exclusively applied to white children, an observation with relevance to other settings as well.
16 Steedman, "Bodies, Figures and Physiology," 32.
17 Wall, *The Nurture of Nature,* 207.
18 Ray Connett, Sunny Trails: A Nudist Call to Canada, *Sunbathing for Health,* July 1947, 10.
19 R.B., CSA eastern secretary, "Report of the Second National Convention of the C.S.A.," Sunny Trails: A Nudist Call to Canada, *Sunbathing for Health,* November 1948, 8.
20 Readers' Page, *Sunbathing for Health,* July 1956, 15.
21 Ibid., September 1948, 19.
22 Ibid., May 1954, 14.
23 "My Naturist Experience," *Sunbathing for Health,* December 1948, 8.
24 Calvert, "Children in the House," 79.
25 R.E. Stone, "Simplicity in Living," *Sunbathing for Health,* March 1954, 6.
26 Gleason, *Normalizing the Ideal,* 87.
27 Brechin, "Danger: Child Growing Up"; Callwood, "Will Your Youngster Turn to Crime?"; Stein, "'Have' Delinquents"; Zoffer, "Psychological Factors."
28 Gleason, *Normalizing the Ideal,* 95.
29 Stearns, *Anxious Parenting,* 3–23; Bakker, "Sunshine as Medicine," 663–64.
30 Thom, "Wishes, Anxieties, Play," 201.
31 Ray Connett, Sunny Trails: A Nudist Call to Canada, *Sunbathing for Health,* January 1947, 269.
32 Mildred Harris, Woman's Page, *Sunbathing for Health,* April 1954, 28.
33 Eric Hammond, "Create a Wholesome Atmosphere," *Sunbathing for Health,* January 1954, 26.
34 Program unknown, CBC Radio, undated [Summer 1957], Sunny Trails Nudist Club collection, T4201:0005, BCA.
35 Mildred Harris, Woman's Page, *Sunbathing for Health,* March 1956, 33.
36 Blatz, *Understanding the Young Child,* 115.
37 Gerald Craig, "Good Citizenship," *Sunbathing for Health,* November 1954, 25.
38 Laycock, *Questions Parents Ask,* 21.
39 Mildred Harris, Woman's Page, *Sunbathing for Health,* August 1948, 17.

40 Blatz, *Understanding the Young Child,* 114.

41 Mildred Harris, Woman's Page, *Sunbathing for Health,* September 1953, 23.

42 R.B. Prosser, "Naturism in Relation to Sex," *Sunbathing for Health,* December 1953, 26.

43 Woman's Page and Readers' Page, *Sunbathing for Health,* January 1953, 21, 28.

44 Notice of Open House, undated (ca. 1960), Sun Valley Gardens file, FCN (emphasis in original).

45 Mildred Harris, Woman's Page, *Sunbathing for Health,* July 1955, 17, and May 1956, 29; *Maritan News,* Spring 1959, Maritan Club file, FCN; *Assignment,* CBC Radio, 19 September 1962, CBC RA.

46 Christabelle Sethna notes that even social purists who promoted sex education for children around the turn of the twentieth century "elided human anatomical, reproductive and sexual detail" out of fear that clear images and frank information would stimulate sexual interest. Sethna, "The Facts of Life," 308.

47 James Welby, "The Commonsense View: The Sex Aspect of Nudism Is Discussed," *Sunbathing for Health,* April 1947, 4.

48 Ray Connett, Sunny Trails: A Nudist Call to Canada, *Sunbathing for Health,* May–June 1952, 9.

49 Adams, "Margin Notes," 138.

50 Ray Connett, Sunny Trails: A Nudist Call to Canada, *Sunbathing for Health,* February 1956, 10.

51 Leon Gilbert, "Accepting the Unsuitable: Leon Gilbert Writes on a Controversial Subject," *Sunbathing for Health,* November 1955, 6 (emphasis in original).

52 E.V. Miller, "Avoid the Modern Scourge – Nervous Debility," *Sunbathing for Health,* April 1949, 7.

53 *Sun Valley News,* December 1961, Sun Valley Gardens file, FCN.

54 Newsletter, January 1959, East Haven Sun Club file, FCN.

55 Egan and Hawkes, *Theorizing the Sexual Child,* 95.

56 Lee, "Three Paradigms of Childhood," 594.

57 Adams, *The Trouble with Normal,* 132.

58 Shah, *Sex Ed, Segregated,* xiii.

59 Adams, *The Trouble with Normal,* 130. Also see Sethna, "The Facts of Life," 248; and Gleason, *Normalizing the Ideal,* 72.

60 Sauerteig and Davidson, *Shaping Sexual Knowledge.*

61 Hustak, "Love, Sex, and Happiness," 453; Egan and Hawkes, *Theorizing the Sexual Child,* 76, 112.

62 Blatz, *Understanding the Young Child,* 88–89 (emphasis in original).

63 Arnold Gesell, *Infant and Child in the Culture of Today: The Guidance of Development in Home and Nursery School* (New York: Harper, 1943), quoted in Low, "'The New Generation,'" 554–55. Also see Gleason, *Normalizing the Ideal,* 104–5, 111.

64 Conover, "Dr. Blatz," 12.

65 Stearns, *Anxious Parenting,* 73. Also see Urwin and Sharland, "From Bodies to Minds," 188. Historic and contemporary critics who see the "permissive parenting" approach as lax would no doubt take issue with Stearns's interpretation.

66 Max Edvold, "Nudism Is Not a Half Truth," *Sun Valley News,* April 1960, Sun Valley Gardens file, FCN; June Lange, "For Children Only!" *Sunbathing for Health,* March 1956, 18.

67 Gleason, *Normalizing the Ideal,* 90.

68 Ray Connett, Sunny Trails: A Nudist Call to Canada, *Sunbathing for Health,* May 1954, 8.

69 Spock, *The Common Sense Book of Baby and Child Care,* 379.

70 Woman's Page, *Sunbathing for Health,* June 1955, 27; Interview Notes, 1964–67, TGS file, FCN.

71 *Sun Valley News,* April 1959, Sun Valley Gardens file, FCN.

72 Mildred Harris, Woman's Page, *Sunbathing for Health,* August 1953, 28.
73 Jack Gray, "Why Not a Naturist Vacation?" *Sunbathing for Health,* July 1956, 13.
74 Ruth Kirk, "A Mother Speaks for Nudism," Woman's Page, *Sunbathing for Health,* February 1955, 20.
75 *The Meadowlark,* July 1970, Meadowbrook Sun Club file, ANRL.
76 Marguerite Bosc, Our Sons and Daughters of Nature, *Sunbathing for Health,* July 1951, 15.
77 Reumann, *American Sexual Character,* 7; Gleason, *Normalizing the Ideal,* 88.
78 Mildred Harris, Woman's Page, *Sunbathing for Health*, August 1948, 17.
79 Sethna, "The Facts of Life"; Adams, *The Trouble with Normal;* Shah, *Sex Ed, Segregated,* xii.
80 *Identities,* CBC Radio, 11 November 1974, CBC RA.
81 Sethna, "The Facts of Life," 309.
82 *Sun-Mor News,* January 1961, London Sun Club file, FCN.
83 *News Round-Up,* CBC Radio, 19 July 1953, Sunny Trails Nudist Club collection, T4201:0004, BCA.
84 Sunny Chinooks Association, *Warm Winds,* 53, Special Collections, Calgary Public Library.
85 Mildred Harris, Woman's Page, *Sunbathing for Health,* July 1955, 17.
86 *Maritan News,* November 1959, Maritan Club file, ANRL; *Sun Valley News,* 1962 Year-End Special, Sun Valley Gardens file, FCN.
87 Rules, 1953, TGS file, FCN.
88 Secretary's Report of Meetings, 1957, TGS file, FCN; *The Meadowlark,* June 1975, Meadowbrook Sun Club file, ANRL.
89 *Sun Valley News,* 1962 Year-End Special, Sun Valley Gardens file, FCN.
90 *Sun Valley News,* April 1959, Sun Valley Gardens file, FCN.
91 Camp Manager's Report, January 1976, Meadowbrook Sun Club file, ANRL.
92 "Ten Camp Rules Everyone Should Know by Heart," undated, Silva Sun Club file, FCN.
93 Holland, *Picturing Childhood,* 16.
94 *Assignment,* CBC Radio, 21 September 1962, CBC RA.
95 Mildred Harris, Woman's Page, *Sunbathing for Health,* January 1953, 29.
96 Eastern Canadian Sunbathing Association, *The Sunshine Family,* 6, Special Collections, Toronto Reference Library.
97 *Sun-Mor News,* January 1961, London Sun Club file, FCN.
98 *Sun Valley News,* January 1958, Sun Valley Gardens file, FCN.
99 "A Positive Attitude to Nudism Given," *Saskatoon Star-Phoenix,* 22 July 1972.
100 Mildred Harris, Woman's Page, *Sunbathing for Health,* March 1955, 26.
101 Comacchio, *The Dominion of Youth,* 19–20.
102 *Update,* CBC Radio, 15 June 1974, CBC RA.
103 American Association for Nude Recreation, "Nudist Family Values," http://www.aanr.com/about-aanr/nudist-family-values.
104 Ray Connett, Sunny Trails: A Nudist Call to Canada, *Sunbathing for Health,* March 1956, 9.

### Chapter 6: Photographs in *Sunbathing for Health* Magazine, 1947–59

1 This phrase is borrowed from *Ways of Seeing,* the influential book by John Berger.
2 According to Connett, because it was retouched *Sunbathing for Health* was more easily acquired by many Americans than the American Sunbathing Association publication, *Sunshine and Health.*
3 Woycke, *Au Naturel,* 12.
4 Abbe Logan, "Notoriety on the Newsstands," *Sunbathing for Health,* August 1957, 25.
5 Ray Connett, Sunny Trails: A Nudist Call to Canada, *Sunbathing for Health,* September 1951, 9.

6 Hoffman, "'A Certain Amount of Prudishness,'" 714.
7 Venereal disease was a problem during the First World War that the Allied forces had no wish to revisit. See Hoffman, "'A Certain Amount of Prudishness'"; and Westbrook, "'I Want a Girl,'" 587–614.
8 McLellan, "Visual Dangers and Delights," 152.
9 Meyerowitz, "Women, Cheesecake, and Borderline Material," 25.
10 Hollander, *Seeing through Clothes,* xii–xiii; Vettel-Becker, *Shooting from the Hip,* 107.
11 Breazeale, "In Spite of Women," 2.
12 Vettel-Becker, *Shooting from the Hip,* 98. For more on *Playboy* magazine, see Fraterrigo, *Playboy and the Making;* and Pitzulo, *Bachelors and Bunnies.*
13 Vettel-Becker, *Shooting from the Hip,* 112.
14 Meyerowitz, "Women, Cheesecake, and Borderline Material," 25.
15 Vettel-Becker, *Shooting from the Hip,* 6. There were exceptions. Bunny Yeager, for example, built a successful career as a pin-up photographer. Her pictures appeared in *Playboy, Esquire, Cosmopolitan,* and *Redbook,* and her collaboration with Bettie Page, *Playboy*'s Miss January of 1955, contributed to Page's rising fame.
16 Marguerite Bosc, 7–11 Morning Exercise Club, *Sunbathing for Health,* January 1954, 18.
17 Readers' Page, *Sunbathing for Health,* July 1949, 20.
18 Mildred Harris, Woman's Page, *Sunbathing for Health,* January 1958, 16 (emphasis in original).
19 Blake McLachlan, Aids for the Amateur Photographer, *Sunbathing for Health,* December 1950, 6.
20 Ibid., October–November 1951, 6.
21 Ibid., March 1951, 6, and September 1950, 9.
22 Ibid., April 1952, 6.
23 Ibid., July 1952, 6, and March 1952, 7.
24 Vettel-Becker, *Shooting from the Hip,* 111; Clark, *The Nude.*
25 Hoffman, *Naked,* 200; Cinder, *The Nudist Idea,* 589.
26 Gary Mussell, "Remembering Elysium," American Association for Nude Recreation – Western Region, https://aanrwest.org/media/attachments/2020/07/02/elysium-remembered-sfw.pdf (accessed 11 March 2022).
27 On the American physical culture movement, see Kasson, *Houdini, Tarzan, and the Perfect Man;* and Whorton, *Crusaders for Fitness.*
28 *Sunbathing for Health*, June 1949, 20.
29 *Sunbathing for Health,* July 1949, 5, 20; and September 1949, 25.
30 The Weiders were also responsible for bringing amateur Austrian weight-trainer Arnold Schwarzenegger to North America in the 1960s to help popularize the sport. Lafrance, "Building a Body," 345–60.
31 Chapman, "Perfection in Chicago," 16.
32 Weiermair, *The Hidden Image,* 10.
33 Waugh, *Hard to Imagine,* 176, 210–22.
34 Clark, *The Nude,* 3–4.
35 Blake McLachlan, Aids for the Amateur Photographer, *Sunbathing for Health,* January 1950, 14.
36 In contrast, a newsletter privately produced by Ray Connett and distributed to CSA members, called *Sunny Trails* (not to be confused with his *Sunbathing for Health* column of the same name), sometimes printed full frontal photos and was occasionally refused by Canada Post.
37 Buszek, *Pin-Up Grrrls,* 245–47.
38 Ray Connett, Sunny Trails: A Nudist Call to Canada, *Sunbathing for Health,* December 1958, 13.

39 Cooper, *Fully Exposed,* 149.
40 Sunshine Book Company v. Summerfield, 128 F. Supp. 564 (D.D.C. 1955); and Hoffman, *Naked,* 182.
41 *Assignment,* CBC Radio, 21 September 1962, CBC RA.
42 Sunshine Book Company v. Summerfield, 128 F. Supp. 564 (D.D.C. 1955).
43 Mildred Harris, Woman's Page, *Sunbathing for Health,* January 1958, 16.
44 Examples of more recent controversies include those surrounding American photographer Sally Mann's 1992 publication *Immediate Family,* featuring pictures of her three young children, and the seizure of shots of adolescents from a 2008 exhibition of artist Bill Henson in Sydney, Australia.
45 Kusz and Verdun-Jones, "From Obscenity to Child Pornography," 150–51. It should be noted that the photos of children in *Sunbathing for Health* would not meet the definition of child pornography under section 163.1, "the dominant characteristic of which is the depiction, *for a sexual purpose,* of a sexual organ or the anal region of a person under the age of eighteen years" (emphasis in original).
46 Ray Connett, Sunny Trails: A Nudist Call to Canada, *Sunbathing for Health,* March 1951, 10–11.
47 Adams, "Margin Notes," 140.
48 Canadian Encyclopedia, "Obscenity," https://www.thecanadianencyclopedia.ca/en/article/obscenity.
49 Ray Connett, Sunny Trails: A Nudist Call to Canada, *Sunbathing for Health,* March 1951, 10–11.
50 Ibid., June 1949, 19.
51 Readers' Page, *Sunbathing for Health,* April 1952, 27.
52 Ibid.
53 Vettel-Becker, *Shooting from the Hip,* 2.
54 *Sun Valley News,* 1962 Year-End Special, Sun Valley Gardens file, FCN.
55 Blake McLachlan, Aids for the Amateur Photographer, *Sunbathing for Health,* September 1950, 8.
56 Ibid., March 1951, 6.
57 Ray Connett, Sunny Trails: A Nudist Call to Canada, *Sunbathing for Health,* April 1952, 8.
58 Tagg, *The Burden of Representation,* 5, 8.
59 Vettel-Becker, *Shooting from the Hip,* 16.
60 Marguerite Bosc, 7–11 Morning Exercise Club, *Sunbathing for Health,* July 1953, 18.
61 Mitchell, *Picture Theory,* 5.
62 Kinsman, "The Canadian Cold War on Queers," 108–32.
63 Readers' Page, *Sunbathing for Health,* February 1954, 25, February 1955, 23, February 1957, 14.
64 Ibid., February 1955, 23.
65 Ibid., September 1955, 14.
66 Ibid., September 1951, 26.
67 Ibid., February 1957, 14.
68 Ibid., March 1956, 14.
69 Ibid., April 1952, 22.
70 Mildred Harris, Woman's Page, *Sunbathing for Health,* October 1955, 17, and December 1955, 21.
71 Mildred Harris, Woman's Page, *Sunbathing for Health,* April 1955, 23.
72 Leon Gilbert, "On Why the Editor May Reject," *Sunbathing for Health,* June 1956, 29.
73 Mildred Harris, Woman's Page, *Sunbathing for Health,* January 1952, 20.
74 Ray Connett, Sunny Trails: A Nudist Call to Canada, *Sunbathing for Health,* April 1952, 9–10.

75 Ibid., July 1948, 9.
76 Ibid., April 1952, 8.
77 Readers' Page, *Sunbathing for Health,* January 1954, 15.
78 Meyerowitz, "Women, Cheesecake, and Borderline Material," 17.
79 Cossman et al., *Bad Attitude(s) on Trial,* 15.
80 Ibid., 20–21.
81 Ibid., 23.
82 Jochelson and Kramar, *Sex and the Supreme Court,* 35–36.
83 Ray Connett, Sunny Trails: A Nudist Call to Canada, *Sunbathing for Health,* February 1957, 10.

Chapter 7: The Pageant Tradition and Miss Nude World

1 Articles in *Sunbathing for Health* frequently noted the occurrence of English and American pageants or printed photos of the winners. Ray Connett, Sunny Trails: A Nudist Call to Canada, *Sunbathing for Health,* November 1954, 11; and photos in *Sunbathing for Health,* March 1954, 31; May 1955, 18–19; October 1955, 28; March 1956, 2–3.
2 Ballerino Cohen, Wilk, and Stoeltje, *Beauty Queens,* 2. Also see Banet-Weiser, *The Most Beautiful Girl;* Watson and Martin, *"There She Is";* and Gentile, "Queen of the Maple Leaf." Pageants were not unique in using the body to convey a message. As Valerie Minnett points out, the female body, in particular, "has been used historically to personify abstract qualities." Minnett, "Public Body, Private Health," 297.
3 Watson and Martin, *"There She Is,"* 8; Gentile, "Queen of the Maple Leaf," 3.
4 Nicholas, *The Modern Girl,* 126–28. Also see Latham, "Packaging Woman," 149–67; and Banner, *American Beauty.*
5 Ray Connett, Sunny Trails: A Nudist Call to Canada, *Sunbathing for Health,* January 1950, 10.
6 Clubs that ran such pageants included Sunny Trails, Sun Valley Gardens, Four Seasons Nature Park, and Paradis Terrestre.
7 For example, "Nudists Defy Showers to Choose Royal Family," *Vancouver Province,* 17 August 1953; and "Guests Watch Nudists Select Year's Best Undraped Mother," *Vancouver Province,* 18 July 1955.
8 Perc W. Cousins, "New Zealand's First Naturist Rally," *Sunbathing for Health,* November 1953, 13; Ray Connett, Sunny Trails: A Nudist Call to Canada, *Sunbathing for Health,* January 1954, 10.
9 Ray Connett, Sunny Trails: A Nudist Call to Canada, *Sunbathing for Health,* January 1954, 10.
10 Mildred Harris, Woman's Page, *Sunbathing for Health,* July 1951, 17.
11 Gilman, *Picturing Health and Illness,* 93.
12 Morris, "Naked in Nature," 283–308.
13 Ray Connett, Sunny Trails: A Nudist Call to Canada, *Sunbathing for Health,* November 1954, 11.
14 *Sun Valley News,* September 1957, Sun Valley Gardens file, FCN.
15 Sunny Chinooks Association, *Warm Winds,* 26, Special Collections, Calgary Public Library.
16 Gentile, "Queen of the Maple Leaf," 51 (emphasis in original).
17 *Maritan News,* March 1963, Maritan Club file, ANRL. New Zealand nudists had not always been dismissive of pageants. A 1953 report on their first convention, written by prominent New Zealand naturist Perc Cousins, recorded the election of a royal family. Perc Cousins, "New Zealand's First Naturist Rally," *Sunbathing for Health,* November 1953, 13.
18 Ray Connett, Sunny Trails: A Nudist Call to Canada, *Sunbathing for Health,* December 1956, 8.

19 *Silva Sun Bulletin,* July 1966, Silva Sun Club file, FCN.

20 Much to the organizers' dismay, on at least one occasion a male reportedly entered the contest and successfully passed through the first rounds. *Variety Tonight,* CBC Radio, 9 June 1980, CBC RA. The Four Seasons Nature Park also played host to a Mr. Nude World Contest, but it took place on a different weekend and did not draw the crowds or receive the publicity that the women's competition did. As a result, sources on that contest are scarce and I have confined my discussion here to Miss Nude World.

21 Lisa Stein, "Everything Is Beautiful," *Bare in Mind,* August–September 1972.

22 Hocker, "Leave the Beauty Contests," 11.

23 *A Contest Run in Good Taste,* Miss Nude World booklet, 1972, Pageants file, ANRL; *Identities,* CBC Radio, 11 November 1974, CBC RA.

24 Winners of these pageants generally had their way paid to the Miss Nude World Contest as part of their prize package, but it was not necessary to have won a qualifying event in order to enter. Despite the name of the contest, the vast majority of entrants were Canadian or American. "Poor Showing as Bookkeeper Crowned Miss Nude World," *Globe and Mail,* 7 September 1970. The contest was moved from September to July in 1971, to increase the likelihood of warm weather for the event.

25 A much hyped appearance by Burt Reynolds as judge did not materialize, reportedly due to "scheduling conflicts." "Area Girl Third in Miss Nude World Contest," *Acton Free Press,* 16 September 1970.

26 *Variety Tonight,* CBC Radio, 9 June 1980, CBC RA.

27 Remsberg and Remsberg, "Here She Comes."

28 Miss Nude Florida Souvenir Program, 1976, Pageants file, ANRL. Affiliated with the Miss Nude World Contest, the Miss Nude Florida Contest used the same system of scoring. The awarding of points for various body parts mimicked the scoring system of the original Miss America contest, in which judges focused on an even larger number of physical attributes.

29 Ray Connett, Sunny Trails: A Nudist Call to Canada, *Sunbathing for Health,* January 1954, 10.

30 Program unknown, CBC Radio, undated [summer 1957], Sunny Trails Nudist Club collection, T4201:0005, BCA.

31 *Identities,* CBC Radio, 11 November 1974, CBC RA.

32 "Miss Nude World 1971 Swiss-Born Montrealer," *Victoria Daily Times,* 26 July 1971; "Miss Nude World Pageant," *Bare in Mind,* August–September 1972.

33 "Area Girl Third in 'Miss Nude World' Contest," *Acton Free Press,* 16 September 1970; Lisa Stein, "Everything Is Beautiful," *Bare in Mind,* August–September 1972.

34 Carl Alkerton, "Promotion and Nudism," *Bare in Mind,* August–September 1972.

35 "Fifty Years at the Ponderosa Nature Resort," Episode 72, Naturist Living Show podcast, 3 December 2014.

36 Miss Nude World Pageant Program, 1971, Four Seasons Nature Park, ANRL.

37 *A Contest Run in Good Taste,* Miss Nude World booklet, 1972, Pageants file, ANRL.

38 "Hard to Bear: Exposure, But Not the Kind She Wanted, Plagued Miss Nude World of 1974," *Globe and Mail,* 28 July 1975.

39 *Identities,* CBC Radio, 11 November 1974, CBC RA.

40 Schrank, *Free and Natural,* 6.

41 Woycke, *Au Naturel,* 171.

42 Ibid., 161, 164.

43 Carl Alkerton, "Promotion and Nudism," *Bare in Mind,* August–September 1972.

44 *Identities,* CBC Radio, 11 November 1974, CBC RA.

45 "Miss Nude Ontario Special Edition," *Summerset Strip,* 1973, Summerset Naturist Society file, FCN.

46 Ramon Williams, "Realism in Pageantry," *American Nudist,* Winter 1965.
47 *A Contest Run in Good Taste,* ANRL; "A Revealing Site at Britannia Hotel," *Barrie Examiner,* undated (1976), Press file, FCN.
48 *Identities,* CBC Radio, 11 November 1974, CBC RA. Decades later, Stein made a similar admission in an interview on the Naturist Living podcast. "Fifty Years at the Ponderosa Nature Resort," Episode 72, Naturist Living Show podcast, 3 December 2014.
49 Mulvey, "Visual Pleasure," 11.
50 Mildred Harris, Woman's Page, *Sunbathing for Health,* November 1954, 17.
51 Nicholas, *The Modern Girl,* 184–210.
52 Gentile, "'Government Girls' and 'Ottawa Men,'" 131–41. Also see Sangster, "'Queen of the Picket Line,'" 83–106.
53 "21-Year-Old Bookkeeper Is Nudist Queen," *Edmonton Journal,* 8 September 1970; "A Sincere Thanks," *Bare in Mind,* August–September 1972.
54 "Area Girl Third in 'Miss Nude World' Contest," *Acton Free Press,* 16 September 1970.
55 Nicholas, *The Modern Girl,* 123.
56 Ibid., 42.
57 "Hard to Bear: Exposure, But Not the Kind She Wanted, Plagued Miss Nude World of 1974," *Globe and Mail,* 28 July 1975.
58 Photo caption, *Edmonton Journal,* 24 July 1978.
59 "The Pickup Artist," Season 3, Episode 2, Sexing History podcast, 25 July 2020.
60 Skolnick, *Embattled Paradise,* 101–2.
61 Janiel Jolley to Miss Canadian University Pageant contestants, 15 January 1970, in Blair, "Miss Canadian University Pageant."
62 "21-Year-Old Bookkeeper Is Nudist Queen," *Edmonton Journal,* 8 September 1970.
63 *The Producer,* Miss Nude World booklet, 1972, Pageant file, ANRL.
64 *Identities,* CBC Radio, 11 November 1974, CBC RA.
65 Peter Jackson, "The International Scene," *Sunbathing for Health,* July 1956, 20.
66 After the Four Seasons stopped hosting Miss Nude World, it staged its own club-based pageant. It included the Miss Four Seasons and Mr. Nude World pageants in its 2009 event calendar. http://www.thefourseasons.com/09events.htm (14 October 2009).
67 Peeters, "Authenticity and Asceticism," 455.

**Chapter 8: Cultivating Nature and Protecting Privacy at the Club**

1 Daley, "From Bush to Beach," 151–52.
2 Gilbert, Matless, and Short, *Geographies of British Modernity,* 3–4.
3 Nicholas, "'A Figure of a Nude Woman,'" 326, 318.
4 Kheraj, "Improving Nature," 66. Also see Dummitt, *The Manly Modern,* 12.
5 "Our Purpose," *Sunbathing for Health,* April 1947, 1; Wayne Johnston, "Nudism Is a Social Need," *Sunbathing for Health,* January 1953, 19.
6 Johnston, "Nudism Is a Social Need," 6.
7 Karl Ruehle, "Where Are You Standing?" *Sunbathing for Health,* July 1956, 31.
8 Draft of story on Lakesun for *ASA Bulletin,* June 1961, Lakesun file, FCN.
9 In *Au Naturel,* James Woycke relays the history of the Canadian clubs largely in these terms, reflecting the emphasis of the leaders themselves.
10 Ibid., 115.
11 Newsletter, Spring 1969, Lakesun file, FCN.
12 *Sun Valley News,* February 1960, Sun Valley Gardens file, FCN.
13 *Identities,* CBC Radio, 11 November 1974, CBC RA.

14 Brochure, 1969, Four Seasons Nature Park file, ANRL; *Sun Valley News,* September 1957, Sun Valley Gardens file, FCN.
15 *Sun Valley News,* December 1959, Sun Valley Gardens file, FCN.
16 Ray Connett, Sunny Trails: A Nudist Call to Canada, *Sunbathing for Health,* January 1953, 9.
17 Kheraj, "Improving Nature," 63–90.
18 Newsletters, Spring 1971 and Spring 1973, Lakesun file, FCN.
19 Merchant, "Reinventing Eden," 134, 147.
20 Ray Connett, Sunny Trails: A Nudist Call to Canada, *Sunbathing for Health,* September 1954, 10.
21 Matless, "Visual Culture," 436.
22 "Old Clubs and a Young Woman in an Old Trailer," Episode 11, Naturist Living Show podcast, 5 September 2009.
23 Newsletter, Spring 1971, Lakesun file, FCN.
24 Newsletter, Spring 1973, Lakesun file, FCN; Woycke, *Au Naturel,* 131.
25 Newsletter, Spring 1975, Lakesun file, FCN.
26 *Sun Valley News,* March 1958, Sun Valley Gardens file, FCN.
27 Woycke, *Au Naturel,* 243.
28 Ibid., 164.
29 Ibid., 247.
30 "Quebec Naturism," Episode 35, Naturist Living Show podcast, 30 September 2011.
31 Cronon, "Introduction: In Search of Nature," 36.
32 "Our Purpose," *Sunbathing for Health,* April 1947, 1.
33 *Assignment,* CBC Radio, 2 August 1960, CBC RA.
34 *Sun Valley News,* April 1959, Sun Valley Gardens file, FCN.
35 Ibid., January 1962.
36 Ray Connett, Sunny Trails: A Nudist Call to Canada, *Sunbathing for Health,* September 1955, 9, and July 1955, 8.
37 Woodall, "The American Nudist Movement," 264–84.
38 "Old Clubs and a Young Woman in an Old Trailer," Episode 11, Naturist Living Show podcast, 5 September 2009.
39 Ray Connett, Sunny Trails: A Nudist Call to Canada, *Sunbathing for Health,* June 1947, 10.
40 *Sun Valley News,* September 1957, Sun Valley Gardens file, FCN.
41 Such episodes also provided fodder for their argument that juvenile delinquency arose from a repression of children's natural curiosity about the body.
42 Max Edvold, "Sound Advice on Sunbathing," *Sunbathing for Health,* November 1948, 6.
43 Bradley, "Managing Wild Behaviour"; Barbour, *Winnipeg Beach;* Bouchier and Cruikshank, *The People and the Bay.*
44 Brochure, undated, Summerset file, FCN.
45 Davis and Lorenzkowski, "A Platform for Gender Tensions," 463.
46 Tabor R. Stone, *Beyond the Automobile: Reshaping the Transportation Environment* (Englewood Cliffs, NJ: Prentice Hall, 1971), 100, quoted in ibid., 438.
47 *Assignment,* CBC Radio, 20 and 18 September 1962, CBC RA.
48 Quoted in Ray Connett, Sunny Trails: A Nudist Call to Canada, *Sunbathing for Health,* October 1955, 10.
49 Newsletters, Spring 1969 and Spring 1971, and Lakesun Pamphlet, undated, Lakesun Club file, FCN.
50 Readers' Page, *Sunbathing for Health,* June 1956, 15.
51 Mildred Harris, Woman's Page, *Sunbathing for Health,* May 1957, 17.
52 *Sun Valley News,* 1962 Year-End Special, Sun Valley Gardens file, FCN.

53 *Close Up,* CBC Television, 5 November 1961, Canadian Broadcasting Corporation collection, V1 8203-0165, LAC.

54 *Maritan News,* March 1960, ANRL.

55 Ray Connett, Sunny Trails: A Nudist Call to Canada, *Sunbathing for Health,* November or December 1950, reprinted in *Sunshine Link,* February 1951, Norhaven file, FCN.

56 Mildred Harris, Woman's Page, *Sunbathing for Health,* May 1957, 17.

**Chapter 9: Defending Nature and Public Nudity at Wreck Beach, 1969–79**

1 Wreck Beach Area Advisory Committee, Annual Report, March 1978, Parks and Recreation fonds, Wreck Beach, 52-F-5, file 9, series 93, City of Vancouver Archives (VA).

2 Loo, *States of Nature,* 211. Also see Kheraj, "Restoring Nature," 577–612.

3 Wreck Beach Area Advisory Committee, Annual Report, March 1978, VA.

4 "Point Grey Cliffs Need Your Help," 12.

5 *Musqueam Declaration, 1976;* "Point Grey Cliffs Need Your Help," 16–17. Also see Susan Roy's work on the Musqueam struggle for political and cultural recognition. Roy, "Performing Musqueam Culture," 55–91; Roy, *These Mysterious People.*

6 A number of scholars have drawn on Victor Turner's notion of liminality and Mikhail Bakhtin's concept of the carnivalesque to explore beaches as sites of escape that "ritualize and contain resistance to the stresses of the social order." Evans, *Paradise on the Margins,* 17; Shields, *Places on the Margin;* Barbour, *Winnipeg Beach.*

7 Barbour, *Winnipeg Beach,* 13.

8 Booth, "Nudes in the Sand," 172. Also see Daley, *Leisure and Pleasure,* 143–59.

9 Booth, "Nudes in the Sand," 183.

10 Daley, *Leisure and Pleasure,* 140.

11 Latham, "Packaging Woman," 149–67; Banner, *American Beauty.*

12 Booth, "Nudes in the Sand," 170.

13 Douglas, Rasmussen, and Flanagan, *The Nude Beach.*

14 Shaffer, "On the Environmental Nude," 135. I use the term "counterculture" cautiously, recognizing its shortcomings. Peter Braunstein and Michael William Doyle highlight the problematic way in which the word is often used to paint in broad strokes a number of disparate movements and trends – political and social – of the 1960s. Braunstein and Doyle, "Introduction," 5–14. I also find Stuart Henderson's definition helpful: "Counterculture is best understood not as an alternate system of social interactions and ideologies existing outside the expected, dominant culture, but rather as the shifting sets of responses, refusals and acceptances performed by actors in the cultural process." Henderson, *Making the Scene,* 5.

15 John, "American Exiles," 33–56. Vancouver's largest Be-In took place at Stanley Park in the spring of 1968, with over six thousand people in attendance. Aronsen, *City of Love and Revolution,* 21.

16 Jim Davies, "Traffic Jams at Wreck Beach: 3,000 Cast Their Eyes on Nude-In," *Vancouver Sun,* 24 August 1970.

17 Ross, "Panic on Love Street," 11–41; Henderson, *Making the Scene.*

18 Aronsen, *City of Love and Revolution,* 70, 75.

19 Jamie Craig, "In Spite of All That ...," *Vancouver Sun,* 29 September 1972.

20 Art Hughes to the Editor, "Is a Nudist Conspiracy Taking Over Vancouver?" *Vancouver Sun,* 10 June 1977.

21 Larry Emrick, "Leave Wreck Beach Alone, Gordon," *Vancouver Sun,* 29 June 1975.

22 Clement, *Canada's Rights Revolution*; and Litt, *Trudeaumania.*

23 "Protest Halts Beach Road," undated; "Protest Halts Beach Project," 11 March 1969; and "Bid Made to Save Beach," 30 April 1970, newspaper clippings in Office of the City Clerk fonds, Beach Development, 79-B-1, file 11, series 20, VA.

24 Mrs. D. Mackenzie to City Council (cc: Park Board and the *Vancouver Sun*), 20 February 1969, Office of the City Clerk fonds, Beach Development, 79-B-1, file 11, series 20, VA.

25 The University Endowment Lands, including the Point Grey beaches, are provincial Crown land and not part of the City of Vancouver, notwithstanding the city's lease of the space. For this reason, the area was policed by the RCMP rather than the Vancouver Police.

26 "Nude Bathers Face Charges," *Vancouver Sun,* 13 August 1970.

27 Kathy Tait, "Wreck Beach Skinny-Dippers Raided," *Vancouver Province,* 13 August 1970.

28 "UBC Beach Nudist Rejects Fine, Takes 10 Days in Jail," *Vancouver Sun,* 19 August 1970; "Sunbather Convicted for Nudity," *Vancouver Sun,* 17 September 1970.

29 *R. v. Beaupre* (1971), 7 C.C.C. (2d) 320 (B.C. S.C.) at 321–22. Note: Section 205A had been re-enacted as Section 159 in 1953–54.

30 Woycke, *Au Naturel,* 191.

31 "Nudists Seek Beach Rights: 'Freedom from Prosecution,'" *Vancouver Sun,* 14 August 1970.

32 Paul Manning, "Gawkers Flock to View Nude-In," *Vancouver Province,* 24 August 1970; Jim Davies, "Traffic Jams at Wreck Beach: 3,000 Cast Their Eyes on Nude-In," *Vancouver Sun,* 24 August 1970; "Nude-In Attracts Crowds to City's Garden of Eden," *Vancouver Sun,* 24 August 1970.

33 Jim McCandlish, "Wreck Beach Revisited: Officialdom Blind to Nudists' Revival," *Vancouver Sun,* 20 July 1971.

34 Donald Gutstein and Peter Chataway, "Why We Must Fight to Save This Beach: 'There Is No Certainty the Plan Will Halt Erosion,'" *Vancouver Sun,* 8 February 1973. Gutstein and Chataway were a faculty member and a student in the UBC School of Architecture, respectively.

35 R.H. Blunden, "Park Board Let Us Down on Wreck Beach: Why No Search for Alternative Schemes?" *Vancouver Province,* 28 March 1974.

36 "RCMP Take No Action after Beach Work Halted," *Vancouver Sun,* 7 March 1974; "Doing What Comes Naturally," *Vancouver Province,* 8 March 1974; Moira Farrow, "'Emotions Delay Erosion Control at Cliffs,'" *Vancouver Sun,* 4 April 1974.

37 "We're Building a Beach for You," *Vancouver Province,* 30 March 1974.

38 Sue Vohanka, "Report Blames 'People Use' for Wreck Beach Erosion," *Vancouver Sun,* 22 August 1975.

39 Korky Day to the Editor, "Why Nudists Moving," *Vancouver Province,* 26 July 1976. This point was corroborated in W.H. Mathews to Colin Leech-Porter, 31 March 1978, Parks and Recreation fonds, Wreck Beach, 52-F-5, file 8, series 93, VA. Mathews was a professor in the UBC Department of Geological Sciences, and Leech-Porter chaired the Wreck Beach Area Advisory Committee.

40 "Beach 'Liberation' Target," *Vancouver Sun,* 24 June 1977; Nate Smith, "Nudists to Get Visitors," *Vancouver Province,* 9 July 1977.

41 Little, *At the Wilderness Edge;* Kheraj, *Inventing Stanley Park;* Tina Loo, *Moved by the State: Forced Relocation and Making a Good Life in Postwar Canada* (Vancouver: UBC Press, 2019).

42 "Washrooms to Be Installed for Wreck Beach Swimmers," *Vancouver Sun,* 22 April 1977. Bathroom facilities had not been installed because beach users opposed it, the lack of road access posed major logistical problems, and the park board had no desire to be perceived as sanctioning nudity by servicing the beach.

43 Wreck Beach Area Advisory Committee, Report, 17 June 1977, Parks and Recreation fonds, Wreck Beach, 52-F-6, file 1, series 93, VA.

44 W.H. Mathews to Colin Leech-Porter, 31 March 1978, VA.

45 Sue Vohanka, "Report Blames 'People Use' for Wreck Beach Erosion," *Vancouver Sun,* 22 August 1975.

46 Wreck Beach Committee Newsletter 2, Summer 1981, Parks and Recreation fonds, Wreck Beach, 242-B-6, file 4, series 93, VA.

47 Doug Bell-Irving to Ian Bain and Park Board Members, 15 June 1977, Parks and Recreation fonds, Wreck Beach, 52-F-5, file 8, series 93, VA.

48 Ted Galay to the Editor, "Bernice, Meet Anita," *Vancouver Sun,* 15 July 1977.

49 Wreck Beach Area Advisory Committee, Annual Report, March 1978, VA; Tom Browne, "Remembering the Pure Sands of Jerry's Cove," *Vancouver Sun,* 3 January 1978.

50 "Bid Made to Save Beach," 30 April 1970; Bernice Gerard to the Editor, "Average Citizen Loses in 'Nudist Takeover,'" *Vancouver Sun,* 9 July 1977; Mrs. Beverley Clark to Ian Bain, 28 July 1978, Parks and Recreation fonds, Wreck Beach, 52-F-5, file 9, series 93, VA.

51 Mrs. E.M. Whitehouse to the Mayor, 4 July 1977; Mrs. D. Wilson to the Mayor, 5 July 1977, both in Mayor's Office fonds, Wreck Beach, 48-G-3, file 119, series 3, VA.

52 G.E. Fordyce to the Editor, "If Nude on the Beach, Why Not on Granville?" *Vancouver Sun,* 16 August 1977. Fordyce was a chaplain at Simon Fraser University.

53 Mrs. J. Oswald to Mayor Jack Volrich and Council, undated, Office of the City Clerk fonds, Wreck Beach, 32-C-1, file 1, VA.

54 T.P. Archer to Mayor, 30 May 1977; Barbara Otteson to the Mayor and Council, 4 July 1977, both in Office of the City Clerk fonds, Wreck Beach, 32-C-1, file 1, VA.

55 Forty-five letters, some of them signed by more than one person, are held in the Parks and Recreation fonds, the Office of the City Clerk fonds, and the Mayor's Office fonds at the City of Vancouver Archives. Local papers printed a few additional examples. I also found a handful that favoured nude bathing. Their small number probably reflects the fact that Wreck Beach was a de facto nude beach by this time, with supporters of the status quo having less motivation to write, and that the advisory committee had been established to represent them.

56 Denise Jarvis to Mayor Jack Volrich, 11 May 1977, Office of the City Clerk fonds, Wreck Beach, 32-C-1, file 1, VA.

57 Dan Gardener to the Mayor, 27 July 1977, Mayor's Office fonds, Wreck Beach, 48-G-3, file 119, series 3, VA; Tim Day to Commissioner Ian Bain, undated (received 30 May 1977), Parks and Recreation fonds, Wreck Beach, 52-F-5, file 8, series 93, VA; Art Hughes to the Editor, "Is a Nudist Conspiracy Taking Over Vancouver?" *Vancouver Sun,* 10 June 1977.

58 A.S. Sheppard to the Mayor and Council, 9 May 1977; Wesley G. Campbell (Minister of the Church of the Nazarene, Vancouver) to Mayor and Council, 10 May 1977; Mr. and Mrs. Hugh T. Stanford to Mayor and Council, 16 May 1977, all in Office of the City Clerk fonds, Wreck Beach, 32-C-1, file 1, VA.

59 Ron Barkley to Mayor Jack Volrich and Council, 14 May 1977; E. Robson to the Mayor and Council, 16 May 1977; also, Miss M. Smith to the Mayor, 22 May 1977, all in Office of the City Clerk fonds, Wreck Beach, 32-C-1, file 1, VA.

60 R.A. Pruner to the Mayor and Council, 11 July 1977, Office of the City Clerk fonds, Wreck Beach, 32-C-1, file 1, VA.

61 Mrs. Barbara Otteson to the Mayor and Council, 4 July 1977 (emphasis in original), Office of the City Clerk fonds, Wreck Beach, 32-C-1, file 1, VA. Similar concerns were raised by Mrs. P.R. Welton to the Mayor and Council, 26 July 1977, in the same VA file.

62 Mrs. L. Irwin to Commissioner Ian Bain, Park Board Office, 14 May 1977, Mayor's Office fonds, Wreck Beach, 48-G-3, file 119, series 3, VA; Elizabeth van der Eerden to the Mayor, 9 August 1977; Ron Barkley to Mayor Jack Volrich and Council, 14 May 1977; M.R. Lueker to the Mayor, 9 May 1977, all three in Office of the City Clerk fonds, Wreck Beach, 32-C-1, file 1, VA.

63 Elizabeth Marocchi to the Mayor and Council, 22 July 1977, Mayor's Office fonds, Wreck Beach, 48-G-3, file 119, series 3, VA.

64 Bernice Gerard to the Editor, "Average Citizen Loses in 'Nudist Takeover,'" *Vancouver Sun,* 9 July 1977.

65 Art Hughes to the Editor, "Is a Nudist Conspiracy Taking Over Vancouver?" *Vancouver Sun,* 10 June 1977.

66 D.W. Martens to the Editor, "No Elite, No Trash at Wreck Beach," *Vancouver Sun,* 18 July 1977.

67 Ron Barkley to Mayor Jack Volrich and Council, 14 May 1977, Office of the City Clerk fonds, Wreck Beach, 32-C-1, file 1, VA; Peter Walls, "Wreck Beach Nudies Eye Passing Parade," *Vancouver Province,* 11 July 1977, quoted in Gerard, *Bernice Gerard,* 192.

68 Aronsen, *City of Love and Revolution,* 26.

69 Quoted in Larry Emrick, "Leave Wreck Beach Alone, Gordon," *Vancouver Sun,* 29 June 1975.

70 Mrs. Frances Fuller to the Mayor, 11 July 1977, Mayor's Office fonds, Wreck Beach, 48-G3, file 119, series 3, VA.

71 Mrs. D. Mansell to the Mayor, 16 July 1977, Mayor's Office fonds, Wreck Beach, 48-G-3, file 119, series 3, VA.

72 Ross, "Panic on Love Street"; Boudreau, "'The Struggle for a Different World,'" 117–33.

73 Evans, "Paradise on the Margins," 7.

74 Ibid., 10. This does not mean that it offers an escape from less institutional forms of regulatory practices and surveillance. It is interesting to note Evans's assertion that "the Wreck Beach Preservation Society maintains a tight discursive control of the beach," made in reference to his own research experience. Ibid., 8. Since the 1970s, the RCMP have not policed nudity at the beach but have sometimes intervened to address open alcohol consumption, drug use, and unlicensed vendors on Wreck Beach.

75 "'Freedom from Prosecution': Nudists Seek Beach Rights," *Vancouver Sun,* 14 August 1970; "Sunbather Convicted for Nudity," *Vancouver Sun,* 17 September 1970; Jim McCandlish, "Wreck Beach Revisited: Officialdom Blind to Nudists' Revival," *Vancouver Sun,* 20 July 1971; *Sunday Supplement,* CBC Radio, 16 July 1972, CBC RA. An exception to this ratio occurred during the Nude-In of 1970, when clothed beachgoers reportedly outnumbered nude ones by ten to one. Jim Davies, "Traffic Jams at Wreck Beach: 3,000 Cast Their Eyes on Nude-In," *Vancouver Sun,* 24 August 1970.

76 "'Freedom from Prosecution': Nudists Seek Beach Rights," *Vancouver Sun,* 14 August 1970.

77 *Sunday Supplement,* CBC Radio, 16 July 1972, CBC RA.

78 Ibid.

79 Jamie Craig, "In Spite of All That ...," *Vancouver Sun,* 29 September 1972.

80 Ingram, "Redesigning Wreck," 192. This seems to have been the case at other North American nude beaches too. A sociological study of a free beach in California noted that gay men used it before it became a popular nude beach, and American nudist Cec Cinder credits the gay community with "play[ing] a pioneering role in establishing free beaches in southern California." Cinder, *The Nudist Idea,* 595–96.

81 Mrs. Beverley Clark to Ian Bain, 28 July 1978, Parks and Recreation fonds, Wreck Beach, 52-F-5, file 8, series 93, VA.

82 Douglas, Rasmussen, and Flanagan, *The Nude Beach.*

83 *As It Happens,* CBC Radio, 11 July 1977, CBC RA.

84 "Fight against Nudity Just Begun – Gerard," *Vancouver Province,* 12 July 1977.

85 *Vancouver Sun* columnist Jamie Craig offered a seemingly frank assessment. He indicated that compared to men, there were "fewer children and fewer women (though still lots of each)." Jamie Craig, "In Spite of All That ...," *Vancouver Sun,* 29 September 1972.

86 Mrs. Emily Sion to the Mayor, 9 September 1977, Mayor's Office fonds, Wreck Beach, 48-G-3, file 119, series 3, VA.

87 Nead, *The Female Nude,* 2.
88 Wreck Beach Area Advisory Committee, Annual Report, March 1978, VA.
89 Ros Oberlyn, "Barely Anybody Around for Gerard's March," *Vancouver Sun,* 11 July 1977.
90 Their reaction echoes the response of Kitsilano residents to the popularity of 4th Avenue as a hippie hangout in the late 1960s. Ross, "Panic on Love Street."
91 "Beach 'Liberation' Target," *Vancouver Sun,* 24 June 1977; "Wrath at Wreck Beach," *Vancouver Sun,* 29 June 1977; Gerard, *Bernice Gerard,* 193 (emphasis in original).
92 Gerard, *Bernice Gerard,* 193.
93 Wreck Beach Area Advisory Committee, Annual Report, March 1978, VA.
94 B. Newell to the Editor, "Nude Stroller Made Convert," *Vancouver Sun,* 28 September 1977.
95 R.A. Pruner to the Mayor and Council, 11 July 1977, Office of the City Clerk fonds, Wreck Beach, 32-C-1, file 1, VA.
96 "Nude Bathing Areas Urged," *Vancouver Sun,* 27 August 1970.
97 R. v. Benolkin et al., (1977), 36 C.C.C. (2d) 206 (SK QB) at 207.
98 Barbour, "Undressed Toronto," 226, 363.
99 R. v. Springer (1975), 24 C.C.C. (2d) 56 (SK QB) at 58.
100 Harvey Oberfeld, "Gardom Refuses to Bare All on Nude-Bathing Problem," *Vancouver Sun,* 14 July 1978.
101 *Identities,* CBC Radio, 11 November 1974, CBC RA.
102 Paul Manning, "Gawkers Flock to View Nude-In," *Vancouver Province,* 24 August 1970.
103 W. Hogarth, "Crusade for Naturism," *Sunbathing for Health,* August 1954, 28.
104 *Sun Valley News,* February 1962, Sun Valley Gardens file, FCN.
105 A tendency to present it in this light appears in the work of both Caroline Daley and Marguerite Shaffer. See Daley, *Leisure and Pleasure;* and Shaffer, "On the Environmental Nude."
106 Cynthia Johnston, "The Naked Truth: Nude Vacations Gaining Popularity," *Calgary Herald,* 16 June 2012, 14.
107 "Wreck Beach," Wreck Beach Preservation Society, http://www.wreckbeach.org/. It should be noted, however, that unofficial "clothing-optional" beaches in Canada far outnumber sanctioned ones. Popular nude bathing sites include Brunswick Beach (British Columbia), Meech Lake (Quebec), and Crystal Crescent Beach (Nova Scotia), tolerated to varying degrees by local authorities.

**Conclusion**

1 "A Day among 'the Bares' at a Nudist Camp in Surrey," *Surrey Leader,* 18 June 1964.
2 *The Meadowlark,* 14 February 1977, Meadowbrook Sun Club file, ANRL.
3 Federation of Canadian Naturists, http://www.fcn.ca/ (accessed 12 July 2012).
4 Howarth, "I Visited a British Columbia Nudist Colony," 63.
5 D'Emilio and Freedman, *Intimate Matters,* vii.
6 Stearns, *Battleground of Desire,* x.
7 Nicholas, *The Modern Girl.* See also Brumberg, *The Body Project.*

# Bibliography


Primary Sources

***Archival Collections***
American Nudist Research Library, Kissimmee, Florida (ANRL)
The ArQuives, Toronto
CBC Radio Archives, CBC Broadcasting Centre, Toronto (CBC RA)
CBC Television collection, Library and Archives Canada, Ottawa (LAC)
City of Vancouver Archives, Vancouver (VA)
Federation of Canadian Naturists, Toronto (FCN)
The Naturist Living Show podcast, https://www.naturistlivingshow.com/
Special Collections, Calgary Public Library, Calgary
Special Collections, Toronto Reference Library, Toronto
Special Collections, Vancouver Public Library, Vancouver
Sunny Trails Nudist Club collection, BC Archives, Victoria (BCA)

***Magazines and Newspapers***
*Bare in Mind*
*Calgary Herald*
*Edmonton Journal*
*Globe and Mail*
*Ottawa Citizen*
*Sunbathing for Health*
*Surrey Leader*
*Vancouver Province*
*Vancouver Sun*

***Published Primary Sources***
Blatz, William E. *Understanding the Young Child.* Toronto: Clarke, Irwin, 1944.
Brechin, M. "Danger: Child Growing Up." *Maclean's,* 15 August 1943.
Callwood, June. "Will Your Youngster Turn to Crime?" *Maclean's,* 15 September 1954.

*Canadian Nudist Profile.* Toronto, 1969.
Conover, Dora. "Dr. Blatz: Child-Care's 'Bad Boy.'" *Saturday Night,* 8 December 1951, 12.
Eastern Canadian Sunbathing Association. *The Sunshine Family: A Guide to Nudism and the Clubs of the Canadian Sunbathing Associations.* Toronto, 1965.
Flugel, J.C. *The Psychology of Clothes.* London: Hogarth Press, 1930.
Gerard, Bernice. *Bernice Gerard: Today and for Life.* Burlington, ON: Welch, 1988.
Hocker, Mel. "Leave the Beauty Contests to the Nudists." *Sundial* 1, no. 1 (1961): 6–13.
Howarth, Jean. "I Visited a British Columbia Nudist Colony." *Liberty,* August 1955.
Jong, Erica. "The Hite Report." *New York Times,* 3 October 1976.
Kinsey, Alfred C., Wardell B. Pomeroy, and Clyde E. Martin. *Sexual Behavior in the Human Male.* Philadelphia: W.B. Saunders, 1948.
Kinsey, Alfred C., Wardell B. Pomeroy, Clyde E. Martin, and Paul H. Gebhard. *Sexual Behavior in the Human Female.* Vol. 1. Philadelphia: W.B. Saunders, 1953. Reprint, New York: Ishi Press International, 2010.
Laycock, Samuel R. *Questions Parents Ask.* Toronto: Ryerson Press, 1952.
Merrill, Frances, and Mason Merrill. *Among the Nudists.* New York: Alfred A. Knopf, 1931.
–. *Nudism Comes to America.* New York: Alfred A. Knopf, 1932.
"Miss Nude World 1971 Swiss-Born Montrealer." *Victoria Daily Times,* 26 July 1971.
Norwood, C.E. *Nudism in England.* London: Noel Douglas, 1933.
Parkes, Peggy. "I'm a Nudist Mother." *Liberty,* August 1958, 16–17.
Parmelee, Maurice. *Nudism in Modern Life: The New Gymnosophy.* 5th American ed., 1927. Reprint, Mays Landing, NJ: Sunshine Book, 1952.
Remsberg, Charles, and Bonnie Remsberg. "Here She Comes, Miss Nude America." *Esquire,* May 1970.
Scott, Jack. "I Went to a Nudist Camp." *Maclean's,* 15 October 1949, 27–28.
Spock, Benjamin. *The Common Sense Book of Baby and Child Care.* 2nd ed. New York: Pocket Books, 1957.
Stein, D.L. "'Have' Delinquents: Why Do They Go Wrong?" *Maclean's,* 25 January 1964.
Sunny Chinooks Association. *Warm Winds on Bare Bodies: A Collection of Stories Chronicling the First Fifty Years of the Sunny Chinooks Association.* 2nd ed. Calgary, 2003.
Webb, Herbert. *Eden Regained: A Challenge to Modern Prudery.* Spokane, WA: Mervin Mounce, 1957.
Welby, William. *The Naked Truth about Nudism.* 2nd ed. London: Thorsons, 1939.
Williams, Ramon. "Realism in Pageantry." *American Nudist,* Winter 1965.
Zoffer, G. "Psychological Factors in Juvenile Crime." *Saturday Night,* 12 January, 19 January, 26 January, and 2 February 1946.

### Secondary Sources

Adams, Mary Louise. "Margin Notes: Reading Lesbianism as Obscenity in a Cold War Courtroom." In *Love, Hate, and Fear in Canada's Cold War,* ed. Richard Cavell, 135–58. Toronto: University of Toronto Press, 2004.
–. *The Trouble with Normal: Postwar Youth and the Making of Heterosexuality.* Toronto: University of Toronto Press, 1997.
Anderson, Benedict. *Imagined Communities: Reflections on the Origin and Spread of Nationalism.* Rev. ed. London: Verso, 1991.
Androsoff, Ashleigh. "A Larger Frame: 'Redressing' the Image of Doukhobor-Canadian Women in the Twentieth Century." *Journal of the Canadian Historical Association* 18, no. 1 (2007): 81–105.

Aron, Cindy Sondik. *Working at Play: A History of Vacations in the United States.* New York: Oxford University Press, 1999.

Aronsen, Lawrence. *City of Love and Revolution: Vancouver in the Sixties.* Vancouver: New Star Books, 2010.

Backhouse, Constance. *Colour-Coded: A Legal History of Racism in Canada, 1900–1950.* Toronto: Osgoode Society for Canadian Legal History, 1999.

Bailey, Beth L. *From Front Porch to Back Seat: Courtship in Twentieth-Century America.* Baltimore: Johns Hopkins University Press, 1988.

Bakker, Nelleke. "Sunshine as Medicine: Health Colonies and the Medicalization of Childhood in the Netherlands c. 1900–1960." *History of Education* 36, no. 6 (November 2007): 659–79.

Ballerino Cohen, Colleen, Richard Wilk, and Beverly Stoeltje, eds. *Beauty Queens on the Global Stage: Gender, Contests, and Power.* New York: Routledge, 1996.

Banet-Weiser, Sarah. *The Most Beautiful Girl in the World: Beauty Pageants and National Identity.* Berkeley: University of California Press, 1999.

Banner, Lois. *American Beauty.* New York: Knopf, 1983.

Barbour, Dale. "Undressed Toronto: The Transformation of Bathing, 1850–1935." PhD diss., University of Toronto, 2018.

–. *Winnipeg Beach: Leisure and Courtship in a Resort Town, 1900–1967.* Winnipeg: University of Manitoba Press, 2011.

Barcan, Ruth. *Nudity: A Cultural Anatomy.* Oxford: Berg, 2004.

–. "'Regaining What Mankind Has Lost through Civilization': Early Nudism and Ambivalent Moderns." *Fashion Theory* 8 (2004): 63–82.

Barman, Jean. *The West beyond the West: A History of British Columbia.* Rev. ed. Toronto: University of Toronto Press, 1996.

Bederman, Gail. *Manliness and Civilization: A Cultural History of Gender and Race in the United States, 1880–1917.* Chicago: University of Chicago Press, 1995.

Belisle, Donica. "Crazy for Bargains: Inventing the Irrational Female Shopper in Modernizing English Canada." *Canadian Historical Review* 92, no. 4 (December 2011): 581–606.

–. *Retail Nation: Department Stores and the Making of Modern Canada.* Vancouver: UBC Press, 2011.

Bell, David, and Ruth Holliday. "Naked as Nature Intended." *Body and Society* 6 (2000): 127–40.

Berger, John. *Ways of Seeing.* London: British Broadcasting Corporation, 1972.

Bernstein, Robin. *Racial Innocence: Performing American Childhood from Slavery to Civil Rights.* New York: New York University Press, 2011.

Blair, Megan. "Miss Canadian University Pageant and Protest, 1970." (Online Exhibit), 2018, Wilfrid Laurier University Archives. https://laurierarchives.omeka.net/exhibits/show/miss-canadian-university-pagea/introduction.

Booth, Douglas. "Nudes in the Sand and Perverts in the Dunes." *Journal of Australian Studies* 53 (June 1997): 170–83.

Bouchier, Nancy B., and Ken Cruikshank. *The People and the Bay: A Social and Environmental History of Hamilton Harbour.* Vancouver: UBC Press, 2016.

Boudreau, Michael. "'The Struggle for a Different World': The 1971 Gastown Riot in Vancouver." In *Debating Dissent: Canada and the Sixties,* ed. Lara Campbell, Dominique Clement, and Gregory S. Kealey, 117–33. Toronto: University of Toronto Press, 2012.

Bourke, Joanna. "The Great Male Renunciation: Men's Dress Reform in Interwar Britain." *Journal of Design History* 9, no. 1 (1996): 23–33.

Bradley, Ben. "Managing Wild Behaviour in Wild Spaces: Rowdiness, Drunkenness, and Misadventure in Canadian Parks." Paper presented at World Congress of Environmental History, Guimaraes, Portugal, July 2014.

Braunstein, Peter, and Michael William Doyle. "Introduction." In *Imagine Nation: The American Counterculture of the 1960s and '70s,* ed. Peter Braunstein and Michael William Doyle, 5–14. New York: Routledge, 2002.

Breazeale, Kenon. "In Spite of Women: 'Esquire' Magazine and the Construction of the Male Consumer." *Signs* 20, no. 1 (Autumn 1994): 1–22.

Brumberg, Joan Jacobs. *The Body Project: An Intimate History of American Girls.* New York: Random House, 1997.

Burman, Barbara. "Better and Brighter Clothes: The Men's Dress Reform Party, 1929–1940." *Journal of Design History* 8, no. 4 (1995): 275–90.

Buszek, Maria Elena. *Pin-Up Grrrls: Feminism, Sexuality, Popular Culture.* Durham: Duke University Press, 2006.

Butler, Judith. *Bodies That Matter: On the Discursive Limits of "Sex."* New York: Routledge, 1993.

–. *Gender Trouble: Feminism and the Subversion of Identity.* 10th anniversary ed. New York: Routledge, 1999.

Calvert, Karin. "Children in the House: The Material Culture of Early Childhood." In *The Children's Culture Reader,* ed. Henry Jenkins, 67–80. New York: New York University Press, 1998.

Campbell, Claire, ed. *A Century of Parks Canada, 1911–2011.* Calgary: University of Calgary Press, 2011.

Chapman, David. "Perfection in Chicago: Lanza Photographs Steve Reeves." *Iron Game History* 6, no. 4 (December 2000): 16–19.

Châtelet, Anne-Marie. "A Breath of Fresh Air: Open-Air Schools in Europe." In *Designing Modern Childhoods: History, Space, and the Material Culture of Children,* ed. Marta Gutman and Ning de Coninck-Smith, 107–27. New Brunswick, NJ: Rutgers University Press, 2008.

–. "Open-Air School Movement." Encyclopedia of Children and Childhood in History and Society. http://www.faqs.org/childhood/Me-Pa/Open-Air-School-Movement.html.

Chenier, Elise. *Strangers in Our Midst: Sexual Deviancy in Postwar Ontario.* Toronto: University of Toronto Press, 2008.

Christie, Nancy. "Sacred Sex: The United Church and the Privatization of the Family in Postwar Canada." In *Households of Faith: Family, Gender and Community in Canada, 1760–1969,* ed. Nancy Christie, 348–76. Montreal and Kingston: McGill-Queen's University Press, 2002.

Cinder, Cec. *The Nudist Idea.* Riverside, CA: Ultraviolet Press, 1998.

Clark, Kenneth. *The Nude: A Study in Ideal Form.* Princeton, NJ: Princeton University Press, 1956.

Clement, Dominique. *Canada's Rights Revolution: Social Movements and Social Change, 1937–1982.* Vancouver: UBC Press, 2008.

Comacchio, Cynthia. *The Dominion of Youth: Adolescence and the Making of a Modern Canada.* Waterloo, ON: Wilfrid Laurier University Press, 2006.

Cooper, Emmanuel. *Fully Exposed: The Male Nude in Photography.* London: Routledge, 1990.

Cossman, Brenda, Shannon Bell, Lise Gotelle, and Becki L. Ross, eds. *Bad Attitude(s) on Trial: Pornography, Feminism, and the Butler Decision.* Toronto: University of Toronto Press, 1997.

Cronon, William. "Introduction: In Search of Nature." In *Uncommon Ground: Rethinking the Human Place in Nature,* ed. William Cronon, 23–67.

–. "The Trouble with Wilderness; or, Getting Back to the Wrong Nature." In *Uncommon Ground: Rethinking the Human Place in Nature,* ed. William Cronon, 69–90. New York: Norton, 1995.

Daley, Caroline. "From Bush to Beach: Nudism in Australasia." *Journal of Historical Geography* 31 (2005): 149–67.

–. *Leisure and Pleasure: Reshaping and Revealing the New Zealand Body, 1900–1960.* Auckland: Auckland University Press, 2003.

Davis, Donald, and Barbara Lorenzkowski. "A Platform for Gender Tensions: Women Working and Riding on Canadian Urban Public Transit in the 1940s." *Canadian Historical Review* 79, no. 3 (September 1998): 431–65.

Davis, Rebecca L. *More Perfect Unions: The American Search for Marital Bliss.* Cambridge: Harvard University Press, 2010.

de Certeau, Michel. *The Practice of Everyday Life.* Trans. Steven Rendall. Berkeley: University of California Press, 1984.

D'Emilio, John, and Estelle B. Freedman. *Intimate Matters: A History of Sexuality in America.* 2nd ed. Chicago: University of Chicago Press, 1997.

Douglas, Jack D., Paul K. Rasmussen, and Carol Ann Flanagan. *The Nude Beach.* Beverly Hills: Sage, 1977.

Dummitt, Christopher. *The Manly Modern: Masculinity in Postwar Canada.* Vancouver: UBC Press, 2007.

Egan, R. Danielle, and Gail Hawkes. *Theorizing the Sexual Child in Modernity.* New York: Palgrave Macmillan, 2010.

Elias, Norbert. *The Civilizing Process.* Rev. ed. Malden, MA: Blackwell, 1994.

Entwistle, Joanne. *The Fashioned Body: Fashion, Dress and Modern Social Theory.* Cambridge: Polity Press, 2000.

Evans, Rhys. "Paradise on the Margins or Paradise Lost? Tolerance, Permissiveness and Conflict on Wreck Beach." *Arkleton Research Papers* No. 5. Aberdeen: Arkleton Centre for Rural Development Research, 2000, 1–33.

Foucault, Michel. *The History of Sexuality.* Vol. 1, trans. Robert Hurley. New York: Vintage Books, 1990.

–. "Technologies of the Self." In *Technologies of the Self: A Seminar with Michel Foucault,* ed. Luther H. Martin, Huck Guttman, and Patrick H. Hutton, 16–49. Amherst: University of Massachusetts Press, 1988.

Fraterrigo, Elizabeth. *Playboy and the Making of the Good Life in Modern America.* Oxford: Oxford University Press, 2009.

Freedman, Estelle B. "'Uncontrolled Desires': The Response to the Sexual Psychopath, 1920–1960." In *Passion and Power: Sexuality in History,* ed. Kathy Peiss and Christina Simmons, 199–225. Philadelphia: Temple University Press, 1989.

Freund, Alexander. "Contesting the Meanings of Migration: German Women's Immigration to Canada in the 1950s." *Canadian Ethnic Studies* 41, no. 3 (2010): 1–16.

–. "Troubling Memories in Nation-Building: World War II Memories and Germans' Inter-Ethnic Encounters in Canada after 1945." *Histoire Sociale/Social History* 39, no. 77 (May 2006): 129–55.

Gentile, Patrizia. "Capital Queers: Social Memory and Queer Place(s) in Cold War Ottawa." In *Placing Memory and Remembering Place in Canada,* ed. John C. Walsh and James Opp, 187–214. Vancouver: UBC Press, 2010.

–. "'Government Girls' and 'Ottawa Men': Cold War Management of Gender Relations in the Civil Service." In *Whose National Security? Canadian State Surveillance and the Creation of Enemies,* ed. Gary Kinsman, Dieter K. Buse, and Mercedes Steedman, 131–41. Toronto: Between the Lines, 2000.

–. "Queen of the Maple Leaf: A History of Beauty Contests in Twentieth Century Canada." PhD diss., Queen's University, 2006.

Gilbert, David, David Matless, and Brian Short, eds. *Geographies of British Modernity: Space and Society in the Twentieth Century.* Malden, MA: Blackwell, 2003.

Gilman, Sander. *Picturing Health and Illness: Images of Identity and Difference.* Baltimore: Johns Hopkins University Press, 1995.

Gleason, Mona. *Normalizing the Ideal: Psychology, Schooling, and the Family in Postwar Canada.* Toronto: University of Toronto Press, 1999.

Goffman, Erving. *The Presentation of Self in Everyday Life.* London: Penguin Books, 1959.

Gordon, Sarah. "'Any Desired Length': Negotiating Gender through Sports Clothing, 1870–1925." In *Beauty and Business: Commerce, Gender, and Culture in Modern America,* ed. Philip Scranton, 24–51. New York: Routledge, 2001.

Grover, Kathryn, ed. *Fitness in American Culture: Images of Health, Sport, and the Body, 1830–1940.* Amherst: University of Massachusetts Press, 1989.

Harris, Richard. *Creeping Conformity: How Canada Became Suburban, 1900–1960.* Toronto: University of Toronto Press, 2004.

Hartman, William E., Marilyn Fithian, and Donald Johnson. *Nudist Society.* New York: Avon Books, 1970.

Hau, Michael. *The Cult of Health and Beauty in Germany: A Social History, 1890–1930.* Chicago: University of Chicago Press, 2003.

Heins, Marjorie. *Not in Front of the Children: "Indecency," Censorship, and the Innocence of Youth.* New Brunswick, NJ: Rutgers University Press, 2007.

Henderson, Stuart. *Making the Scene: Yorkville and Hip Toronto in the 1960s.* Toronto: University of Toronto Press, 2011.

Hoerder, Dirk. "Local, Continental, Global Migration Contexts: Projecting Life Courses in the Frame of Family Economies and Emotional Networks." In *Beyond the Nation? Immigrants' Local Lives in Transnational Cultures,* ed. Alexander Freund, 21–43. Toronto: University of Toronto Press, 2012.

Hoffman, Brian. "'A Certain Amount of Prudishness': Nudist Magazines and the Liberalisation of American Obscenity Laws, 1947–1958." *Gender and History* 22, no. 3 (November 2010): 708–32.

–. *Naked: A Cultural History of American Nudism.* New York: New York University Press, 2015.

Holland, Patricia. *Picturing Childhood: The Myth of the Child in Popular Imagery.* London: Tauris, 2004.

Hollander, Anne. *Seeing through Clothes.* Berkeley: University of California Press, 1975.

Howell, Colin D. *Blood, Sweat, and Cheers: Sport and the Making of Modern Canada.* Toronto: University of Toronto Press, 2001.

Hustak, Carla. "Love, Sex, and Happiness in Education: The Russells, Beacon Hill School, and Teaching Sex-Love in England, 1927–1943." *Journal of the History of Sexuality* 22, no. 3 (September 2013): 446–73.

Iacovetta, Franca. *Gatekeepers: Reshaping Immigrant Lives in Cold War Canada.* Toronto: Between the Lines, 2006.

Ilfeld, Fred, Jr., and Roger Lauer. *Social Nudism in America.* New Haven, CT: College and University Press, 1964.

Ingram, Gordon Brent. "Redesigning Wreck: Beach Meets Forest as Location of Male Homoerotic Culture and Placemaking in Pacific Canada." In *In a Queer Country: Gay and Lesbian Studies in the Canadian Context,* ed. Terry Goldie, 188–208. Vancouver: Arsenal Pulp Press, 2001.

Jackson, Paul. *One of the Boys: Homosexuality in the Military during World War II.* Montreal and Kingston: McGill-Queen's University Press, 2004.

Jasen, Patricia. *Wild Things: Nature, Culture, and Tourism in Ontario, 1790–1914*. Toronto: University of Toronto Press, 1995.

Jeffries, Matthew. "For a Genuine and Noble Nakedness? German Naturism in the Third Reich." *German History* 24, no. 1 (2006): 62–84.

Jochelson, Richard, and Kirsten Kramar. *Sex and the Supreme Court*. Halifax: Fernwood, 2014.

John, Henry Richard Lawrence. "American Exiles beyond the Politics of the Draft: Nudity, Feminism, and Third World Decolonization in Vancouver, 1968–71." *BC Studies* 205 (Spring 2020): 33–56.

Johnson, Donald. *The Nudists*. Spokane, WA: Outdoor American Corporation, 1959.

Kasson, John F. *Houdini, Tarzan, and the Perfect Man: The White Male Body and the Challenge of Modernity in America*. New York: Hill and Wang, 2001.

Kheraj, Sean. "Improving Nature: Remaking Stanley Park's Forest, 1888–1931." *BC Studies* 158 (Summer 2008): 63–90.

–. *Inventing Stanley Park: An Environmental History*. Vancouver: UBC Press, 2013.

–. "Restoring Nature: Ecology, Memory, and the Storm History of Vancouver's Stanley Park." *Canadian Historical Review* 88, no. 4 (December 2007): 577–612.

Kincaid, James R. *Child-Loving: The Erotic Child and Victorian Culture*. New York: Routledge, 1992.

Kinsman, Gary. "The Canadian Cold War on Queers: Sexual Regulation and Resistance." In *Love, Hate, and Fear in Canada's Cold War*, ed. Richard Cavell, 108–32. Toronto: University of Toronto Press, 2004.

–. *The Regulation of Desire: Homo and Hetero Sexualities*. Montreal: Black Rose Books, 1996.

Kinsman, Gary, and Patrizia Gentile. *The Canadian War on Queers: National Security as Sexual Regulation*. Vancouver: UBC Press, 2010.

Korinek, Valerie J. "'We're the Girls of the Pansy Parade': Historicizing Winnipeg's Queer Subcultures, 1930s–1970." *Histoire sociale/Social History* 45, no. 89 (May 2012): 117–55.

Kruger, Arnd. "There Goes This Art of Manliness: Naturism and Racial Hygiene in Germany." *Journal of Sport History* 18, no. 1 (1991): 135–58.

Kruger, Arnd, Fabian Kruger, and Sybille Treptau. "Nudism in Nazi Germany: Indecent Behaviour or Physical Culture for the Well-Being of the Nation." *International Journal of the History of Sport* 19, no. 4 (December 2002): 33–54.

Kuffert, L.B. *A Great Duty: Canadian Responses to Modern Life and Mass Culture, 1939–1967*. Montreal and Kingston: McGill-Queen's University Press, 2003.

Kusz, Jennifer, and Simon Verdun-Jones. "From Obscenity to Child Pornography: An Analysis of Canadian Court Cases." *Canadian Criminal Law Review* 23, no. 2 (June 2018): 132–70.

Lafrance, Marc. "Building a Body, Building a Life: Men, Masculinity, and the Birth of Bodybuilding Magazines in Montreal." In *Canadian Men and Masculinities: Historical and Contemporary Perspectives*, ed. Christopher J. Grieg and Wayne J. Martino, 345–60. Toronto: Canadian Scholars Press, 2012.

Laqueur, Thomas. *Making Sex: Body and Gender from the Greeks to Freud*. Cambridge, MA: Harvard University Press, 1990.

Latham, Angela J. "Packaging Woman: The Concurrent Rise of Beauty Pageants, Public Bathing, and Other Performances of Female 'Nudity.'" *Journal of Popular Culture* 29, no.3 (Winter 1995): 149–67.

Lee, John Alan. "Three Paradigms of Childhood." *Canadian Review of Sociology and Anthropology* 19, no. 4 (November 1982): 591–608.

Litt, Paul. *Trudeaumania*. Vancouver: UBC Press, 2016.

Little, J.I. *At the Wilderness Edge: The Rise of the Anti-Development Movement on Canada's West Coast*. Montreal and Kingston: McGill-Queen's University Press, 2019.

Loo, Tina. *States of Nature: Conserving Canada's Wildlife in the Twentieth Century.* Vancouver: UBC Press, 2006.

Lorenzkowski, Barbara. *Sounds of Ethnicity: Listening to German North America, 1850–1914.* Winnipeg: University of Manitoba Press, 2010.

Low, Brian J. "'The New Generation': Mental Hygiene and the Portrayals of Children by the National Film Board of Canada, 1946–1967." *History of Education Quarterly* 43, no. 4 (Winter 2003): 540–70.

Macdonald, Charlotte. *Strong, Beautiful and Modern: National Fitness in Britain, New Zealand, Australia and Canada, 1935–1960.* Vancouver: UBC Press, 2011.

Maeder, Pascal. "Germans into Europeans: Expellees in Postwar Canada." In *Beyond the Nation? Immigrants' Local Lives in Transnational Cultures,* ed. Alexander Freund, 227–46. Toronto: University of Toronto Press, 2012.

Matless, David. "'The Art of Right Living': Landscape and Citizenship, 1918–39." In *Mapping the Subject: Geographies of Cultural Transformation,* ed. Steve Pile and Nigel Thrift, 93–122. London: Routledge, 1995.

–. *Landscape and Englishness.* London: Reaktion Books, 1998.

–. "Visual Culture and Geographical Citizenship: England in the 1940s." *Journal of Historical Geography* 22, no. 4 (1996): 424–39.

Matthews, Jill Julius. "'They Had Such a Lot of Fun': The Women's League of Health and Beauty between the Wars." *History Workshop* 30 (Autumn 1990): 22–54.

McLaren, Angus. *Trials of Masculinity: Policing Sexual Boundaries, 1870–1930.* Chicago: University of Chicago Press, 1997.

McLaren, John. "The Law and Public Nudity: Prairie and West Coast Reactions to the Sons of Freedom, 1929–32." In *Laws and Societies in the Canadian Prairie West, 1670–1940,* ed. Louis A. Knafla and Jonathan Swainger, 309–22. Vancouver: UBC Press, 2005.

–. "The State, Child-Snatching, and the Law: The Seizure and Indoctrination of Sons of Freedom Children in British Columbia, 1950–60." In *Regulating Lives: Historical Essays on the State, Society, the Individual, and the Law,* ed. John McLaren, Robert Menzies, and Dorothy Chunn, 259–93. Vancouver: UBC Press, 2002.

McLellan, Josie. *Love in the Time of Communism: Intimacy and Sexuality in the GDR.* Cambridge: Cambridge University Press, 2011.

–. "State Socialist Bodies: East German Nudism from Ban to Boom." *Journal of Modern History* 79 (March 2007): 48–79.

–. "Visual Dangers and Delights: Nude Photography in East Germany." *Past and Present* 205 (November 2009): 143–74.

McTavish, Lianne. "Learning to See in New Brunswick, 1867–1929." *Canadian Historical Review* 87, no. 4 (December 2006): 553–81.

Meeker, Martin. *Contacts Desired: Gay and Lesbian Communications and Community, 1940s–1970s.* Chicago: University of Chicago Press, 2006.

Merchant, Carolyn. "Reinventing Eden: Western Culture as a Recovery Narrative." In *Uncommon Ground: Rethinking the Human Place in Nature,* ed. William Cronon, 132–69. New York: W.W. Norton, 1995.

Meyerowitz, Joanne. "Women, Cheesecake, and Borderline Material: Responses to Girlie Pictures in the Mid-Twentieth-Century U.S." *Journal of Women's History* 8, no. 3 (Fall 1996): 9–35.

Minnett, Valerie. "Public Body, Private Health: *Mediscope,* the Transparent Woman, and Medical Authority, 1959." In *Contesting Bodies and Nation in Canadian History,* ed. Patrizia Gentile and Jane Nicholas, 286–304. Toronto: University of Toronto Press, 2013.

Mitchell, W.J.T. *Picture Theory: Essays on Verbal and Visual Representation.* Chicago: University of Chicago Press, 1994.

Mitchinson, Wendy. *The Nature of Their Bodies: Women and Their Doctors in Victorian Canada.* Toronto: University of Toronto Press, 1991.

Möhring, Maren. "The German Nudist Movement and the Normalization of the Body 1890–1930." In *Normalising Diversity,* EUI Working Paper HEC No. 5 (2003): 45–62.

Morris, Nina J. "Naked in Nature: Naturism, Nature and the Senses in Early 20th Century Britain." *Cultural Geographies* 16, no. 3 (2009): 283–308.

Mosse, George. *Nationalism and Sexuality: Respectability and Abnormal Sexuality in Modern Europe.* New York: Howard Furtig, 1985.

Mulvey, Laura. "Visual Pleasure and Narrative Cinema." *Screen* 16, no. 3 (Autumn 1975): 6–18.

*Musqueam Declaration, 1976.* https://www.musqueam.bc.ca/wp-content/uploads/2018/06/musqueam_declaration.pdf.

Nead, Lynda. *The Female Nude: Art, Obscenity, and Sexuality.* London: Routledge, 1992.

Nicholas, Jane. "'A Figure of a Nude Woman': Art, Popular Culture, and Modernity at the Canadian National Exhibition, 1927." *Histoire sociale/Social History* 41, no. 82 (November 2008): 313–44.

–. *The Modern Girl: Feminine Modernities, the Body, and Commodities in the 1920s.* Toronto: University of Toronto Press, 2015.

Owram, Doug. *Born at the Right Time: A History of the Baby Boom in Canada.* Toronto: University of Toronto Press, 1997.

Paris, Leslie. *Children's Nature: The Rise of the American Summer Camp.* New York: New York University Press, 2008.

Parr, Joy. *Domestic Goods: The Material, the Moral, and the Economic in the Postwar Years.* Toronto: University of Toronto Press, 1999.

Peeters, Evert. "Authenticity and Asceticism: Discourse and Performance in Nude Culture and Health Reform in Belgium, 1920–1940." *Journal of the History of Sexuality* 15, no. 3 (September 2006): 432–61.

Petigny, Alan. "Illegitimacy, Postwar Psychology, and the Reperiodization of the Sexual Revolution." *Journal of Social History* 38, no. 1 (Fall 2004): 63–79.

Pierson, Ruth Roach. *"They're Still Women After All": The Second World War and Canadian Womanhood.* Toronto: McClelland and Stewart, 1986.

Pitzulo, Carrie. *Bachelors and Bunnies: The Sexual Politics of Playboy.* Chicago: University of Chicago Press, 2011.

"Point Grey Cliffs Need Your Help." UBC/Pacific Spirit Park Cliff Erosion Management Planning Consultation Discussion Document, 31 July 2000. http://web.viu.ca/earle/pt-grey/gvrd-pg-document-full.pdf.

Putney, Clifford. *Muscular Christianity: Manhood and Sports in Protestant America, 1880–1920.* Cambridge, MA: Harvard University Press, 2001.

Razack, Sherene, ed. *Race, Space, and the Law: Unmapping a White Settler Society.* Toronto: Between the Lines, 2002.

Reumann, Miriam G. *American Sexual Character: Sex, Gender, and National Identity in the Kinsey Reports.* Berkeley: University of California Press, 2005.

Ross, Becki. *Burlesque West: Showgirls, Sex and Sin in Postwar Vancouver.* Toronto: University of Toronto Press, 2009.

Ross, Chad. *Naked Germany: Health, Race and the Nation.* Oxford: Berg, 2005.

Ross, Daniel. "Panic on Love Street: Citizens and Local Government Respond to Vancouver's Hippie Problem, 1967–68." *BC Studies* 180 (Winter 2013–14): 11–41.

Roy, Susan. "Performing Musqueam Culture and History at British Columbia's 1966 Centennial Celebrations." *BC Studies* 135 (Autumn 2002): 55–91.

–. *These Mysterious People: Shaping History and Archaeology in a Northwest Coast Community.* Montreal and Kingston: McGill-Queen's University Press, 2010.

Rugh, Susan Sessions. *Are We There Yet? The Golden Age of American Family Vacations.* Lawrence: University Press of Kansas, 2008.

Sangster, Joan. "Creating Social and Moral Citizens: Defining and Treating Delinquent Boys and Girls in English Canada, 1920–65." In *Contesting Canadian Citizenship,* ed. Robert Adamoski, Dorothy E. Chunn, and Robert Menzies, 337–58. Peterborough, ON: Broadview Press, 2002.

–. *Girl Trouble: Female Delinquency in English Canada.* Toronto: Between the Lines, 2002.

–. "'Queen of the Picket Line': Beauty Contests in the Post-World War II Canadian Labour Movement, 1945–1979." *Labor: Studies in Working-Class History of the Americas* 5, no. 4 (2008): 83–106.

–. *Regulating Girls and Women: Sexuality, Family, and the Law in Ontario, 1920–1960.* Don Mills, ON: Oxford University Press, 2001.

Sauerteig, Lutz D.H., and Roger Davidson, eds. *Shaping Sexual Knowledge: A Cultural History of Sex Education in Twentieth Century Europe.* London: Routledge, 2009.

Schrank, Sarah. *Free and Natural: Nudity and the American Cult of the Body.* Philadelphia: University of Pennsylvania Press, 2019.

Segel, Harold. *Body Ascendant: Modernism and the Physical Imperative.* Baltimore: Johns Hopkins University Press, 1998.

Sethna, Christabelle. "The Facts of Life: The Sex Instruction of Ontario Public School Children, 1900–1950." PhD diss., University of Toronto, 1995.

–. "The University of Toronto Health Service, Oral Contraception, and Student Demand for Birth Control, 1960–1970." *Historical Studies in Education* 17, no. 2 (2005): 265–92.

Shaffer, Marguerite S. "On the Environmental Nude." *Environmental History* 13, no. 1 (January 2008): 126–39.

Shah, Courtney Q. *Sex Ed, Segregated: The Quest for Sexual Knowledge in Progressive Era America.* Rochester: University of Rochester Press, 2015.

Shields, Rob. *Places on the Margin: Alternative Geographies of Modernity.* London: Routledge Chapman Hall, 1991.

Skolnick, Arlene. *Embattled Paradise: The American Family in an Age of Uncertainty.* New York: Basic Books, 1991.

Smith, Michael B. "'The Ego Ideal of the Good Camper' and the Nature of Summer Camp." *Environmental History* 11, no. 1 (January 2006): 70–101.

Stearns, Peter. *Anxious Parenting: A History of Modern Child-Rearing in America.* New York: New York University Press, 2003.

–. *Battleground of Desire: The Struggle for Self-Control in Modern America.* New York: New York University Press, 1999.

Steedman, Carolyn. "Bodies, Figures and Physiology: Margaret McMillan and the Late Nineteenth-Century Remaking of Working-Class Childhood." In *In the Name of the Child: Health and Welfare, 1880–1940,* ed. Roger Cooter, 19–44. London: Routledge, 1992.

Steele, Valerie. *Fashion and Eroticism: Ideals of Feminine Beauty from the Victorian Era to the Jazz Age.* Oxford: Oxford University Press, 1985.

Stevens, Peter A. "Cars and Cottages: The Automotive Transformation of Ontario's Summer Home Tradition." *Ontario History* 100, no. 1 (2008): 26–56.

Strong-Boag, Veronica. "Home Dreams: Women and the Suburban Experiment in Canada, 1945–60." *Canadian Historical Review* 72, no. 4 (December 1991): 471–504.

Sugiman, Pamela. "Unmaking a Transnational Community: Japanese Canadian Families in Wartime Canada." In *Transnational Identities and Practices in Canada,* ed. Vic Satzewich and Lloyd Wang, 52–86. Vancouver: UBC Press, 2006.

Tagg, John. *The Burden of Representation: Essays on Photographies and Histories.* Minneapolis: University of Minnesota Press, 1988.

Terry, Jennifer. *An American Obsession: Science, Medicine, and Homosexuality in Modern Society.* Chicago: University of Chicago Press, 1999.

Thom, Deborah. "Wishes, Anxieties, Play, and Gestures: Child Guidance in Inter-War England." In *In the Name of the Child: Health and Welfare, 1880–1940,* ed. Roger Cooter, 200–19. London: Routledge, 1992.

Tillotson, Shirley. *The Public at Play: Gender and the Politics of Recreation in Post-War Ontario.* Toronto: University of Toronto Press, 2000.

Toepfer, Karl. *Empire of Ecstasy: Nudity and Movement in German Body Culture, 1910–1935.* Berkeley: University of California Press, 1997.

Urwin, Cathy, and Elaine Sharland. "From Bodies to Minds in Childcare Literature: Advice to Parents in Inter-War Britain." In *In the Name of the Child: Health and Welfare, 1880–1940,* ed. Roger Cooter, 174–99. London: Routledge, 1992.

Van Slyck, Abigail A. *A Manufactured Wilderness: Summer Camps and the Shaping of American Youth, 1890–1960.* Minneapolis: University of Minnesota Press, 2006.

Vertinsky, Patricia. "'Building the Body Beautiful' in the Women's League of Health and Beauty: Yoga and Female Agency in 1930s Britain." *Rethinking History* 16, no. 4 (December 2012): 517–42.

Vettel-Becker, Patricia. *Shooting from the Hip: Photography, Masculinity, and Postwar America.* Minneapolis: University of Minnesota Press, 2005.

Wall, Sharon. *The Nurture of Nature: Childhood, Anti-Modernism, and Ontario Summer Camps, 1920–1955.* Vancouver: UBC Press, 2009.

–. "They're 'More Children than Adults': Teens, Unmarried Pregnancy, and the Canadian Medical Profession." *Canadian Bulletin of Medical History* 31, no. 2 (Fall 2014): 49–69.

Walsh, John C., and Steven High. "Rethinking the Concept of Community." *Histoire sociale/Social History* 32, no. 64 (November 1999): 255–73.

Watson, Elwood, and Darcy Martin, eds. *"There She Is, Miss America": The Politics of Sex, Beauty, and Race in America's Most Famous Pageant.* New York: Palgrave Macmillan, 2004.

Waugh, Thomas. *Hard to Imagine: Gay Male Eroticism in Photography and Film from Their Beginnings to Stonewall.* New York: Columbia University Press, 1996.

Weiermair, Peter. *The Hidden Image: Photographs of the Male Nude in the Nineteenth and Twentieth Centuries.* Trans. Claus Nielander. Cambridge, MA: MIT Press, 1988.

Westbrook, Robert B. "'I Want a Girl, Just Like the Girl That Married Harry James': American Women and the Problem of Political Obligation in World War II." *American Quarterly* 42, no. 4 (December 1990): 587–614.

Whorton, James. *Crusaders for Fitness: The History of American Health Reformers.* Princeton, NJ: Princeton University Press, 1982.

Williams, John. *Turning to Nature in Germany: Hiking, Nudism, and Nature Conservation, 1900–1940.* Stanford, CA: Stanford University Press, 2007.

Woloshyn, Tania Anne. *Soaking Up the Rays: Light Therapy and Visual Culture in Britain, 1890–1940.* Manchester: Manchester University Press, 2017.

Woodall, Ellen E. "The American Nudist Movement: From Cooperative to Capital, the Song Remains the Same." *Journal of Popular Culture* 36, no. 2 (2002): 264–84.

Woycke, James. *Au Naturel: The History of Nudism in Canada.* Etobicoke, ON: Federation of Canadian Naturists, 2003.

Zelizer, Viviana. *Pricing the Priceless Child: The Changing Social Value of Children.* Princeton, NJ: Princeton University Press, 1994.

Zweiniger-Bargielowska, Ina. *Managing the Body: Beauty, Health and Fitness in Britain, 1880–1939.* Oxford: Oxford University Press, 2010.

# Index

*Note:* "(i)" after a page number indicates an illustration. For abbreviations, please see page xiv. In subentries, "Connett" refers to Ray Connett, "Harris," to Mildred Harris, and "Ruehle" to Karl Ruehle.